Potomac Fever

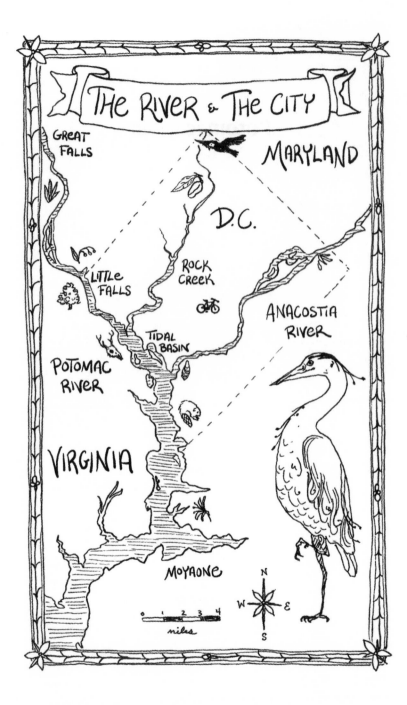

THE RIVER & THE CITY

GREAT FALLS

MARYLAND

D.C.

LITTLE FALLS

ROCK CREEK

ANACOSTIA RIVER

TIDAL BASIN

POTOMAC RIVER

VIRGINIA

MOYAONE

0 1 2 3 4
miles

N
W E
S

Potomac Fever

Reflections on the Nation's River

Charlotte Taylor Fryar

Bellevue Literary Press
New York

First published in the United States in 2025
by Bellevue Literary Press, New York

For information, contact:
Bellevue Literary Press
90 Broad Street
Suite 2100
New York, NY 10004
www.blpress.org

Library of Congress Cataloging-in-Publication Data
Names: Fryar, Charlotte Taylor, author.
Title: Potomac fever : reflections on the nation's river / Charlotte Taylor Fryar.
Description: First edition | New York : Bellevue Literary Press, 2025. |
    Includes bibliographical references.
Identifiers: LCCN 2024013280 | ISBN 9781954276345 (paperback ; acid-free
    paper) | ISBN 9781954276352 (ebook)
Subjects: LCSH: Fryar, Charlotte Taylor. | Ecology--Potomac River Valley. |
    Washington Metropolitan Area--Social conditions--21st century. |
    Washington Metropolitan Area--Race relations--History. | Potomac River.
Classification: LCC HN80.W3 F793 2025 | DDC 305.8009752--dc23/eng/20241129
LC record available at https://lccn.loc.gov/2024013280

Bellevue Literary Press would like to thank all its generous donors—individuals and
foundations—for their support

 This publication is made possible by the New York State
Council on the Arts with the support of the Office of the
Governor and the New York State Legislature.

Book design and composition by Mulberry Tree Press, Inc.

Bellevue Literary Press is committed to ecological stewardship in our book production practices, working to reduce our impact on the natural environment.

♾ This book is printed on acid-free paper.

Manufactured in the United States of America.

First Edition

1 3 5 7 9 8 6 4 2

paperback ISBN: 978-1-954276-34-5

ebook ISBN: 978-1-954276-35-2

To those who have been lost in the city,
or found on the river

Contents

Preface

Washington isn't the same place as D.C. D.C. isn't Virginia. And Virginia sure as hell isn't Maryland. One of the most confounding things about living in the Washington, D.C., metropolitan area—or what is sometimes called the DMV, referring to the District, Maryland, and Virginia—is that you can live across the street from your neighbor and also in another state. Your neighbor may have two senators who represent her in the United States Congress, while you have none. If you work in Georgetown and are earning the minimum wage, you make fifteen dollars an hour, but if you work for the minimum wage a quarter mile across the Potomac River in Rosslyn, you make little more than half that. Your sister out in Fairfax may have a harder time finding an abortion provider than if she lived in Bethesda or Brookland. If you live in Anacostia, you will pay far more in income taxes than your colleague who lives in Falls Church.

This city is a deeply divided place, with significant political and social implications as to which side of the Potomac River (or Southern Avenue) you live on. With the hardest line of division undoubtedly that of statehood for the District, where over 700,000 people are denied representation in Congress, you would think that more residents of the city would be eager to erase these borders, even if just rhetorically. And yet most people who live here are more than eager to shore up the perimeters between the various states and jurisdictions. When an Alexandrian says he lives in D.C., real Washingtonians scoff. The Takoma Park resident who does not fess up to the crime of living in Maryland is dismissed as an urban aspirant. The idea of someone who lives in Gaithersburg, Maryland, or, God forbid, Fredericksburg, Virginia, claiming that they live in the DMV is inanity to a resident of Capitol Hill.

I understand why D.C. residents want to preserve the boundaries of the District. During the era of white flight, in which white people fled the District to create so many of the Maryland and Virginia suburbs, Black Washingtonians stayed in place. These are the folks responsible for creating the idiosyncratic sense of place that the city is now losing as it modernizes, gentrifies, and whitens. Thus, when a white ranch-house resident of Arlington asserts a personal relationship to the original "Chocolate City," it can feel like appropriation, even theft.

Today, rampant housing inequality has turned the city and its suburbs into a patchwork of stratified segregation. Longtime Black residents of D.C. live next to white newcomers, sharing the same streets but no longer the same sense of place. As economic pressures force many Black Washingtonians out of the District and into the surrounding counties, the lines between a Black city and white suburbs are not quite as sharp as they once were. Still, for people who love this city, the impulse to protect it from newcomers understandably remains.

I am one of these newcomers. When I first arrived in D.C., I lived in a studio in Petworth; later, my partner and I rented an unusual cottage on the Potomac River in McLean, Virginia, where I began writing this book. Two years after that, we returned to the District and lived for a time in Park View. For a few months during the COVID-19 pandemic, we moved to North Carolina, where we are both from, to see whether we could or even wanted to live anywhere else but this city. We could not, and soon returned to live in Glen Echo, Maryland, a small town on the Potomac two miles up from the District line, where I still live now.

Having lived in all three places (notice I didn't say states) over the last seven years, I have become attuned to the various sensitivities of what counts as the nation's capital. I understand that there will be District residents who will roll their eyes at the idea that a person could live in Glen Echo and pretend to understand the city. But this book is premised on the belief that the state lines that make and break the nation are part of what prevents us from building relationships of care and reciprocity with regard to the places we live. I consider myself to be a voting resident of Maryland but a citizen of the Potomac River. Our fractured democracy ties me to Montgomery County, but my allegiance is to the city of Washington, D.C., and the future state of the Douglass Commonwealth, the nation's potential fifty-first state.

Nevertheless, the experience of living along the Potomac is still defined by those sharp state lines, and because of this, I would like to clarify my use of a few place names. When I use the name Washington, I refer to the version of this city typified by the presence of the federal government and the flocks of lobbyists and lawyers that surround it. Washington, as I experience it, is the oblong strip of the National Mall, and the federal buildings, museums, and monuments around it. D.C. is the part of the District where people actually live—where they eat, walk, garden, cry, and sleep. This includes everything from Bellevue in the Southeast quadrant to Shepherd Park in Northwest, and from Ivy City all the way down to the Palisades. The District is just that—the disenfranchised lop of land surrounded by Maryland and the Potomac. When I talk about "the nation's capital,"

I refer to the place included within the geographic bounds of the District but seen from the perspective of people who do not live here.

When I talk about "the city," though, I mean a place more expansive than the boundaries of the District or whatever constitutes Washington or D.C. or the nation's capital. The city is a porous, amorphous place that extends out to include as vast a stretch of the suburbs and exurbs as necessary for the individual. My own sense of the city begins to ebb away somewhere near Laurel, Maryland, but for you, it might stretch all the way up to Baltimore or out to Upper Marlboro. For me, this city is defined by the people who live here and care for it, regardless of whether they are, by virtue of statehood (or not), Virginians or Marylanders or Washingtonians.

Over time, I came to understand that my geographic sense of what constituted the city was largely concurrent with a map of the drainage area of the Potomac River. Everyone who lives in this city has a relationship to the river, whether they recognize it or not, and my broad view of what counts as Washington, D.C., is grounded in that fact. It is my hope that readers will remember this as they encounter the lines of division that I have tried to both map and erase in this book.

My thinking on this point and my geographical allegiance to the Potomac over that of the jurisdiction in which I live has been informed by the teachings of people indigenous to the banks of this river. Before the state of Maryland claimed possession over the Potomac, this river and the land it made were occupied and cared for by the Piscataway and Nacotchtank peoples. Upriver, past Great Falls, where the Potomac was known to Algonquin-speaking peoples of the region as the Cohongarooton, or "honking geese," the Susquehannock, the Massowomeck, and the Manahoac learned and loved the intimacies offered by the great oxbow curves of low water. Because this book is concerned with belonging, how and where one may feel and enact it, it is vital to understand that this river belongs first to the Indigenous peoples of this region.

At various times, Washington, D.C., has struck me as both a piddling village and dizzying megalopolis. There are only so many places in this city that I have been to, and fewer still that I know well enough to reflect on and write about. Readers may protest that I have given short shrift to the parts of this city they know and love; I agree, and hope to read a hundred more books written about the nuances and niches of our enigmatic city. There are not enough.

To these readers, and to conclude these introductory remarks, I humbly offer these words from Frederick Douglass, a onetime newcomer to the city who came to care for and critique it in equal measure: "You may know much, and I may know little. Nevertheless, having spent in Washington several of the most eventful, stormy, and perilous years of the Republic . . . I have naturally enough thought it might be well for me to tell my story about our National Capital."

Potomac Fever

Sycamore

THE NEW YEAR CAME IN COLORLESS. The wash of whites and grays and browns and blacks, with little reprieve for a blue sky or a pine green, stupefied me the first winter I lived on the Potomac River. All the leaves had fallen, baring the beech trees as the river coursed down beyond the line of silver maples on the rocky Virginia bluffs. A week into January, a night of bitter rain spilled into an icy morning, and the smell of frost drew me out of my house and down to the floodplain. The wrack line had come up and then receded, and the river swept murky and quick, south and east toward Washington, D.C., leaving behind a thread of muck on the bank. My face stung in the cold, but I could not close my eyes to the stark, hard pitch of the Potomac.

On the far shore, ancient sycamores spread their limbs, paler than the sky. More than any other tree along the Potomac, sycamores grow wider and taller. For some stretches of the plain just up from the District line, they account for over half of the trees within thirty feet of the river's edge. In the littoral zone between land and water, sycamores grow to epic sizes, sinking their roots deep into the silt. Hundreds of skeletal trunks lean forward toward the current, and their boughs grasp out against the sky like frayed nerves.

I passed the sycamore I had once measured to be six feet in diameter. Dozens of feet above my head, its limbs extended far out over the water in the direction of its Maryland kin on

Sycamore Island. Later, when this tree leafed out in May, it absorbed so much sunlight that little else but wood nettles grew around it. Sycamores are watery trees, and their bodies mimic the meanders of the rivers that feed them. In spring, they are among the last trees to put out leaves, and in the fall, they are the first to cast them off. For over half the year, these white titans twist naked on the bank in contorted poses.

The tree we call an American sycamore—or, if we are feeling fanciful, a buttonball tree—has lived on the land now known as the Potomac River valley for 95 million years. The Potomac is a bit wet behind the ears by comparison, a mere 3.5 million years old. Cretaceous sycamores grew beside other trees you can still put your hands on here today, including willow, tulip, elm, and oak. Together, these deciduous trees once formed a quarter of the valley's flora, and sycamores themselves, less than a quarter of that. Walking under the sycamores' waxy limbs, I found it difficult to imagine a time when the river was not dominated by a tree so wraithlike that Indigenous peoples across the continent called it the "ghost tree."

"No one was white before he/she came to America," James Baldwin explained in "On Being 'White' . . . and Other Lies." No one but the sycamore tree: Its vulnerable limbs endure through the winter, while its trunk sheds curled, frangible sticks of bark, exposing their tender insides. Sycamore wood is difficult to split, and when beamed or columned, it swiftly warps and decays. When old sycamores fall in the woods, their lower cores are often hollowed out with rot. Thomas Jefferson confirmed the sycamore's lack of esculent or utilitarian purposes by placing the tree at the top of his list of native ornamental trees in *Notes on the State of Virginia;* presumably, sycamores were to be planted by enslaved people for the enjoyment of enslavers.

The sycamore was so prized for its general hardiness and

good looks that twentieth-century city planners lined America's streets with these trees. Now, sycamores, along with their hybrid offspring, London plane trees, are an omnipresent feature of almost every major American city east of the Rocky Mountains. Unlike so many other native trees across the country, chopped and blighted into blackout, sycamores are ubiquitous, irrefutable in their number and color.

Flaunting their age in swollen trunks and weighty branches, some sycamores have become national landmarks, the ultimate witness tree of the past. There was a sycamore tree, or at least a faint legend of one, on Wall Street in New York City, under which the nation's early stockbrokers signed in 1792 the Buttonwood Agreement, forming the New York Stock Exchange; in the shade of that sycamore, twenty-four men created an economic apparatus that would do much over the centuries to integrate whiteness and wealth. The Burnside Sycamore still grows beside a bridge that crosses Antietam Creek, a run that soon after empties out into the Potomac; in one afternoon in September 1862, almost four thousand men died at Antietam as they slaughtered one another to preserve or break the nation over slavery. The sycamore beside the bridge was still a sapling when it drank water running red with blood.

There are other witness sycamores without formal names.

There was once a sycamore in Emporia, Virginia. In its limbs, a white mob lynched together Walter Cotton, a Black man, and his companion, Brandt O'Grady, described in white newspapers as a "white tramp."

There was once a sycamore in front of the old Baltimore County jail. In its limbs, the white elite of that city lynched a fifteen-year-old Black child, Howard Cooper.

There was once a sycamore on the south bank of the Potomac, a few dozen miles upriver from Washington, D.C. In its limbs, a mob of two hundred white masked men and women from Loudoun County, Virginia, lynched Page Wallace, a young Black man, and left him hanging from winter white branches for days.

In "How It Feels to Be Colored Me," Zora Neale Hurston wrote, "I feel most colored when I am thrown against a sharp white background. . . . 'Beside the waters of the Hudson' I feel my race. Among the thousand white persons, I am a dark rock surged upon, overswept by a creamy sea. I am surged upon and overswept, but through it all, I remain myself." The winter I moved to Washington, D.C., I walked beside the waters of the Potomac under the sycamores. They appeared to grow whiter and whiter under my scrutiny, and I became fixated on how this color, or really a lack of one, could turn harder and sharper the longer I stared, cutting through this city made by a river that, in turn, reflected an impassive white sky.

🔆

WASHINGTON, D.C., EXISTS in the minds of Americans as one amorphous place that operates on behalf of and at the behest of the rest of the United States. In Federalist No. 43, James Madison harped on the political imperative to create a detached federal district, separate from the power and influence of formal states. This new, discrete district, he wrote, would "exercise . . . authority over all places purchased by the consent of the legislatures of the States . . ." From its origins, the District was meant to be a distinct place set apart from the nation.

This perspective on the capital city is deeply embedded within the national consciousness. As such, most Americans believe that Washington, D.C., is, at its best, a democratic amalgamation and centripetal composite of all the stuffs and isms and convictions and vices that make up a nation. It is comprised of people from all over the country who have come to live on approximately sixty-eight square miles of land along the Potomac River so that they might represent the interests of citizens and corporations located in places defined by their utter unlikeness to the nation's capital. It is a permanent tabula rasa, swept clean every four or eight years by the power of democracy, this perpetual renewal marking it in contrast to the rest of the country.

So many Americans have conflated Washington, D.C., with notional ideas about the functions of democracy that the very name of this city has become a sobriquet for the swirl of political operations around and within the three branches of the federal government, instead of a descriptor for the land covering over forty thousand acres between the Potomac River and its tributaries. Washington is understood to be a city, yes, but it is more so the capital, the place that represents and contains every other place, and therefore has no particular locality or regionality unto itself. Washington, D.C., is the nation's geographic void.

Before I lived here, I might have said that Washington lacked a meaningful identity beyond its relation to a democratic history and culture, which may take its final shape here but finds its origins elsewhere. By virtue of its representative relationship to the nation, not to mention that regretful matter of its lack of representation in the United States Congress, Washington could be understood as fundamentally placeless. I would have argued then that while its placelessness was unfortunate, it was not all together important. If this country was, in the manifest destiny–inflected words of Walt Whitman, "always the continent of Democracy," why should those in the rest of the United States concern themselves with this severed square of land cut off from participation in their shared republic?

If Americans today know anything about D.C.'s long

plight of disenfranchisement, it is from the District's license plates, which now pointedly and almost plaintively read "End Taxation Without Representation." Given the small number of citizens who read and retain information found on license plates, it is no surprise that even fewer understand how and why federal lawmakers and the citizens they represent have forced the District's residents to play the infuriating role of something less than full American citizens.

The absence of a voting representative in Congress—a position necessary to advocate on behalf of the nearly 700,000 people who live within the boundaries of the District—further exacerbates the pervasive view of Washington as placeless, made impotent and submissive by legislators who own houses here but do not live here. Washington's colonized political condition extends the belief that the District, through vast governmental, bureaucratic, and diplomatic systems, operates solely to keep the rest of the country (and, in its more jingoistic moments, the rest of the world) operational. It matters little where the center of operations is placed, and whether its residents participate in American democracy.

There is another concomitant way in which the rest of the nation has rendered the District placeless, and it is through the cultural identification of this city with Black people. From 1957 until 2011, the majority of D.C.'s residents were Black, and today, it remains a Black-plurality city. Though D.C. is now bleaching white with new residents, racist stereotypes persist in the white American imagination of this city. The division between white capital and Black city materializes rhetorically. If you speak of the place where policy is set and corporations lobby, you are talking about Washington; if you speak of the place where whiting is fried and go-go is king, you are talking about D.C. Washington is white; D.C. is—and, to some, *was*—Black.

The District's geographical location, set by Thomas Jefferson, James Madison, and Alexander Hamilton—though largely determined through the political will of George Washington—confirmed its future as a place of racial division. "Since the city's inception," historians Chris Myers Asch and George Derek Musgrove write in *Chocolate City: A History of Race and Democracy in the Nation's Capital,* "race, racial tensions, and the changing racial demographics of the city's population have been the animating force in the lives of capital city residents." George Washington himself sliced the District from the two states that together held half the nation's enslaved people in 1800, and the city has, for centuries now, been a port of asylum for freedom seekers from all over the country.

Within these few square miles along the Potomac, D.C. was the only place in the nation where enslaved people were freed immediately in place by law in the spring of 1862. For those who emancipated themselves before and after the Emancipation Proclamation in 1863, the city became a beacon, a place to steal away to and make yourself anew, liberated. For Black Americans, D.C. has never been placeless; it has been, in multiple ways, a mecca for freedom within the Black nation, a place where, as Frederick Douglass said in his "Lecture on Our National Capital," "men breathe freer here than ever they did before," though he would not "pretend to say that Washington is at all perfect."

During the Great Migration, tens of thousands of Black southerners and a handful of their white neighbors left the South, following the flare of freedom and opportunity in D.C. The majority came from Virginia, South Carolina, or North Carolina, my home state, traveling up the corridor of what would become I-95 North. The culture of the eastern Carolinas, built on a foundation of solidarity, still runs deep in D.C.

If you are familiar with its origins, you can feel its contours all over the city.

My grandfather, the son of white sharecroppers in South Whitakers, North Carolina, moved to D.C. for an entire decade to ride out the Great Depression, flipping burgers on Pennsylvania Avenue, blocks from the White House. He eventually returned home, but a decade after that, he moved his family to a far-out Maryland suburb of the District, where he ran a dairy farm that supplied milk to D.C. residents. My grandfather's movement from inner city to outer suburb (with an atypical stop back home in North Carolina) maps a general pattern followed by many white D.C. residents. By the time of the March on Washington for Jobs and Freedom in 1963, the Census Bureau confirmed that since 1950, D.C. had lost a third of its white population and was now the nation's first Black-majority city.

Five years later, white fear of the uprisings that followed the assassination of the Reverend Martin Luther King, Jr., drained almost every mixed-race neighborhood east of Rock Creek Park of its remaining white residents. White boomers in the affluent suburbs of Falls Church, Virginia, and Chevy Chase, Maryland, still shudder when describing their escape from the city following the destruction of Columbia Heights, Shaw, and U Street, during which thirteen people were killed. Lines of division—streets you don't cross and suburbs you never enter—went up across the city that year, demarcations that remain in place.

The underlying logic of white flight works on the purportedly benign exchange of cause and effect: The anger and violence of Black people forced out white people, helpless innocents still sorting through the latent trauma of the sixties. But white flight, as the writer Ta-Nehisi Coates explains, "implies a kind of natural expression of preference. In fact, white flight was a triumph of social engineering, orchestrated by the shared racist presumptions of America's public and private sectors." Because the center of America's racist public sector of policymaking was and is located in Washington, there is a way in which the white abandonment of D.C. was manifested materially, in the lived experience of the city's neighborhoods, and also symbolically, in the white American psyche. The true fact of an increasing Black population in the city was conflated with the perception of a rising tide of urban poverty and violence associated with Blackness across the entire nation.

White flight thus transformed D.C. in the minds of white Americans into a Black place—perhaps the Blackest place. Its former status as the "murder capital" of the nation in the 1990s and the infamy of the old open-air drug markets in Mount Pleasant and H Street bled into the national, racist, and paradoxical perception of Washington, D.C., as the Black capital city of a white settler nation.

The national identification of D.C. as a Black city, enclosed almost totally by a ring of white suburbs and a muddy river, fixed Black residents in certain neighborhoods and designated this entire city as placeless, a national erasure of the nation's own capital. Within D.C. itself, though, the city's Black residents opposed the identification of the city as placeless, fostering spaces for democratic aspirations, advocating for full and equal citizenship. The band Parliament immortalized the dynamic Black community that grew in the wake of white flight in the 1975 hit "Chocolate City," still the city's unofficial "state" song.

Following a nationwide pattern of a white millennial relocation to urban areas, D.C. crossed over the threshold to become a Black-plurality city in 2011. I moved here myself in 2016, when my partner began a new job. It is a hackneyed remark these days to describe D.C. as a cappuccino city, and it is indeed becoming more caffè latte as the city continues to gentrify, driving up housing prices and driving out longtime Black residents. (It is ostensibly lost on everyone that these coffee metaphors applied to D.C.'s population never include the original ingredient: chocolate.) The Latino and Asian populations of D.C. have also increased alongside that of whites, complicating the narrative of Black displacement by solely white means. Today, at least 14 percent of D.C.'s population was born in another country, another important change in the question of who calls the city home.

As D.C. has whitened and globalized over the last two decades, the debate over the first fact of the city that renders it placeless—the refusal to grant the District full representation in Congress—has intensified. Generations of Black activists have led a century-long movement to grant D.C. statehood, and thus representation in Congress, arguing that the continued disenfranchisement of District residents is the result of patronizing, racist ideologies held by members of Congress on both sides of the aisle. In 2021, after several noncommittal decades, the Democratic majority in the House of Representatives finally passed a bill that would grant D.C. statehood, though at the time of this writing, it has yet to pass the Senate. The movement for D.C. statehood may have more support than ever before, and yet it is hard to ignore that the disenfranchisement of the District was accepted as a simple fact of place until white folks, born in alignment with the guarantees of the republic, moved back to town, blanching the voter rolls.

If you follow the logic that the continued disenfranchisement and a cultural association with Blackness is what has coded D.C. as placeless in the nation's imagination, then the movement for D.C. statehood as well as the District's overall whitening should work to return a sense of place to the city. But as gentrification unfurls through all eight wards and all four quadrants, Black residents—the people who made D.C.

into what might be called a placeful place, defined by the kind of deep, abiding love of community that only comes with time and care—are being forced out. Many have moved to suburban Prince George's County, Maryland, where the remaining vestiges of Chocolate City have taken on a new shape.

In the wake of Black displacement, D.C. is losing its Black sense of place—though it has not yet lost it completely. A postracial haze has settled in over the city, clouding the protracted reality of gentrification with the gauzy language of diversity. The city may appear from afar to be diverse, the kind of fictitious global melting pot that makes a metropolitan area, but once you step in, you see division stiffening and segregation hardening.

To live in this city is to live in a constant state of disorientation. I mean this literally as well as figuratively, spatially, and temporally: I often find myself lost in neighborhoods that even I, a white newcomer, once knew my way around. Signposts of place—a neon carryout sign, the funeral parlor with bright green window trim—have disappeared, and I find myself unable to remember where to make my next turn, or indeed what year it really is.

To orient myself in a city that felt at once to be perpetually new and still heavy with history, I tried, particularly during the first years I lived here, to transform Washington, D.C., into a memory palace—a method of mnemonic retrieval many historians rely on to maintain a detailed recollection of the past. In my memory palace, each street and trail became associated in my mind with some aspect of the city's history. To retrieve these stories later in order to make sense of them, I had only to imagine walking down Florida Avenue or the tip of Kingman Island and I was there, somewhere in the past.

For a time, I found this to be a useful strategy for locating myself in both place and time in a city that seemed to struggle with both concepts. Soon, though, I became overwhelmed. D.C. is, of course, quite a large city, and there are more histories here than one mind can wrangle. But there is also a unique dual feature to retrieving memories laid down in place here. For D.C. is not only home to its own history—what might, in any other place, be called local history; it is also the repository for the nation's history. The struggle over which layer should rise to the surface makes the already unsettled terrain of the capital even trickier to navigate.

This contested aspect of the city's past has meant that D.C. has always been a place with a split psyche: It belongs to the nation but not to itself. The belief that Washington, D.C., the imagined Black capital city, belongs only to the white settler nation has transmuted into a widespread, national relationship to the city predicated on ownership, though this relationship is not always interpreted in racial terms. The idea of the capital as a national cynosure and cipher, where every American may stake a claim, has long been celebrated. Even Frederick Douglass could not help but to join in on the patriotic and proprietorial feelings such an understanding of the capital can inspire: "The poor man should feel rich and the rich man should feel richer by reason of his relationship to it and his ownership in it, for the capital of the nation belongs alike to all." But when the capital belongs to the nation, Washington, D.C., becomes, of course, property. And in this way, it ceases to be a real place, where its residents might seek their own sense of belonging—or indeed a sense of safety.

There is an inherent and underdiscussed danger to District residents embedded in this possessive consideration of the capital, which was on display during the white supremacist siege of the Capitol Building on January 6, 2021. Terrorists directed their attack that day not only at members of Congress but also at the idea of Washington, D.C., a place they conflated with a federal government they saw as depraved. As the rioters poured into the symbolic center of American democracy, a group of white men shouted, "We own you now," a threat I heard first on CNN while texting with friends who lived in Capitol Hill to make sure they were alive and safe. I understood that claim of ownership to be aimed not only at legislators but at my city and my neighbors, a place and its people that these Americans believed, as a right of their citizenship, they could claim as property. Later, I learned that terrorists had placed bombs around the city and attacked my neighbors on our streets, violent affirmations of the seemingly harmless belief that D.C. belongs not to the people who live there but to all Americans.

Washington, D.C., carries wounds it cannot cauterize, and this city suffers from the ineffable pain of exile, which permeates its history as a place of racial division, displacement, and violence. The permanent alienation of the nation's capital from the nation has meant that D.C.'s critical narrative, the story that repeats over and over, circling like a vulture, is whether we can ever find a way to belong to this place together.

Even a cursory look over the landscape of this city would suggest, more often than not, the answer is no; the place that is supposed to hold together all places and all people has, in practice, broken them up and organized them into a cartographic mosaic of citizenship, neighborhoods, and states. The place where we are supposed to come home to the nation is instead a place denied a home by the nation. The place that is supposed to unite us is instead the place that divides us.

But in that place, there is a river, and in that river remains the possibility of common belonging.

⚹

MY FIRST ENCOUNTER WITH the Potomac River was a well-spring experience, a coalescence of self, nation, and water from which all future encounters with this city would flow. It was also appallingly typical: In the summer of 2008, my family traveled to Washington to spend five hot days shuffling through museums choked with stale air-conditioning and walking heat-baked concrete around the monuments, memorials, and ponds stocked with goose shit. Like most tourists, we did not cross north of K Street or east of the Capitol.

I was a teenager, too embarrassed to show how thrilled I was to be with my family in the nation's capital, still cresting on the high of new knowledge I had accumulated in a recent American history course. After that class, I felt tethered to my nation as a citizen, a relationship I had never before been asked to consider beyond mouthing the Pledge of Allegiance each morning at school. I believed in the singularity of certain American ideals—equality, freedom, civil rights—and still also believed in the great forever-unfinished project of American democracy. As I watched a throng of tourists crowd into the pronged shadow of the Washington Monument in search of a respite from the heat, I imagined the obelisk bending, like the arc of American history, toward justice.

At the end of our last day in the city, I drifted away from my parents and siblings inside the chilled marble of the Lincoln Memorial to read the text of President Lincoln's Second Inaugural Address. I was surprised to feel a lump at the back of my throat as I read the words "with malice toward none, with charity for all, with firmness in the right as God gives us to see the right, let us strive on to finish the work we are in, to bind the nation's wounds . . ."

Standing in the cool stone temple of the man who I was taught held together the nation, I watched streams of tourists from around the country spill through the space, calling to one another to come here, to look at this statue, to read these words. Some wore pins and carried tote bags with the face of the Democratic candidate then running for the presidency. The sight of all these people gathered in this secular yet holy space, holding against their bodies symbols of the hope they had in the nation's democratic project, overwhelmed me. Emotions swelling at the prospect of real social change against the sweep of America's racial history, I slunk through the crowds to the back of the monument in search of a space to be alone, then sat down and rested my face in my arms.

When I lifted my head, I saw the sun sinking into a glowing haze across the Potomac, the blue river stained orange, now red, now pink, the elegance of a white-columned house atop a far hill to the south, a wide bridge ferrying people across the water, flanked with golden statues of men on winged horses, and again, the blue water, flowing east toward the bay and out to the ocean. I was awestruck by the sight, and even more so by the fact, confirmed by my isolation, that I was the only one to have ever taken in this breathtaking view. For several years into my young adulthood, I maintained a false belief, easily overturned if seriously considered, that I had discovered that space, and thus the view from the back of the Lincoln Memorial remained uniquely mine.

I had little sense then of how deeply my racial identity informed my relationship to that space, to that view over the Potomac, and to D.C. itself. To visit a place you have never been before, a place so obviously constructed and cared for by other people, to see it as beautiful and righteous, to believe you alone understand the worth of it, and to claim it as your own—this is the way of white settlers. I did not know that the bridge dominating the scene was purposefully placed there to symbolize the connection between the North and the South, linking a monument to President Lincoln with another kind of monument, the former residence of the Confederate general Robert E. Lee. Without this knowledge, sitting at the back of the closest thing that the United States has to a shrine to its own unity, I held close the prospect of my nation's ability to bind its own wounds and, perhaps soon, change.

From this moment, the Potomac River, which offered a specific geographical location for the placeless mixture that was the nation's capital, became for me the ultimate manifestation of American coalescence, a watery bond across difference.

Soon after I moved to D.C., my perception of the Potomac as a place of national unity shifted. It was December 2016, a time of intense social and political division, and several friends from my hometown in North Carolina had come to visit for the weekend. As we walked in the raw cold around the monuments, we bundled up close to one another, the sun falling in front of us as we walked west across the Mall. I was joyful to be in the company of old friends, but I recognized the same sorrow in each of them that I felt within myself. It was impossible for us to be visitors to this commemorative landscape without reflecting on the moral failings of the nation that the most recent presidential election had exposed.

We made our way to the Lincoln Memorial and around to the back of the monument to take in what I confess I still thought of, in some way, as my view. We stood apart and stared. There was no room for reverence for me. I studied a sycamore slashing through the sky on the far shore, and I saw the river then not as a place of unity, but of division. One of my friends took my arm, and we soon left, but in that reversal of feeling, any prior memory of the Potomac as a place of civic convergence splintered.

I saw in the river then a mirroring of the national mood, as well as my own. My desk at that time faced a set of windows turned southwest toward a woodland slope and a stony run, which emptied several hundred yards later into the Potomac above Little Falls. I would sit down to write the manuscript I was supposed to be working on and stop within an hour, distracted by the sycamores on the bank as well as the national news headlines. I met an acquaintance for coffee in Petworth, and as I walked down Georgia Avenue, I sensed the construction and redevelopment projects rising up from the ground like red lines, every new apartment building a partition. On my way back to the house I was renting in Virginia, I crossed the Potomac, a horrible ease sliding through me as I returned to democratically represented ground.

At that time, there was a sense that American society was dissolving, a sentiment that, if anything, has only grown more acute in the years since. Liberal white people often described a sense of disillusionment with their country following the 2016 presidential election. Their disillusionment, though often born of their anger with white friends and family who voted for the Republican candidate in states across the nation, was nevertheless focused on a place they called "Washington." I am sure I also used the word *disillusionment* to describe my own loss of bearings, though it never seemed to be quite the right word. It was not that my relationship to my country had been proven false so much as it had shattered, the result of a fissure that had developed between the history I had been taught and the landscape I experienced.

Faced with the shards that remained of my relationship to this country, I sought out water. Unable to write, I would stand up and leave the house, wander across the lane and into my neighbor and landlady's backyard, and there, standing on the ridge above the river, I would stretch out my neck to see the very site where the geopolitical borders of Maryland, Virginia, and Washington, D.C., converged in the water. The invisibility of these borderlines, covered and dissolved by the river, did not restore my civic bond with the nation. To borrow from Henry David Thoreau at the moment of his break following Massachusetts's enforcement of the Fugitive Slave Law: I had lost my country, and I was not interested in finding it again.

To have a country that you might lose is a privilege for those born with an affinity for the identity of their country. To be born a white citizen in a white settler nation is to be born with a single national consciousness. It does not cause me pain or confusion to say that I am an American; it is a fact. But for those born beyond the pale of white American identity, the bounds of the nation are at once both loose and tight. No one has ever described this with greater clarity than W. E. B. Du Bois, who explained this "peculiar sensation, this double-consciousness, this sense of always looking at one's self through the eyes of others, of measuring one's soul by the tape of a world that looks on in amused contempt and pity. One ever feels his two-ness,—an American, a Negro; two souls, two thoughts, two unreconciled strivings . . ." Dr. Anna Julia Cooper, a longtime resident of D.C., described, even before Du Bois, what might be called triple consciousness, the intersection of her identities as a Black woman in America.

Multiple consciousness, or at least refusing the singular national consciousness tied to white identity, can be redemptive for the white individual. Far more important, though, losing your country orients you away from national ideologies and toward a restorative path of reciprocity with the land you live in, with the place you inhabit and make, and within your communities of kin and labor. When I stood at the top of the ridge above the Potomac with my eyes fixed on the spot in the rills where D.C. began and Maryland, Virginia, and democracy ended, I was searching for something beyond and more important than the nation: a place to belong.

❊

THE NEXT SEVEN YEARS I spent by and in the Potomac, learning how it cuts and mends, breaks and brings together this city. It is one of the last so-called wild rivers on the East Coast, having survived numerous attempts by speculators and even presidents to dam and levee its flow. With a drainage area of almost fifteen thousand square miles, the Potomac regularly throws itself over its banks in open rebellion against the best-laid plans of private enterprise before shriveling into a thin streak pocked by boulders. Due to its unpredictable current, the banks of the Potomac are far less developed than other tributaries of Chesapeake Bay, and at least 184 contiguous miles along one side form a national park.

Flowing for its entirety between Virginia and West Virginia on one shore, and Maryland and the District on the other, the Potomac is one line that divides North from South, and decides who is granted representation in Congress and who is not. Though the distinction is far less visceral in the era of globalism, the riparian landscape of the District once marked the boundary between the East and the West on this colonized continent. If you drive fifteen miles from D.C. along the Potomac on either bank, you can clearly observe how the river determines whether places are agrarian or urban or industrial as geological zones blur from piedmont to plain.

The District is bound and formed by the Potomac and its tributaries. To the west spill Little Falls and Rock Creek, to the east sweeps the Anacostia River, and to the south flows the

Potomac. Underneath the city run Tiber Creek and dozens of other subterranean streams, now sown under the earth into culverts and drains. The Potomac's tributaries form hydrous boundaries that segregate Black residents from white. These forks and their own branches also separate the rich from the poor, people with power from those they subjugate. Potomac waters form some of our most unyielding intranational borders.

And yet, along and in these waterways is a seemingly endless fount of astonishments. In what other major American city could you expect to see dolphins finning the water as bald eagles soar overhead? Where in New York or Chicago or Atlanta will you find roaring waterfalls, ferny ravines, and sandy beaches, all in the same zip code? Along the Potomac and its tributaries, narrow strips of public land, some no wider than five hundred feet, protect the region's rarest species and preserve some of its most striking landscapes. In this way, *city* and *nature* are largely concurrent in D.C., eroding a dichotomy that defines the dominant American relationship to public lands. In many neighborhoods across the city, you can leave your twenty-story apartment building or step out of the liquor store with a six-pack, walk a single block, and there you are: already deep into a network of forested trails, lost in the woods, and so, lost in the city.

Though today the Potomac is an apparent model of ecological urban stewardship, judging by the number of hikers, bikers, climbers, and kayakers who flock to its verdant trails, for most of the twentieth century the river sloshed with acid mine drainage, raw sewage, and erosive sediment. In 1954, the only creatures that could be found living on the bed of the river were sewage worms, and in 1967, a river fountain gifted by Lady Bird Johnson had to be removed after it was found to be spraying coliform bacteria across a nearby park. For decades, fish kills and algae mats heralded the start of every summer in the capital. By the early 1970s, industrial development, coal-mining pollution, and municipal neglect—each supported by narratives rooted in white supremacy and myths of boundless capitalist progress—had very nearly destroyed the Potomac River.

The river's legal road to ecological recovery may have begun with the enforcement of the Clean Water Act, but the Potomac's most dedicated protectors have consistently been people who love the river they live on. In my own anecdotal experience, I have found that for those Washingtonians who already have a relationship with the Potomac, their love for the river comes not in spite of the river's impurity, but because of it, even its occasional foulness, when high tides reek and floods crust the shore with gunk. For city dwellers, the Potomac offers a vision of nature that is less than pristine and therefore open and approachable. Neither fully wild nor fully urban, not pure but not yet ruined, the Potomac and its tributaries are liminal spaces within the city; everyone, I believe, may find a crook or cove along the banks that speaks to them.

Today, the Potomac has traveled a long way from its past as a twentieth-century cesspool, and is now an imperfect but remarkable metropolitan oasis. Though the Potomac still faces the old problems of pollution and erosion, it is now climate change and its harbingers—flooding and sea-level rise, extinctions and nonnative species, and the widespread displacement of the city's Black and Native residents—that are the critical issues threatening the health of the river. Whether and how the nation will rally to protect the Potomac and its people remains to be seen.

The Potomac's epithet, formally given by Lyndon Johnson in 1965, is the Nation's River, which has previously signified little more than its location by the nation's capital. But the longer I walked its banks and the farther I waded in, the more I understood this moniker as evocative not just of the Potomac's symbolic position by the capital but also of what its actual place on Earth reveals about that symbolic position. The river's geography and ecology are the terrain and living material that have made the nation's history, rooted in white supremacy, colonialism, capitalism, and land depredation. Our national myths about the founding and functions of the country are almost always emptied of these oppressive systems, but a walk by the Potomac restores the truth of the nation to the false stories we tell about it.

What would the nation make of its reflection in the nation's river? This book is that reflection, a national and intimate reorientation of this city on the Potomac, and an exploration of how the nation's history has come to reside within the landscape of its capital city. "The life of a nation is secure only while the nation is honest, truthful, and virtuous," wrote Frederick Douglass, who might one day become the namesake of the Douglass Commonwealth, the nation's fifty-first state. The Potomac, the Nation's River, keeps the nation pointed in the direction of what is honest, true, and virtuous, if only we can will ourselves to follow it.

Late into my first winter in D.C., there was a skift of snow, the kind of light white that falls like feathers. "The old woman is picking her geese," the old folks from North Carolina still living up on Upshur Street might say about a snowfall this slight. By the time the sun cracked over the east ridge, I was out on the trail, the snow turning to slush under my feet. I had just crossed over the no-name run I had taken to calling "Wood Duck Run," after the birds I often startled there, when I was blocked by a downed tree. I followed the trunk up to where its branches lay over the bank, dangling into the water, and I saw the familiar white limbs. Here lay a sycamore, cracked at its rotten base, its body sunk deep in rich black mud as its limbs drowned in the slate chops of the river. I climbed over and walked on, a new longing, even hope, stirring within me.

The name Potomac is an English spelling of Patawomeck, an Algonquin word thought to mean "a place where people trade." It's there in the name: The Potomac is a place where people of different tribes meet and exchange, a place of mutual encounter—and, potentially, a place of mutual belonging. If rivers are the veins of the Earth, then the Potomac is the heart of this landscape, bringing waters down from the crests and folds of the mountains, through piedmont pine hills and clay banks past the city to the wide tidal wash of the bay. If nothing else, our shared dependence on the river gives us the foundation of interdependence. The land holds and divides us, but this river made the land.

Bald Eagle

THE FIRST TUFTS OF CHICKWEED had sprouted in the south-facing nooks of creek beds, and crowds of bluebells pushed their purple heads through the silt and litter. The morning was brisk and wet and not quite warm as I slid down the trail, which was slick with mud from nighttime showers. Everywhere along the path, I could see traces of the river's early risers: the tapered pads of red foxes, the tiny hands of raccoons, the matchstick hooves of white-tailed deer, the grooves of other humans' hiking boots. Everyone was out searching for an end to winter.

The Potomac was up and murky, thundering over the Little Falls Dam. As the sun capped High Island, the mist on the surface began to burn, and songbirds launched into their trills and chirps. Cardinals whistled, jays shrieked, and wrens twittered, crying out for spring. I was so in tune with this message and so eager for green myself, I closed my eyes to listen. I felt relaxed, loose, and easy, the rays of a new sun thawing me out, when I heard a screech and opened my eyes in time to see a bald eagle. It snatched into the water and rose up empty-taloned before landing in the distant crook of a sycamore, glowering.

This was the first bald eagle I had seen outside of captivity, and I could not contain my shock and delight. I screeched myself and ran off the trail in the bird's direction. Hushing as I approached, I squelched my way toward the sycamore, and there, I stared up at the bald eagle and the broad cross-stitch of its nest for what felt like an elastic, unbound epoch.

The sight of a bald eagle was so novel, I was startled by the angled razor of its beak and the size and color of its head, so bright that it appeared peroxided. The bird flustered on the high branch, the twin daggers of its eyes turned hard on the river. It seemed exasperated, seething from the unsuccessful catch. Despite my continued rapture at witnessing a rare bird for this area, the eagle's sharpness and my perception of its anger pricked me momentarily with fear. This unease expanded the longer I stared, mixing with my surprise, until I was no longer sure how I felt.

The paradox of the bald eagle is that despite its dramatic decline in population throughout the majority of the nation's history, most Americans have only known the creature's ubiquity: Its likeness coats silver dollars, state flags, and the United States seal, among other symbols of American nationalism. Chosen by the Continental Congress in 1782 for its expression of "supreme power and authority," the bald eagle has served since the nation's founding as its central emblem and even allegory. Soaring over broad waters and bays, crying out in raucous, insurgent tones, the bald eagle represents a nation of boundless opportunity and access.

Though the bald eagle is known to survive by scavenging, the national imagination of the bird is rooted in the ideal of rugged individualism. Aggressive and territorial, the bald eagle evokes the mythos of American liberty found in the open expanse of a forever-future frontier of prosperity and freedom. Commanding itself against the harsh elements of the natural world, the bald eagle is often pictured as I saw it: flying over a raging river, seeking out its livelihood against the perils and richness of a wild, untamed landscape.

On the national seal, the bald eagle stands for a uniquely American mixture of isolationism and aggression. Its body spread wide and facing front, it holds in its dexter talon an olive branch, representing the peace that follows victory, and in its sinister talon, a bundle of thirteen arrows, symbolizing the rebellion of the original thirteen English colonies and the nation's continued readiness for war. In its beak, the eagle clutches a banner reading *E Pluribus Unum*, a reference to the concord of an idealized American union.

Along the Tidal Basin, just a few miles south of where I stood transfixed with awe and alarm at this very real bald eagle, vendors peddle hats and sweatshirts emblazoned with the national seal. To walk the National Mall is to be confronted with hundreds of identical bald eagles, each a symbol of the nation's supreme power. The iconography of the bald eagle is so omnipresent throughout D.C., it is easy to forget that, across the District, these birds are almost totally absent. The fact that I was able to witness one at all is largely a testament to one prior resident of the Potomac River.

Sixty years before and twelve miles north of where I saw my first bald eagle, the biologist and writer Rachel Carson began writing a book in the sylvan suburb of Silver Spring, Maryland. This book, *Silent Spring,* famously begins with the fable of a fictional town suddenly gone sick and silent: "There was a strange stillness. The birds, for example—where had they gone?"

Following that prelude, Carson described the dangers of dichlorodiphenyltrichloroethane (DDT), a substance marketed as a panacea for any pest problem in the post–World War II era of domestic chemical control. Soon after its introduction to the market, scientists revealed how DDT trickled through ecological communities, killing not just insects but also reptiles, fish, mammals, and birds. Though the implications of these studies were clear, it was not until Carson argued that the use of DDT should be limited that the American public began to pay attention to the dangers of pesticides.

Though Carson documented the rising human death toll associated with DDT exposure, her most enduring arguments involved the prospect of a birdless world. The fertility of bald eagles in particular, she explained, had radically decreased over the last decade. DDT absorption caused their eggshells to become so thin that incubation crushed the eggs, leaving behind soupy nests of embryonic eagles.

Already imperiled due to habitat loss and hunting, bald eagles suffered a reduction in population so substantial that by 1963, the year after the publication of *Silent Spring*, as few as one thousand bald eagles were left in the United States. This number was compared repeatedly in the national press to an estimated 100,000 bald eagles that existed when the bird became the national emblem in the late 1700s. If nothing was done to reverse their population decline, Carson wrote, the trends in DDT use "may well make it necessary for us to find a new national emblem."

The legacy of *Silent Spring* is, of course, legendary and vast. As the catalyst for the modern environmental movement, Carson's findings precipitated a wave of new policies, some of which were specifically focused on the plight of the bald eagle. In 1967, bald eagles were declared an endangered species in all areas south of the fortieth parallel, and the Environmental Defense Fund launched a campaign to ban DDT. In 1970, the Environmental Protection Agency was founded with the power to regulate pollutants entering U.S. waterways, and two years later, DDT was banned. The media narrative surrounding the bald eagle's plummeting population soon pressed Richard Nixon to sign the Endangered Species Act. By 1995, the bird's status had been upgraded from endangered to threatened, and in 2007, the Department of the Interior removed the bald eagle from the Federal List of Endangered and Threatened Wildlife.

The return of the bald eagle is one of the most awe-inspiring stories that followed national environmental regulations implemented in the late twentieth century. The Chesapeake Bay region in particular saw an extraordinary recovery in bald eagle populations. In 1977, there were an estimated sixty-four bald eagles throughout that region; today, there are over three thousand bald eagles spread across Maryland, Delaware, and the upper watersheds of Virginia.

But in Washington, D.C., where the human population is dense and threats to birds are more numerous, the return of bald eagles has been far less spectacular. From 1947 to 2015, there were no recorded nestings in the District, and since 2015, the one pair that has deigned to make their home here—in an old tulip tree in the National Arboretum—has not produced offspring every year. The nest I stood underneath near Little Falls was one of only a half dozen or so that have been located along the Potomac west of the District over the last five years. Craning back to find a better angle to stare, I felt transported to some earlier era, when I would be the strange creature, out of place and worthy of ogling, rather than this fearsome eagle.

❊

I WASN'T SURE IF IT WAS MY BREATH or blinking or weight shifting on wet leaves, but the eagle heard me, turning its head in my direction before lifting off toward the north shore. I watched it vanish into the tree line before making my way to the base of the sycamore to better study its nest. At once both meticulous and slipshod, this nest, like the eagle itself, astonished me by its size. If I had curled up into a ball, I am sure that I could have fit inside.

Rounding the tree in an attempt to get a view of the nest's interior, I became aware of the luminescent signs tacked onto the birches around me: PRIVATE PROPERTY, NO TRESPASSING. As I turned to face the embankment, I found myself looking up at one of the largest houses I had ever seen. In my scramble to reach the eagle, I had veered south off the blue-blazed trail of public lands, and, it would appear, onto property owned by a Washington billionaire.

The mansion roosted on the bluff as though with outstretched wings. It seemed to be hovering on the hill, supported by a vast net of rough-cut stones. A yawning terrace engulfed the back of the house, casting a heavy shadow over the knolls of eroded rocks fifty feet below. Out on the veranda were an assortment of opulent frills: an infinity pool, a children's splash pad, a six-foot-tall daisy-shaped fountain, and dozens of sun-shaded chaises and other plush furniture.

I had known there were large houses along this stretch of the river, but I had not known there were palaces. Epic glass windows framed the back of the house, and all the slants and angles of the structure pointed toward the river. Lights lodged into the ground around my feet were aimed toward the tops of the three trees remaining along the riverfront, and other lights situated in the tops of those trees pointed down and across at the river. The artificial light show illuminating the bald eagle's nest and the water for the benefit of whoever lived in the house grated at my sense of justice.

I began to read the PRIVATE PROPERTY signs as a personal attack. The house and its implicated occupants seemed to refuse acknowledgment of the place in which it was located. How could you excuse an infinity pool when there was a river just a few steps down the hill? More infuriating than the house's dissonant aesthetics, though, was its spatial scope and the seemingly exclusive access these residents had to a bird I was desperate to get to know.

If I could do nothing else to refute the existence of this house and all the possessive authority it represented, I would, at least, refuse to leave. For a half hour, I sat in the sun with my back against a tree, thinking about the freedom-to-roam or "everyman's right" laws cherished in many European countries, which ensure the public's access to privately owned lakes, rivers, and oceans for recreational purposes. With my eyes closed and jaw set, I concocted a passionate speech I would deliver to anyone who attempted to haul me off about the early republic's capitalist ethics, which had prevented these laws from ever taking root in the United States.

When the sun moved, the shade and chill returned. Still smug and angry, I pulled myself up and back toward the trail and home, shaking my head at the mansion, if only because shaking my fist would have been too ridiculous an act to conduct without an audience.

I felt safe and moral in my trespassing, assured by the ultimate goodness that was my desire for further study of the bald eagle, which had led me onto private property in the first place. If I had been found and questioned, I would likely not have delivered my speech, but feigned ignorance of the posted signs. I sensed my intrinsic right to access what was wild and decent in the world being infringed upon by the rich and powerful, and a quiet riot of seated protest seemed the only honest option. Only in retrospect did I understand that the sight of that bald eagle had stirred something in me, something American, entitled, and white.

As I sat there scowling at the very concept of private property,

I had not once considered my race, though my refusal to be governed by the posted signs was a racial act as much as a political one. In another body, I might have encountered those signs and immediately heeded them to avoid potential aggression or violence. In another body, I might not have been guided by a belief in my own moral virtue at all times. In another body, I might not have been out on the trails that run through the suburbs of northern Virginia at all. But in my whiteness, I used the presumed guilt of another—to me, this meant the ostentatious wealth that limited my access to the bald eagle's nest—to maintain not only an expectation of my safety but my right to be there, out in nature.

White Americans demand spatial dominance, assuming all spaces that read to us as natural or wild should be ours to access, without constraint or question. In the white American psyche, nature flatters us and belongs to us, and our sense of ownership over natural landscapes feeds our expectation of access to land. When we encounter an object that limits that access, we believe these obstacles not only deserve our indignation but occasionally warrant our violence against them. This was the case in 2016, when Ammon Bundy, a far-right white terrorist, led an occupation of the Malheur National Wildlife Refuge, arguing that federal ownership of public lands in southeastern Oregon was morally bankrupt. During their weeks-long takeover of the refuge, Bundy and his followers desecrated Native heritage sites and destroyed federal buildings, guided by the logic that their claims to unfettered access to public lands had guided them to the moral high ground. They were patriots fighting a necessary war against a federal government they had found guilty, an oppositional stance that necessarily cast them as innocent.

Bundy's actions—which mirrored that of the Capitol insurrectionists five years later—were widely denounced by white progressives. Beyond such extreme cases, though, white Americans rarely question how our faith in the sanctity of our racial privilege allows for our access to and ownership of land. In her *Harvard Law Review* article "Whiteness as Property," the legal scholar Cheryl I. Harris argues that "the set of assumptions, privileges, and benefits that accompany the status of being white have become a valuable asset that whites sought to protect." White people rely so much on the benefits afforded by whiteness, Harris explains, that our expectations of these privileges and benefits, including access to and ownership of land, inform the interpretation of American law, ensuring our morality and, thus, our innocence.

White people are perhaps at the peak of their racial innocence when they encounter landscapes they perceive as natural or wild, and thus are emptied of the identity-based demands of modern society. Only in nature do we believe that we can slip all the way through the veil of ignorance and forget our own whiteness in the dazzling emptiness of an imagined, nonhuman wilderness. But in a nation whose history has been defined by colonization and enslavement, systems based on exclusion and exploitation, few places remain empty as a matter of coincidence.

The false utopia of a wide-open wilderness continues to inform white Americans' search for a timeless, ahistorical frontier. And we will settle for whatever kind of frontier we can find, as long as it means that once there, we can forget the self-reproach of being white. When we are fenced in and shown a sign that limits the boundaries of our imagined frontier, we fume and rebel. In this way, Bundy, in his violent protest against public lands, and I, in my silent one against private lands, were following an established pattern of racial innocence, even if our beliefs were rooted on far opposite political poles. My sycamore sit-in was fueled, at least in part, by an unconscious recognition that my own whiteness was a form of property, which is to say, an expectation to access what I believed I ought to have the right to access.

I confess that I crossed those NO TRESPASSING signs a half dozen times before I began to think about how this repeated action was an incarnation of the white innocence that I supposedly disavowed. Even then, it would be disingenuous to suggest that a new sensitivity to my whiteness is what ended my rebellion. Though I kept a long watch for the rest of the nesting season, I never saw a bald eagle in that nest again. Eventually, I stopped trekking off-trail through the greened-up woods to stare at the nest. But I still walked through public lands by the river, firm in my freedom to be there, possessing a silent privilege to access this place I still understood to be nature and, therefore, to be mine.

❊

EACH BRICK-BLOCKED SPLIT-LEVEL house in Silver Spring, Maryland, is somehow both modest and ample. They stand at the back of deep front lawns, dotted with plastic playgrounds and fenced-in kitchen gardens. As I drove down the broad streets of Rachel Carson's former neighborhood, the towering black walnuts were still bare, though strands of cherries were starting to bud. In Carson's yard, shaded with spruce, hemlock, and pine, a stream ran off the side of the property and under the road, flowing underground into the Northwest Branch of the Anacostia River, which, some fifteen miles later, empties into the Potomac.

The day I visited was muted by cold showers, but when they slackened off, I got out of my car and walked to Carson's home, a single-story structure that she designed as a writing retreat in 1956. Today, it is a national landmark and private residence.

I stood in front of it for a minute, trying to find some sign of its former inhabitants, but the quiet closeness of suburban living does not encourage rubbernecking. I quickly made my way down the blacktop to the intersection of Quaint Acres and Apple Grove Streets and onto the trail that skirts the river.

I would be astonished if this woody, verdant neighborhood were not the exact place that Carson envisioned as she wrote the first pages of *Silent Spring*. "There was once a town in the heart of America where all life seemed to live in harmony with its surroundings," the first chapter begins. Returning to the opening salvo and the euphonic town gone silent, I hear Silver Spring all over the pages.

But at the end of the fable, Carson tells her readers that "this town does not actually exist, but it might easily have a thousand counterparts in America or elsewhere in the world." The nonspecificity of the fictional town, dying as pesticides leached through it, was key to the success of *Silent Spring*. In Carson's descriptions of barking foxes and shady trout-filled pools, many white Americans heard echoes of the suburban developments where they had recently moved.

Silent Spring was published during the era of white flight, a period in which white Americans, fueled by a powerful racist cocktail of redlining, restrictive covenants, and government housing incentives, left urban areas for the suburbs. Carson spoke largely to this audience, with whom she shared a common suburban interest. The letter that first sparked her commitment to write the book came from a woman in suburban Boston, who described how a recent DDT spraying had decimated birds in her and her neighbors' backyards. For the "suburbanite who derives pleasure from birds in his garden," Carson later wrote, "anything that destroys the wildlife of an area for even a single year has deprived him of a pleasure to which he has a legitimate right."

Among scholars, there is little doubt that Carson's many domestic responsibilities informed this backyard focus; when she began her research in 1957, Carson served as the main caretaker for both her elderly mother and her recently adopted five-year-old grandnephew. Nevertheless, with her book homed in on the "legitimate right" of suburban residents to the pleasures of nature, Carson omitted research on pesticides in urban areas, in industrial contexts, and in communities of color, choosing instead to focus on people who lived in towns more like her own.

When Carson and her family lived there in the late 1950s and early 1960s, Silver Spring was strictly segregated. Drawn from a dozen subdivisions that had formerly been farmland, Silver Spring was a "sundown suburb," a white-majority community that enforced its prejudice primarily through racially restrictive housing covenants that refused the sale of houses and businesses to Black citizens. In 1967, three years after the passage of the Civil Rights Act, *Washingtonian* magazine reported on the appeal of Silver Spring for white people: "They love it because it's easy to commute to Washington. . . . And, they love it because Negroes, so far, have been safely left behind at the District line. Virtually everybody says so, one way or another." Another resident told the reporter that she had moved to Silver Spring to "get away from certain neighbors."

Jim Crow laws were rigorously observed, and few, if any, businesses accepted Black customers in their shops. While Black people could not legally live in Silver Spring, they were nevertheless a part of the community. They worked in white homes as domestic servants, they raised white children, and they maintained the town's neat gardens and expansive lawns. Black people built the stores in downtown Silver Spring that they were later barred from and the homes that they legally could not buy. Black workers used buses that conveniently ran between whites-only neighborhoods in the northern Maryland suburbs and Black communities in Northwest D.C. The bus schedule aligned with sunset and the arrival of darkness.

The northwest Maryland suburbs were touted as "the natural heart of Washington's future home development," a place with a "strategic location . . . surrounding parks and excellent boulevards . . . high elevation and natural scenic beauty." Silver Spring was promoted for its proximity to Rock Creek Park and its location in the valleys created by Sligo Creek and the Northwest Branch of the Anacostia. With access to both rural and urban spaces, Silver Spring offered its white residents both the conveniences of a close-knit community and access to the natural settings they sought in exurban landscapes.

In Silver Spring, Carson had close access to the research institutions she relied on to gather evidence and data for *Silent Spring*, and she was also part of a pleasant neighborhood in which she could easily care for her family. And, of course, Silver Spring offered access to the kind of natural spaces that Carson loved and had written about for almost two decades. When her domestic duties and health permitted, she often went bird-watching in Rock Creek Park, where she was particularly fond of veeries, a kind of thrush.

Access to public lands and parks was a critical component of selling the suburbs to white Americans, but even this supposedly natural aspect of suburban living was deeply racialized. As white residents retreated from the city, provoked by racist fears that D.C. was growing dirtier as the population became more Black, the subdivisions in which they bought their new homes were perceived as clean and green. Park spaces were understood to be buffers that both protected white suburbanites from the filth associated with urbanity and blackness and affirmed the purity associated with nature and whiteness. Carson may have challenged some assumptions about the healthful, natural state of the suburbs, but she did so without challenging the racism embedded in those beliefs.

About a mile up the Northwest Branch from where I had parked my car, the clouds split open and I got drenched by a bone-chilling rain. Forced to retreat or risk freezing by the Anacostia, I turned around, annoyed by the absent tree canopy that might have protected me from the rain in any other season. I was frustrated by the prevailing winter weather but also felt an outsized impatience with my surroundings—the privacy fences made of bamboo, the paved driveways and blighted boxwoods.

Trudging up the dirt trail and onto asphalt, I splashed through small streams of runoff toward Carson's old home. In her front yard, shaggy evergreens hosted a whole clan of sparrows, hiding under lush cover from the rain, and I made note of a multitude of native shrubs and trees, which would soon leaf out. I imagined Carson standing at her living room window to admire the first daffodils and the jade tips of spring azaleas before retiring to her study to write that her new home had "all the special things that I need." The comfort she felt here, tucked away in her retreat, must have been immense. During the eight years she lived here, she raised her niece's orphaned son, nursed her dying mother, fell in love with a woman she could not openly be with, fought with that same woman about the importance of her work, researched and wrote a book about the potential death of the planet, discovered cysts in her left breast, underwent a mastectomy and radiation therapy, and died, right here, at home.

It is heretical to fault Carson for anything, her sorrows so multiple, her legacy so extensive and undeniably vital; every person on Earth owes a part of whatever health they may have to her commitment to making a different world. And still, in front of her home—a house so similar to one that I grew up in, to the houses my friends and family have lived in—I felt boxed in, though all around me were wide yards and towering trees, inviting me into a community built for people like me.

I warmed up at an Ethiopian restaurant in downtown Silver Spring, which, with its faintly cosmopolitan commercial appearance, bore little resemblance to the white suburb of Carson's time. White people are no longer the majority population here, and over a third of Silver Spring's residents were born outside of the United States. It is powerful to know how much this one community has changed, rejecting—if only in its demographics—the white supremacy on which the town was founded. I paid for the meal with cash, and received, as part of my change, an old Washington Eagle quarter. On one side was the bust of George Washington, and on the other, the bald eagle, wings outstretched. I thought of Carson and all she did not live to see, including the return of bald eagles in the sky over Silver Spring.

⁂

A WEEK AFTER I SAW that first bald eagle, a wet snow fell and dissolved on warm soil, leaving only an inch of white when the clouds passed. During the snowfall, I trekked down the same trail with my dog, who was more than happy to leave the confines of our house to go splashing in the creeks, unfazed by the temperature. All was quiet around us except the speckling snow, and in that silence, the seclusion and beauty of the river seemed especially prominent. To feel that you have intimate access to nature and to watch another creature so sincerely enjoy the freedom made possible by that access is exhilarating.

Before we turned home, I spotted the bald eagle with its mate, cresting over the swell of the river above the dam. Almost as soon as I had seen them, the birds disappeared through blinds of snow. Set against the silver-white of the landscape, the feature that appeared most striking was not their white heads but their brown-black bodies and wings, stretched four feet wide. From that moment, the bald eagle became for me the perfect national emblem, split by color but specified by its whiteness.

An integral part of being white in nature is the expectation that, once there, one can be freed of an awareness of one's racial identity and associated privileges. When I am in whatever I consider to be nature, I can entertain the fantasy that I have access to public land because of luck, not wealth; that my morality is constant, rather than wayward; and that in a fundamental way, I belong to nature and thus, nature belongs to me. When I am in nature, I can forget that I am white, and I simply become myself. It's an illusion, and a dangerous one at that, but it is also the wellspring of the white American relationship to land. That the mansion I encountered had shown me the limits of my privilege, and the Silver Spring suburbs had reflected the ugliness of that privilege back to me, was unsettling, hence my indignation.

I knew then I had a problem with expectations of what lands I had a right to access, but I confess I didn't think those expectations were completely flawed. Everyone should have the right to access nature and to feel the kind of unmitigated joy I had felt as my dog pulled me down the trail through the snow. I became curious about who actually had access to the region's parks, and whether that corresponded, as I reckoned it might, to residents of the city's white neighborhoods and suburbs. I was surprised to learn that in 2023, the Trust for Public Land named Washington, D.C., the number-one city in the country for parks and public lands. (Just across the Potomac, Arlington, Virginia, is the third city on the list.) Almost a quarter of D.C.'s total acreage is devoted to public lands, and 98 percent of D.C.'s residents live within a ten-minute walk of a park, a number that does not vary by more than one percentage point when residents are divided into racial categories.

Yet this data did not match my own experience of public parks in D.C. Zooming around an online map that showed in different gradients of green where parks are located and which neighborhoods are within walking distance, it became obvious how detached this data was from the reality of the city. Massive dark green swatches colored the portions of the map that represented Northwest, the wealthier white quadrant of the city, while in Southeast, where many neighborhoods remain working class and majority Black, the map was spotted with just a few small parks. Pale green blotches traced the sharp boundaries of Fourteenth Street, Georgia Avenue, and the Anacostia River—all familiar historic lines of racial segregation.

Undoubtedly, though, the starkest line on the map was Carson's beloved Rock Creek Park, which spread out like a split vein across almost two thousand acres of Northwest. To the west of Rock Creek, the map was verdant; to the east, noticeably less so. Established in 1890 as the nation's third national park, Rock Creek (or simply "the park" in local parlance) cut the city into two unequal halves. The timing of its creation by President Benjamin Harrison coincided with both a massive real estate boom in the capital and the nationwide entrenchment of Jim Crow. Many of the city's most familiar and beloved neighborhoods in Northwest, including Dupont Circle and Chevy Chase, were constructed around the turn of the century to attract white employees of the expanding federal government.

The developer of Chevy Chase, Nevada senator Francis G. Newlands, was explicit about using Rock Creek as a boundary to keep both Black and Jewish citizens on "the wrong side of the park," thereby "protect[ing] property holders against the encroachment of undesirable elements." With a white stranglehold on the neighborhoods surrounding the park, Rock Creek became, from its very establishment, a de facto white space; in the decades following, it became a de jure white space, with the National Park Service enforcing a strict ban on Black people using the park, which was not legally overturned until 1949. The final desegregation of the park was not enforced until the 1970s.

Now, decades after so many of the city's neighborhoods have shifted from all-white to all-Black to a modern mixed-race category of subtle segregation, Rock Creek Park remains one of the most fixed racial boundaries in the city. Today, D.C. residents still casually talk of living "east of the park" or "west of the park," without an understanding of how it was, and still is, used to bisect and segregate the capital. Although the act creating Rock Creek Park had decreed the lands to be "perpetually dedicated and set apart as a public park or pleasure ground for the benefit and enjoyment of the people of the United States," the park continues to serve its original implicit purpose: a boundary beyond which to place Black residents.

Returning to the park access map, I traced the meanders of Rock Creek from its outfall south of Silver Spring down to its confluence with the Potomac, then trailed the creek back upstream, each curve of the waterway slipping into the landscape alongside the affluent alcoves of Washington. The stone-cobbled, tony feel of upper Georgetown, the swanky, parvenu vibe of Kalorama, and the postbohemian splendor of Mount Pleasant each passed through my mind as I thought of all the walks I had taken down the trails that run through these neighborhoods. Our lived experience of public lands in the capital maintains the racist myth that nature exists only for white people. In this way, the line between city and nature has become concurrent with the color line, boundaries between democratic ideals and the practice of those ideals.

There is a photograph I return to now and then: Rachel Carson, in a long pleated skirt and smart blazer, sits on a lichen-dappled stone in Rock Creek Park, a book in one hand, a notebook open to a blank page beside her. She has binoculars around her neck and a scarf covering her tightly coiled hair. In the background is the creek, midsummer greens framing her as the water swirls onward to the Potomac. Taken in 1962 for a *Life* magazine story, the photograph is posed, her body language, conveying dutiful study and attention, obviously feigned.

But looking into her lined dark eyes, I cannot help but think how very natural she looks there, how at ease she seems by those waters, *these* waters, as if she knew, in a way beyond mere fact, that this land belonged to her. It's more than a comfort with place or affection for nature or her deep love for the world depicted in this photograph. I see, in the way Carson occupies a needle of sunlight and the way in which she leans forward to deliver an inscrutable stare, how her unconscious ownership of land might manifest in her own posture as a facet of her whiteness.

I return to this photograph because to me it is totemic, a reminder to ask myself whether it is possible to love and care for nature while knowing that your love, predicated on a certain exclusive intimacy, necessarily prevents others from access. How do I make sure my love for the world—its people, its rivers, its eagles—is not used to exclude and destroy? This is a question Carson cannot help me answer.

Months later, I was walking in the dusk-pink hours through Columbia Heights, a formerly majority Black and Latino neighborhood located "east of the park," an area that has been gentrified, though not completely. Making my way down the

Fourteenth Street strip, I happened to look up to the top of an old firehouse, and there I saw a bald eagle roosting on the roof-line like a gargoyle. I paused, almost disbelieving, and we held each other's eyes for seconds, long enough for me to become conscious of my own breath. A young man, laden down with plastic bags of groceries from the Giant, stopped next to me to stare up.

Soon enough, the eagle lifted off the building and away, heading south in the direction of the river. The man and I said nothing, but we smiled at each other. His face was a candid expression of utter joy. I turned away, filled with quiet awe both at the eagle and that man's smile. The bald eagle was there, and then it wasn't. The man was with me, a momentary "us," and then we weren't. Nothing belonged to me but the memory of the encounter.

I kept walking, past a *pupusería* and a storefront church, past the Target and Starbucks, the T-Mobile and the community health clinic, the women selling bagged mango slices from carts, the men hawking roses, the Trader Joe's, a West Elm, a wine bar. As I walked, I imagined I could feel the city cleave and break around me.

Ephemerals

By early February, the mouse-brown layer of leaf duff, once ironed out by the weight of winter snow, began to pucker and wrinkle. As plants split through their sheath of seed coat and silt, riffles and waves surfaced across the floodplain. A month later, the first seedlings pierced the roiling stretch of litter, then paused with a late cold snap, appearing to reconsider their plans. As the ephemerals poked and crept toward their bloom, I sensed a restlessness rippling along the river as my anticipation of spring swelled into a desperation for it.

Then there was a long rain and a few warm days, and the Potomac was a riot of color. Virginia bluebells burst forth in colors ranging from snow white to powder blue. Milk-white bloodroot unfurled from a single handlike leaf. Wild violets broke into a splash of purple blossoms, and trilliums tendered their single sanguine blooms.

Speaking to a friend from college, I compared the prismatic frenzy of colors and precipitous arrival of the season to the energy of a rave, and more specifically to the moment in electronic dance music when, after a period of rhythmic buildup and heart-pounding anticipation, the beat drops, the body jolts, and then all liquifies into phosphorescent waves of sound. Redbud trees went berserk with lurid blooms. Phlox congregated in stands of electric blues, whirling above the creamy buds of the delightfully named squirrel corn and Dutchman's-breeches.

As I walked along the river toward Scott's Run one morning, I wondered briefly whether I had been slipped a psychedelic with my coffee. The colors were so intense and multiple, the air hummed. Whatever invisible lines normally separated my sensory perception dissolved, and now I tasted green on my tongue—sharp, bitter, and alkaline.

As the ephemerals erupted in bloom, I met such a seeming infinity of new flora that I formed my own fictional genera to keep them all ordered in my mind. A group of plants I called "the dudes" carried men's names, like Solomon's seal and Jacob's ladder, Jack-in-the-pulpit and golden Alexanders. A crew of charlatans included false Solomon's seal and false indigo. The group of plants that I ironically dubbed "the grocery store" were the "wild" versions of produce, including wild strawberry, wild turnip, wild parsnip, and wild lettuce. I met heartleaf and twinleaf, pennywort and ragwort, dame's rocket and yellow rocket, and more oddballs than I knew what to do with. There was, honest to goodness, a plant out there named honesty, and clumps of humble bluets you could instead address as Quaker ladies. You could make lunch with butter and eggs toadflax, cheeseweed, and corn salad, or you could start up a petting zoo with pussytoes, coltsfoot, and cow vetch.

On every walk, even just to drop a letter in the mailbox or take out the dog, I saw from the corner of my eye some beguiling stranger crawling up the fence line or bursting forth at the edge of woods. If I went out for an hour-long walk, I was guaranteed to meet no fewer than ten new plants, and then after all those introductions, I would spend another hour at home investigating their names and families, favored homes and neighbors.

All this research led me to a number of pressing questions, which I experienced less as curiosities than as real exigencies: Why did wild blueberries seem to grow only under the shade of pine trees? How could there be this many prickly pears, a cactus I associated with the deserts of the Southwest, thriving in soggy Maryland? But the most urgent question of all: Why were all these different forms of life here, along the Potomac River, in Washington, D.C., of all places? How could this sprawling city with its scores of peopled suburbs also be a place with such a diversity of plant life that it had collapsed and melded my very senses?

This contradiction was rooted in something deeper than any erroneous expectation of where a city should be and where nature should be. It was more so that until the ephemeral bloom, my experience of living in D.C. had been defined by a profound sense of disorientation. I had spent my first winter dissecting every slicing line of segregation through the city in an attempt to understand where, exactly, it was I lived. Now I was at a loss as to how to reconcile a divided city made of boundaries and borders with the abundance and beauty of life that seemed to coalesce here in perfect accordance.

❊

ON A FLIGHT HOME from a cousin's wedding, the pilot overshot the descent into Reagan National Airport; perhaps we were forced to dawdle before the plane was allowed to land. Riding low over the river, we circled the airfield and the Washington Monument, then headed northwest, the Potomac growing thinner as we flew against the current. Fifteen miles and half a minute later, we cruised over an epic set of rapids. White water shot through the rocky gorge of Great Falls, and spectacular cliffs hung over the waterfalls, creating a craggy, almost alpine scene that brought to mind some place more akin to Yosemite than the nation's capital.

The pilot then turned us southeast, back in the direction of our destination, and I watched the river transform from frothing white to stone-studded green to a final muddy churn as we again passed over the airport without landing. A minute later, the Potomac had turned wide and flat, without so much as a pebble ruffling the surface. I saw George Washington's family home and slave-labor camp, Mount Vernon, resting alone on its pleasant hill, looming over the tidal water below.

Pressing my nose against layers of glass, I had watched the terrain shift from mountains to sea, the District a bridge between them. The pilot made one final turn and, our impromptu tour of the various geographies comprising the greater Washington, D.C., metropolitan area now complete, we finally landed, though I could have flown those thirty miles forever, watching the Potomac shrink and spread.

Disembarking, I caught a whiff of gasoline and salt, and I felt gripped with a desire to know every inch of every mile between the rugged drama of Great Falls and the seagull-studded beaches near Mount Vernon. I made a plan on the metro ride home: By walking as much of this concise stretch as I could, I would learn what was responsible for the abundance and diversity of the city's plant life.

That one prolonged touchdown had provided a ten-thousand-foot-high vantage on one aspect of the Potomac's varied ecology. The District is situated on the Atlantic Seaboard Fall Line, a strip of land that stretches from Tuscaloosa, Alabama, to Paterson, New Jersey. Here, the Piedmont plateau of hard, erosion-resistant rocks at the foot of the Appalachians meets the coastal plain of gravel, shells, and sand as rapids emerge among new snags of stone. The fall line on the Potomac is the stretch between Great Falls, where the escarpment begins to drop through a long ravine, and Washington, D.C., where it concludes in a still, salty expanse.

As the river descends through those fifteen miles that comprise the Potomac Gorge, its shifting geology creates a series of diverse and rare ecologies. The rock cliffs immediately south of the falls quickly give way to fluvial terraces, within which form a number of distinct habitats: vernal ponds that pool in potholes; arid, cactus-covered outcrops; riverside prairies of grasses rarely found outside the Midwest; and acidic, piney arbors enveloped by blueberries. Farther down the gorge, closer to Little Falls, these terraces break into eroded boulder fields, full of hydrophilic shrubs at the shore. As the Capitol dome comes into view, wetland star grasses and water lilies bloom. By the time you reach Mount Vernon, the river tosses full tidal, the smell of the air now a flood of brine.

For my first official Potomac walk, I clambered down the Potomac Heritage Trail south of Chain Bridge after a night of steady rain but found the path swallowed by the river, which had easily risen six feet over the past twelve hours. The angle of the bluff was too steep to forge my own path, so I returned home, but this failed first hike was a lesson in how the river's propensity to flood contributes to its expansive ecology. With its headwaters far in the reaches of the Appalachians, the Potomac carries seeds from mountain plants in its current. During extraordinary surges, the current can shoot over the edge of the eighty-foot-high gorge. Scouring the tops of the terraces, the river clogs old oxbows, rearranges soil, and deposits new seeds. As a result, the gorge is home to several dozen species of plants that are native to neither the piedmont nor the plain, but to the high mountains.

I pieced this together on a drier hike later that week up the same trail, where I found northern maidenhair ferns and black cohosh, two endangered plants that thrive in the mossy coves of the mountains. Farther up the path, I scratched at a sweet birch to release its wintergreen scent, before tripping over the rooted knees of a bald cypress. Located in the Mid-Atlantic, between the geographic South and North, the Potomac also crosses the divide between plants like sweet birch that flourish in the boreal forests of New England and those such as cypress, more likely to be found in the backwater sounds of the southern Sea Islands.

With species converging on the Potomac from every direction, the Washington-Baltimore area, which is defined as the fifty-mile radius around the nation's capital, is home to over 2,800 native plant species. That number is modest compared to the biodiversity hot spots of the Alabama coast or North Carolina's mountains, but compared to other major cities on the East Coast, D.C. is a veritable wonderland of plant life.

The Potomac itself is also a niche for rare plants. Across the three square miles that comprise the ribbon of land along the gorge, scientists have classified thirty-six plant communities, three of which are not found anywhere else in the world. Nearly three hundred plant species found here are listed as species of concern, and many of these are so rare to Maryland, Virginia, and the District that they are found only in the gorge, and even then, only on certain islands.

On the next Saturday evening, I left the house to wade out to Plummers Island, a twelve-acre whale-shaped rise in the river. Home to 885 native or naturalized plant species, a significant number considering its small size, the island thrummed with life. The plain, sandbars, and rocky rises above were all a billowing mass of color. More and more kinds of unusual plants flourished in the microcontact zones of this island where plant communities across the Mid-Atlantic met, creating an ecology not just more dense but more vibrant. As dusk descended, I watched a fox pup on the far side of the river sit down on a spit of rocks and close her eyes in a last slit of sun, tapping into some matrix of energy I could then only feel myself at the boundaries of.

Only later did I learn there is a word for those places where different energies meet and exchange across spaces of constant flow. Ecotones are transitional areas between ecosystems, distinctive in that they are richer in species than the habitats on either side, with overlapping forces combining to create a place more dynamic than those adjacent to it. In these ecotonal contact zones, diverse assemblages of species form outside their comfort zones, building an abrasive magnetism as life agitates and merges along the edges.

As I plodded on with my Potomac plan of daily walks, I began keeping a journal filled with lists of plants and plaintive ruminations on the pleasures of piecing together the landscape across ecotones. I reported on a Monday that while hiking through the boulder fields of Scott's Run, I ate an apple under an eastern hemlock, a tree far more common to the northern United States than to the southern piedmont. On Tuesday, I scrambled around the prairies and ponds of Bear Island, admiring the dryland little bluestem grass, which grew next to the lime-green spark of water-loving jewelweed. On Wednesday, as I listened to wood frogs croak in the pools of Roosevelt Island, I touched the sticky buds of a pinxter azalea, a species not unknown to the piedmont but more common to the Appalachians. On Thursday, I saw the first leaves of spatterdock, a creamy yellow water lily, in the mudflats near Roaches Run. And on Friday, I looked out my living room window and noticed for the first time just how many sugar maples there were on the hill, adding yet another more mountainous species to the botanical blend that constituted life here.

When I had thought of D.C. before I instituted my Potomac plan, I saw a map of the city grid in my mind, with certain streets rising like stark barricades. Now I sensed those lines going soft as ecotones blurred the borders. My daily walks had revealed that the place I lived was not quite the North and not quite the South, not quite the East and not quite the West. It was not quite the mountains, not quite the piedmont, and not quite the coast. It was all of these and none of these, and in this liminal space, there were bluffs and beaches, ponds and prairies, wooded floodplains and tidal marshes, freezing ravines and sunny shores. There were lines without borders, edges without corners, and in between was the capital city, teeming with six and a half million people stretched out across two states and the District, an immense mass of life, all of it humming, churning, and shifting.

❈

MY NONAGENARIAN LANDLADY, a woman well versed in the timeworn ways of Washington, informed me that I had a disease called "Potomac fever." "You will find that this city has ways of grabbing hold of you," she explained.

I googled *Potomac fever* when I returned home from drinking gin rickeys in her sitting room, and after scrolling through a number of entries on Potomac horse fever, a bacterial infection that causes equine colic and depression, I found what I thought she was referring to instead. Potomac fever is a condition endured, but not suffered, by bureaucrats who arrive in the city with the intention of staying just four years but instead find themselves lingering, drawn in by power and money, or else by the city itself. If you contract Potomac fever, the surest symptom is an obsession with Washington, D.C.

My landlady's diagnosis was confusing. I am not a bureaucrat, nor am I involved in the federal government in any way, and my partner and I had moved to D.C. with the intention of staying for a long time. Moreover, I did not feel so much drawn to the cosmopolitan swirl of the city as plagued by its paradoxes.

It is unclear when the term, at least as it is now used to describe federal appointees, first originated, but it owes something to George Washington, a man who became so obsessed with the Potomac River that he believed it was destined to be the center of the entire nation, if not, eventually, the entire world. Although he was born not far from the Potomac's tidal inlets, Washington's preoccupation with the river only began when he crossed the fall line for the first time in the late 1740s.

Tasked with surveying the colonial interior of what would become Virginia, West Virginia, Ohio, and Maryland, Washington scrambled over boulder fields and across the fluvial terraces of Great Falls, awed by the scene. The experience of seeing the weathered rapids and soft mountains of the upper Potomac after a lifetime spent in the Tidewater shifted something in him. Washington was no longer interested in the Potomac, which had previously been another line on an expanding map; he was now infatuated by it—its beauty, its wildness, and its potential. This was a river, he thought, that matched the spirit of America.

It was from these youthful upriver romps that Washington first identified a space of exchange in the landscape between the falls and the marshes, a place where all things, plants and animals and people, converged. The stretch between Great Falls and the Potomac's Eastern Branch (now the Anacostia River) was such a singular landscape that Washington never forgot it. Throughout the remainder of his career as a statesman, enslaver, and commander in chief, and despite extensive travel between the nation's cities and its backcountry, Washington held fast to his belief that there was no other river on the continent like the Potomac.

In the years immediately after the American Revolution,

as the nation undertook the task of figuring out what it would become, Washington transformed his memories of adolescent adventure into an ideology, based on his sense of the river's geographic destiny. The core tenet of his belief system was that the political and economic center of the nation should be located in the exact middle of the country, which Washington identified as the postfalls stretch of the river: "Potomac River then, is the centre of the Union," he proclaimed. "It is designated by law for the seat of Empire; and must, from its extensive course through a rich and populous country become, in time, the grand Emporium of North America."

Washington envisioned the Potomac as the foundation for a new American empire. The river would serve as the axis of democracy and economy, from which trade, industry, and slavery would spin outward in all directions. He would accomplish this by two means: developing a western trade route along the river and constructing a grand capital city on its banks. This twin doctrine became known informally as the Potomac plan.

Blinded by riparian monomania, Washington overlooked the considerable obstacles to inland navigation that the Potomac presented, including massive cataracts, irregular flow, and the unknown extent of what lay beyond its headwaters. At a time when all land beyond the fall line was considered the distant wilderness, the idea that the Potomac, rather than the larger Hudson or gentler James, would be the economic future of the nation was, to Washington's peers, not just eccentric but foolish. Nevertheless, Washington retained his faith in the Potomac and its fate to connect the capital city in the East to the yet uncolonized West.

Like most forms of zealotry, Washington's belief in the Potomac was partly motivated by fear. The nation he had just fought a war to create was prepared to splinter—either between the enslaving South and the quasi-free North or between the urban East and backcountry West. With the United States still then more an aspiration than reality, Washington sought in the Potomac not only a center for a united country but a way to "bind those people to us [in the West] by a chain which never can be broken."

As the first step in his Potomac plan, Washington chartered the Patowmack Company in 1785, following a long process of negotiations between Maryland and Virginia. Enslaved workers, artisan rock cutters, and mechanical engineers would spend the next twenty-five years hacking away at the sides of the gorge as they tried to build a canal that would fulfill Washington's dream to unite the country through trade. Traveling east across the Ohio Territory and through the Appalachians would come the resources of the interior: furs, timber, and perhaps even gold and silver. Traveling west from the capital up the banks of the river, filling in its fertile valleys, would spread agriculture, slavery, and commerce. The Potomac would hold these industries together, and in turn, those industries would form a unified nation.

The Compromise of 1790—a clandestine dinnertime deal between New Yorker Alexander Hamilton and Virginians Thomas Jefferson and James Madison—is usually identified as the single event in history that confirmed the capital's future location on the Potomac River. But the critical context surrounding that compromise is just how unremitting Washington had been over the last decade in his efforts to convince Jefferson, Madison, and anyone else who would listen to him to throw their support behind the Potomac plan.

And on July 9th, 1790, when Congress passed the Residence Act, his efforts paid off: The newly elected president, George Washington, was given the singular power and responsibility to select the exact location of the nation's capital. Though he entertained other possibilities, Washington had long known the approximate spot he would choose: ten square miles of land and water, just up from Mount Vernon and just south of the falls. I imagine, as he ordered the borders drawn and stone markers placed, he still believed the rest of the Potomac plan would fall into place.

Blasting through colossal rocks and navigating the turbulent rapids proved challenges to the progress of the Patowmack Canal, but Washington remained undeterred by the company's lack of initial success. The Potomac was the only route that could connect the nation. "There is such an intimate connection in political and pecuniary considerations between the federal district and inland navigation of the Potowmac, that no exertions, in my opinion, shou'd be dispensed with to accomplish the latter," Washington wrote in 1792.

In the last years of his life, beset by financial troubles at Mount Vernon and the setbacks of the canal, Washington became so obsessed with fixing forever the relationship between the Potomac and the rest of the nation that people around him began to describe his fanaticism not as a quaint quirk of the old general, but as a disease colloquially known to Virginia's elites as Potomac fever.

Washington did not live to see the failed outcome of the Potomac plan. The river itself ensured that the Patowmack Canal and its successor, the Chesapeake and Ohio Canal (C&O), would never be a thoroughfare to economic prosperity, let alone a route that would unify the nation. The Potomac flooded, mudded, and refused to be chiseled into tiny channels. The costs for company investors swelled into the millions as the years went on, and as those years turned into decades, railroads overtook canals as the vanguard of trade and transportation. By the time the entire canal had been completed in 1850, over sixty years after the first stones were blasted away at Great Falls, Americans had found other ways into and across the continent.

And as far as the capital city went, there were few Americans in the early nineteenth century who would have confused the mud-splattered, malaria-plagued outpost on the Potomac with a thriving commercial city. A stonemason hired to cut marble for the first federal buildings described the still speculative city as a project of Washington's ego, a place at "the mere whim of the President of the United States . . . as soon as he is defunct, the city, the boasted monument of his greatness, will also be the same." Abigail Adams described the fledgling cityscape more succinctly: "the very dirtiest Hole I ever saw." There was not much, at least in the built landscape, to suggest that the Potomac had intentionally been chosen by Washington as the place that would unify the nation. Perhaps only in spring, when the ephemerals bloomed and an indistinct feeling of connection saturated the landscape, could its residents recall Washington's lost dream for the Potomac as the spot on the map where everything came together.

✳

How, EXACTLY, DID WASHINGTON's peers diagnose the first known case of Potomac fever? Was it enough for the infected to speak incessantly of the river's unifying potential? What if you awoke every morning with a desperate need to see the object of your obsession and to walk along its banks? Were you sick if you dreamed of a vast alluvial fan covering the map of the city in your mind, a thin flood that brought all together in the water?

And what if that cover of unity cracked? Was it the river that infected you, or was it the silences around its story? How hard would you have to look at the past for your fever to break?

As I learned of Washington's goal of national unification through the failed Potomac plan, I was disturbed by the absences in the story. I sensed Washington's focus on the Potomac's uniting potential to be a distraction, if not an erasure. What, exactly, besides a river, was the nation destined to unify over?

Slavery so often exists in our telling of American history not as the ubiquitous societal force it was, but as a single distressing detail, creating a convenient distance between the atrocities of the past and our own enlightened times. In the nation Washington founded, the slave economy was so enmeshed in every facet of life that the presence of enslaved people was implicit in his proclamations that the Potomac and the nation shared a destiny. When Washington proclaimed that the river would, in his own words, "chain" the yet unexploited West to the open ports of the East, the textile factories of the North to the cotton fields of the South, he did not have to explain that an economic system built on the dehumanization of Black people wasn't just part of the Potomac plan; it was the Potomac plan.

And when that plan is viewed through the logic of national unity through chattel slavery, Washington's argument that the Potomac was the definite center of the nation quickly collapses. Frederick Douglass explained that the capital site had been chosen not because the Potomac was the geographic heart of the new republic, but because it was "sandwiched between two of the oldest slave states, each of which was a nursery and a hot-bed of slavery . . . [and] pervaded by the manners, morals, politics, and religion peculiar to a slaveholding community." As a result of their allegiance to the slave society, Douglass explained, "the inhabitants of the National Capital were, from first to last, frantically and fanatically sectional. It was southern in all its sympathies and national only in name." The idea that the Potomac was the midpoint of the nation had always been a convenient geographical lie, used to extend the power of southern enslavers in the creation of the United States and its capital.

By 1800, the year President John Adams moved into the White House, Washington, D.C., was not only the putative center of democracy but also a hub for the nation's booming southern slave trade. Even as the flood-prone Potomac impeded the westward expansion of trade up the canal, slaving ships carrying captured Africans regularly docked at the Potomac ports of Alexandria and Georgetown, both subsumed into the District by the Residence Act. After the international slave trade was abolished in 1808, the two towns became important domestic slave-trading centers because of their crossroads location between the worn-out tobacco lands of the Chesapeake and the fertile cotton fields of the lower South. The District, along with the rest of Virginia and Maryland, soon became what white supremacist Virginian Thomas Dew called "negro-raising states," engaged primarily in the trafficking of enslaved people, rather than in agriculture alone.

In the "Yellow House," a slave jail located just blocks away from the Capitol and made notorious in Solomon Northup's memoir *Twelve Years a Slave,* slave traders held captured Black people in jail cells before they were sold "down the river" (a phrase that usually refers not to the Potomac, but to the Ohio or the Mississippi). The landscape that would eventually become the National Mall was, as journalist Jesse Holland describes it in *Black Men Built the Capitol,* simply "the best place in town to sell slaves," and by 1840, there were over a dozen slave pens surrounding the structure that supposedly represented the idea that "all men are created equal."

The sight of coffles of enslaved people marching from the Potomac ports to slave pens across the front lawn of the Capitol offended several northern congressmen, who began agitating to end the domestic slave trade in the District. This effort was supported considerably by an increasing number of free Black citizens who had found their way to D.C. and begun the city's abolitionist movement. Southern congressmen, intent on maintaining Washington's status as a convenient center for the slave trade, countered by proposing retrocession, which would return the majority of the District (minus a few federal buildings) to the slave states of Maryland and Virginia.

The residents of Alexandria, a city that had relied on slave trafficking as a critical component of its economy for over a century, were particularly flustered by the prospect of the end to the capital slave trade and vigorously campaigned for Virginia retrocession. The federal government had yet to build on the southern side of the Potomac, Alexandrians argued. Why not return the Virginia portion of the District to the South so that Alexandrians could continue to reap the profits of selling people, and the rest of the District, on the north side of the Potomac, could keep up their moral pretenses?

In 1847, Congress relented and returned to Virginia thirty-one square miles of the original one-hundred-square-mile plot, drawn by Washington himself. While the sale of humans in the District eventually ended in 1850, just across the river slave ships arrived weekly until the end of the Civil War. And if an enslaver didn't want to take the five-minute boat ride across the Potomac, they could always force their slaves to walk a few miles into Maryland, where trading enslaved people was also still legal.

The presence of slavery in Washington, D.C., had the effect not of bringing together the nation along the Potomac, but of transforming the river into a border between places free and unfree. By the start of the Civil War, the notion that the Potomac might have served as a unifying, even federating, landscape had been long forgotten. The river had instead been recast into a hard line between the illusion of freedom represented by the capital and the rest of the vast slave society that surrounded it.

If George Washington was the first fatality of Potomac fever, then I understood my own diagnosis to be, if not quite an indictment, then certainly troubling. It had become impossible for me to spin the ecotonal energies of the Potomac into any illusion that D.C. was a place of natural coalescence. The conflux of the biodiverse landscape of the Potomac with the nation's capital was not a geographical coincidence, I realized, but one inevitable outcome of a plan rooted in brutal violence. My daily walks, which I had instituted as part of my own Potomac plan, had been not only a way to learn the local ecology but also a latent personal, and certainly impossible, effort to repair a landscape severed by the legacy of slavery.

❖

AFTER A WEEK OF WARM, almost sultry weather, the bluebells that had lit up the woods on the other side of my study window disappeared. The bloodroot flowers had faltered, and even the violets were beginning to fade. I was so unwilling to say goodbye to the ephemerals that I decided to drive an hour north up the river to Harpers Ferry, West Virginia, in hopes of outrunning the end of the season at the edge of the mountains. I was unable to admit to myself how desperate I was to catch a last high of ephemeral euphoria and the warm feelings of ecotonal convergence.

Walking toward the mist-shrouded confluence of the Shenandoah and Potomac Rivers in Harpers Ferry, I found a few ephemeral stragglers, but not many: a handful of trilliums that hadn't yet molded into the ground and a stand of squirrel corn going brown about the edges. By the old train station, the

box elders had leafed out, and even the slow-sprouting sycamores were budding.

When I reached the Point, a small peninsula that extends
between the two rivers, I paused to look out around the hills
surrounding the town, my eyes resting on land that belonged
to Maryland, then to Virginia, while I stood in West Virginia,
a state that seceded from Virginia in 1861 rather than remain
in the Confederacy. Preserved largely as it existed in the mid-
nineteenth century, Harpers Ferry is today a motley tourist
trap for all manner of backpackers, tubers, and bird-watchers.
A historic park, which tells the history of Harpers Ferry's role
in everything from the coal industry to Black higher education
and celebrates the legacy of everyone from Stonewall Jackson to
W. E. B. Du Bois, occupies the majority of the town. Every ten
feet, a placard, sign, banner, monument, or fluttering pamphlet
alerts you to some fact of the town's bizarre blend of histories.

John Brown, a white abolitionist and revolutionary, arrived
here in 1859 to lead a national movement of self-emancipation.
(Enslavers would have called it a slave rebellion.) With a twenty-
one-strong biracial "army of liberation," Brown seized the federal armory to arm enslaved people, who he believed would rise
up behind him and fight for their own freedom. After two days,
during which enslaved people from the surrounding farms
failed to join his revolt, the U.S. Marines, headed by future
Confederate general Robert E. Lee, stormed the armory and
captured Brown, who was quickly tried and hanged for treason.

Brown's raid was short, a blip in the town's history, but its
significance to the nation is indisputable. The raid at Harpers
Ferry struck a chord of terror in the hearts of southerners and
renewed the urgency of abolition for northerners, culminat-
ing in the start of the Civil War a year and a half later. Before
Harpers Ferry, most Americans believed the widening division

between North and South would eventually coalesce into compromise. After it, the schism was revealed to be a vast chasm that, apparently, only war could bridge.

Approaching the former armory, now called John Brown's Fort, I thought how well the landscape of Harpers Ferry reflected Brown's plan. At the meeting of the Shenandoah, along which the rest of the South lay, and the Potomac, which led in one direction up to the Allegheny Mountains and in another to Washington, D.C., Brown imagined a revolution of armed slaves and their white advocates pressing their battle for freedom forward in three directions: first, to the south to liberate the millions of people enslaved beyond the Blue Ridge; then to the north and up the Alleghenies, where legions of self-emancipated people would find freedom in the lands across the Potomac; then eventually to the east to exert political pressure on the capital city, where freedom for all would finally be enshrined. For this plan, the Potomac was exactly the right place.

As I walked west, staring across the rocky stretch of the river to the remains of the C&O Canal, I thought how Washington's Potomac plan to unify the nation over slavery had, in a way, led to Brown's Potomac plan to break the nation over slavery. By inciting a rebellion of self-emancipation, Brown's goal had been to rupture the complacency of white Americans, smashing to smithereens the slave society they relied on for their economy and comforts. The Potomac was the setting for this plan, but it was also the tool, a place in which the inherent convergences of people and energies could activate the broad redistribution of power across the entire country. By cracking the country at Harpers Ferry, Brown transformed the Potomac into the nation's fault line.

Perhaps, then, the river as a line of national fracture was not such a terrible thing. I had imagined the Potomac to be a lodestone, drawing to itself by force of nature all diversity of people and plants. But it was also a line in the sand across which a nation steeped in slavery could go no farther. There was no need to reconcile the two.

I felt compelled then to cross to the other side, as though in crossing I myself might serve as a bridge across difference. The temperature of the water made this an impossible undertaking, but the current was such that I could hop across a short channel to Byrnes Island. I struggled up the slick embankment, but when I reached the hilltop and looked up, I saw that the island was covered in a multicolored haze of late-blooming ephemerals.

Here, where the nation broke in half over slavery, I felt an all-consuming connection with the Potomac at the same time that I was overcome by the inexorable rending of history. The air vibrated with tension as these two sensations—one of coalition and one of division—rose from the river as materially as mist. I sat for a long while on that island, letting my senses gather and meld, then rend and divide. I could not tell whether my fever had broken or whether a sickness had just begun.

Ramps

THERE IS A SOGGY SPOT OF SOIL on the trail near Little Falls, made soft by an underground rill flowing close to the surface. A haphazard mesh of bark and branches lies over this stretch, which allows hikers to pass through without sinking into the mud. Skunk cabbage reigns in the shade, and elder hovers over the clutter. For most of the year, even into the freeze of winter, this plot has an earthy scent, loamy with the funk of fertility and decay. But for two weeks in April, it smells different. The scent is piquant, and there's a sharpness, even spiciness to the air.

Thrusting up through the leaf litter are the reeking culprits: ramps. Blooming from a slim bulb, ramps (or wild leeks) poke through the forest floor as petite purple shoots. Within a week, they split their casing into two green leaves, their oniony aroma wafting through the floodplain. A month after their advent, they loll about like long tongues, their stench intoxicating.

It's not just the smell of this plant that entrances but also the taste, stirring the blood with its vernal tang. I first tasted ramps when a colleague picked a bag of leaves from their family's farm in western North Carolina, then carried them hundreds of miles east to share with their office mates in the rampless piedmont. I remember the shock of flavor, the certainty that I was tasting spring in Appalachia distilled to perfection.

Sprawling across forested ravines, ramps shelter under sycamores, among other ephemerals like bluebells and bloodroot.

Within this intimate woodland community, ramps play a critical role in the mineralization of the shared forest soil. During the very early spring, a time when most trees still remain dormant and few other understory herbs have begun to grow, ramps conduct a temporary uptake of nitrogen, which prevents mineral leaching. As the season progresses, ramps release stored nitrogen back into the soil for use by other plants, their role as so-called nitrogen sinks complete. It is not figurative to say that a ramp leaf contains the life of every other plant in its community; in this very literal way, ramps embody interdependence.

Slow to mature—perhaps as an antidote to the hastiness of the ephemeral season—ramps can take a decade to set out enough seed to be considered fully grown. A subsequent decade will need to pass before a full ramp stand of a dozen or more plants is established. Digging up a ramp by its roots kills the plant and slows the growth of the entire stand; fewer ramps mean fewer seeds, which take years to germinate. During that time, the remaining ramps in a stand might be dug up, their postage stamp of soil overtaken by some other plant, rendering return all but impossible. Because ramps play an essential role in the yearlong health of their communities, the stakes of displacing them could not be higher.

I made my way down the trail toward a dry run, making note of which stands off-trail looked particularly abundant to pick from. I was about to curve down the hill to reach the run when a man, older and bearded, appeared, carrying two weighted-down grocery bags. I recognized the hairy rootlets extending from bone-white bulbs at the rim of his bags, and felt a surge of unexpected anger.

"What are those?" I asked, wanting to draw this man into some kind of conversation, if not confrontation.

"They're wild leeks," the man replied cheerfully. "Have a

great hike." He nodded as he passed, leaving the air behind him scented with onions and me stunned. This man had just decimated an entire ramp stand.

Though they grow alongside other delicious, plentiful spring greens, ramps are prized among chefs for their vibrant, versatile taste. Ripped up by their roots, ramps are a precious and expensive delicacy for home cooks, as well. A bundle of just six plants easily costs twenty dollars at D.C.'s high-end Dupont Circle farmers' market. I watched the man lumber down the trail, carrying enough ramps to earn him over a thousand dollars at market.

When people forage for ramps, they hunt *le goût de terroir,* or the taste of a place. The *terroir* of a certain food or wine evokes not only the sensory evidence of the plants, soil, and climate of the region from which a dish or vintage hails but also the cultural knowledge of that food or bottle, passed down through generations. Though their range across the continent was once quite wide, today ramps are most commonly found in a specific stretch of wet, mountainous geography between north Georgia and southern Maine, an area roughly concurrent with the Appalachians and the riverbanks that flow out from their folds.

In the mountains, a region still coded in the minds of many Americans as a wilderness, there is a long tradition of digging ramps and going "dry-land fishing" for morel mushrooms, which pop up at the same time each spring. Many folks from the mountains know where and in which valleys and southern slopes to dig and fish, and their local knowledge of place informs the cultural association of ramps with a kind of wild *terroir.*

For urbanites up and down the East Coast, ramps have thus become the most local of all local foods and the wildest of all wild foods. Once associated with the make-do dishes that defined Appalachian cuisine, ramps have been vaulted from the dinner plates of poverty and necessity to become one of the most popular ingredients a chef can use to reflect their commitment to locally sourced foods. Valued as a virtue signal of agrarian rural ethics as much as for their distinctive taste, ramps have taken on a certain tokenized status in the world of fine dining.

It may seem counterintuitive, then, to see ramps on the menu of restaurants in places as far-flung as Los Angeles and San Francisco, where chefs have been known to import ramps from as far away as West Virginia. But as scholar Gina Rae La Cerva explains in *Feasting Wild,* "weeds have become a delicacy only in the context of wealth, a luxury because access is limited. This is a meal for those most benefiting from the economic and social structures of modern-day capitalism, itself responsible for the vast destruction of species and ecosystems. Having consumed everything else civilization has to offer, we fetishize the wild because, in many ways, it no longer exists." In this way, ramps offer the ability to eat not just a plant but a place.

To forage for ramps, then, is to eat oneself into an imagined culture of what is natural and wild. When city dwellers head to the hills to dig ramps, we fantasize ourselves into spaces of local, tight-knit community and idyllic nature, grubbing in the dirt after a sense of place that gratifies our hunger to belong without our having to take responsibility for the living things that have made the place we are consuming. But as we dig, we eat ourselves into the ground, destroying the places where we long to belong.

Though I had learned not to dig up the plant by the roots, I had no idea who else might be digging in the same patches I planned to pick leaves from, and I wondered if I should pick them at all. Maybe I should have just gone home then. But the scent caught me again, and instead of letting guilt or hunger sway me, I decided to ask the ramps.

⁂

THE WEEK BEFORE, I HAD BEEN OUT on the trail with a friend to ogle over the last ephemerals. As we walked, we gathered garlic mustard, an enterprising plant that often moves into the soil left when ramps have been dug up. My friend asked how I became interested in wild foods. Was it something I had grown up doing in North Carolina? I told her no, that aside from picking honeysuckle and a few wild berries, foraging was something I had only become interested in since moving to D.C., where the whole landscape around me appeared to be edible.

As I pushed my way to the ramp patch, the yellow blossoms of spicebush dropping onto my shoulders, I knew I had lied to my friend by omission. I had become interested in wild foods after I moved to D.C. because I was hungrier than I had ever been in my life—and not just for food. During my first ephemeral season, I had become captivated by the Potomac's plant life, but I still found the landscape confusing and the climate vexing. A creek could be both full of massive sharp rocks and quicksand silt. Late April could be stifling or there could be an ice storm.

I had also come to resent D.C. as a sprawling megalopolis of national government and global capitalism that nevertheless felt stiflingly small. The city's inconsistent size seemed underscored by the fact that there were only so many roads into it; at the end of my life, as I stood at the pearly gates and my days and works were tallied, would I be reminded that I had spent three years of my life stuck in traffic trying to cross the Fourteenth Street Bridge? With a horizon that notably lacked smokestacks or skyscrapers, the city didn't seem like a city at all, but rather like a series of neighborly villages gathered around a federally occupied front lawn. People grew fig trees and vegetables in their front yards and out in the alleys, sights that both warmed my heart and reinforced my belief that D.C. had an ironically provincial edge that rendered it almost boondocky.

It seemed I was constantly running into academic acquaintances in coffee shops all over the city and on the trails of Rock Creek Park, lending the city a chummy, and at times claustrophobic, atmosphere. Though I was living in one of America's largest metropolitan areas, it often felt smaller than the tiny college town I had just moved from. Still, I thought constantly of the community I had been a part of in North Carolina, and how much I had relied on my relationships with friends and colleagues to help me make sense of that particular place. Since I knew only a few people in D.C., I was adrift, longing for connection.

Then I smelled them—pungent but not overpowering, decidedly leeklike. I followed my nose to a patch of ramps, which resembled the plant my colleague had once brought into our office. I took a photograph and went home to verify my identification. When I had decided that, yes, I had indeed found ramps, I hurried back to that spot on the trail and dug a filthy fistful. (I didn't know the sustainable way to harvest ramps at the time.) Back at home, I pickled the bulbs and fried the leaves, and by the time I had done that, I wanted to eat every single green thing growing outside my living room window.

I began with what was right outside my front door: dandelion, violet, chickweed, and purple dead nettle, four common lawn "weeds," spring tonics full of vitamins and minerals, that are also, respectively, bitter, soapy, grassy, and hairy. When I had learned how to cook each of these plants beyond palatability, I slid on my garden gloves to harvest stinging nettles. Despite my attempt at defense, the toothed leaves stung my wrists, raising welts across my arms. It hurt as badly as any burn I had received from cooking, and I plunged my arms into the river. When I pulled them out of the chilly water, the lines across my wrists gently pricked, as if the nettles had tattooed themselves onto me. After I learned how to harvest nettles properly (always wear long sleeves), my partner and I stuffed ourselves with them: risottos, raviolis, frittatas, and far too many soups.

Can one claim to have followed one's nose into a mania? I ate cattail catkins like corn on the cob, butter dripping from the sides of my mouth. I made lilac honey, cherry-blossom sugar, forsythia syrup, and wisteria sorbet, enraptured by the balmy, aromatic flavors of edible flowers. I stir-fried daylily shoots with soy sauce and chili crisp and ate them with fried rice, each grain glistening with red oil in lurid contrast to green leaves. I sautéed Japanese knotweed shoots in ghee and served them on toast with a poached egg.

These were the epicurean meals. There were far more bitter pestos and grassy salads than I care to admit, but I was learning, reading field guides and scouring cookbooks for new recipes. As my confidence in identifying and preparing wild foods grew, I asked those few acquaintances I did have to come to dinner, to bring their partners and friends, and my partner did the same. A good way to make a new friend, I learned, is to feed them weeds for dinner and flowers for dessert.

One night, an evening breeze blew up the ridge and sent smoke into the eyes of all ten of us seated around the fire pit in our yard, starting up a fit of coughs and laughter. We had spoken over dinner of how we had all come to live in D.C., a few of us locals, most of us newcomers, and now we asked one another what it was to feel that you were a part of a community. As we rethreaded the strands of our conversation, I looked around at the faces of these people becoming my friends, then down at my feet in the grass. Community is such an ethereal thing, I thought, and even though the memory of this night is a happy one, I remember I had little to contribute to what was otherwise a deeply considered conversation. Foraging had led me into a new affinity with the plants and place around me, and now, too, I was building new human relationships. But I could not, as many of my friends said they could, claim D.C. as the place where I felt I belonged.

On a muggy, miserable afternoon not long after, I went out to harvest stinging nettles. As I bent to snip off one of the stringy tops, a nettle plant reached out and bit me. I had forgotten to wear long sleeves, and I winced in pain before returning to my task. I had taken only a few limp tops when I was stung again, even sharper than before. It hurt as much as the worst bee sting, and I cried out, "Why are you doing this to me?" I looked over the whole patch, which I only now noticed had set seed and were past their prime, and I swear, these plants said back to me, *Why are you doing this to us?* I took their point and went home.

In her essay "The Serviceberry," Potawatomi botanist and scholar Robin Wall Kimmerer writes, "To name the world as gift is to feel one's membership in the web of reciprocity. It makes you happy—and it makes you accountable. Conceiving of something as a gift changes your relationship to it in a profound way, even though the physical makeup of the 'thing' has not changed." The plants I foraged fed me and my partner, gave me an undue amount of pleasure as I worked them into delicacies, and even aided in forging new friendships. At their essence, though, wild foods were to me then wild-sourced commodities, vegetal material for consumption. To the degree I could claim any meaningful relationship to these plants, it was one based on my own desperation for connection, never on what might be required of me in return.

I was slowly learning the tenets of what Kimmerer has termed the *Honorable Harvest,* a set of ethical guidelines for foraging, and also for belonging to a place. When I went out to gather wild foods, I began, at Kimmerer's suggestion, by asking permission of the plants I harvested, self-consciously at first, then with ease, as though I was simply talking with a friend: *How are you doing? Can I take home a few blossoms? Would that be okay?* I almost always received a yes from these plants, though I confirmed their affirmations by studying what other plants or animals they were in community with and how their presence or absence might affect their surroundings. This act of basic ecological observation made me feel accountable not just to a particular plant but to the place in which we both lived.

Kneeling now at the edge of a lush stand of ramps, I touched their curving leaves. I thought of the first time I had harvested this plant, how insatiable my desire was for the ramps. I remembered the sight of my fingernails stained black with humus from clawing into the soil. Why was I still harvesting this plant at all? For everything I had learned about foraging ethically, for every species I had learned the name and relations of, it was still difficult at times for me to hold myself accountable to this place. My hunger to belong, it seemed, could still get the best of me.

⚙

I HAD BECOME ENOUGH of an evangelical about wild foods that my family had taken notice, and for my birthday, I received a gift certificate to eat at a Michelin-starred restaurant in D.C.'s Shaw neighborhood that specialized in foraged Mid-Atlantic cuisine. I made a reservation several weeks in advance, and as my partner and I walked to the restaurant, we admired the last of the saucer magnolias that seemed to decorate the entire city in April, and stopped to people-watch as we passed the many bustling outdoor bars of the neighborhood.

Shaw was ground zero in the city's urban renewal efforts in the 1990s and the gentrification boom of the 2000s. Emerging after the Civil War from encampments of formerly enslaved people, Shaw was the center of D.C.'s Black cultural, social, and economic life in the early twentieth century. Langston Hughes, Carter Woodson, Alain Locke, and Duke Ellington all once made their homes here, but decades of municipal disinvestment after the 1968 uprisings sent the neighborhood's population and resources plummeting. Like so many D.C. neighborhoods, Shaw was a Black-majority and working-class neighborhood until white people came to covet this community's stately Victorians and convenience to downtown. Multimillion-dollar redevelopment projects followed. By 2010, the Black population of Shaw had fallen to 30 percent, a dramatic decrease from 80 percent in 1980.

The restaurant was tucked into the back corner of Blagden Alley, a series of cobblestoned side streets behind the lines of elegant row houses on the main street. A century ago, Blagden largely housed Black workers, who either labored in the homes of their wealthier Black neighbors on the main street or operated liveries, carriage workshops, and illegal distilleries located in the alley. By the 1930s, Blagden had developed enough of a hard-knock reputation that First Lady Eleanor Roosevelt referred to the enclave as "the most despicable in the country," expressing her disgust with the bootlegging, prostitution, and poverty. Through the late twentieth century, Blagden was notorious as a haven for drugs and muggers, known to some residents as the city's "most infamous backstreet."

Like the rest of Shaw, gentrification swept Blagden Alley clean of crime, but this nook of bars and restaurants has retained an aesthetic association with its history. Except for the interiors of the retail shops it contains, of course, Blagden has stayed much the same as I imagine it was before urban renewal, just a little spiffier. Entering the alley, the warmth of early evening disappeared as the brick walls blocked the sun, and we marveled at the many striking murals and people taking photographs in front of them. Turning the corner toward the restaurant, the air smelled of herby hops and burning cedar.

We checked in and were seated at our table, a dark wood two-top close to a central stone cooking fireplace. In front of the hearth, which warmed the room like one too many cocktails in the company of old friends, half a dozen white cooks chopped and stirred and seared, pushing cast-iron pans of fish and greens in and out of the fire. It was a midsize restaurant that felt as though all sixty or so patrons, the vast majority of us white, were in a cozy hand-hewn cabin, awaiting the cook's return from the river with a catch of rockfish and a basket of sochan for our dinner.

Gentrification eases into modern cities in a way that often appears inevitable. Within this logic of predetermination, there is something that feels natural and irresistible to liberal white people about Black community; they will do what they can to live in proximity to a sense of authenticity, grit, and coolness that they associate with Black culture. Over the last two decades, tens of thousands of young and progressive non-Black people have moved to D.C., seeking a diverse living experience, which they believe will lead to an increase in their quality of living and feeling of belonging. In neighborhoods like Shaw and H Street, and even into Anacostia and Barry Farm, non-Black people have moved into Black communities in search of not just lower rents or proximity to their workplaces but also cultural markers of place: the famous soul food restaurant, the record store with the great Motown selection, the gritty back alley filled with Instagram-ready murals. These commodities are not always what drives the initial wave of gentrifiers, but it is what keeps them there and keeps them coming.

Creating and confirming the consumption requirements of new white residents are a whole host of commercial enterprises that use aesthetic and cultural markers of Blackness—edginess and tempered exoticism mixed with a communitylike feel—as a proxy to convey a diverse living environment. With millions in investment capital, a deliberate commercial ecology of speakeasy bars, jazz clubs, Eastern-inflected wellness spaces, and local eateries have proliferated in these neighborhoods, trafficking in the illusion of authentic placefulness.

In this way, D.C.'s small-town sense of place, which has largely been created and determined by Black residents who have made their homes here, is now up for sale. Gentrifiers' search for diverse, placeful living environments perversely contorts Blackness away from Black people and places, turning Blackness into a stimulating consumer good that stands in contrast to the austerity of white-collar jobs that brings many newcomers to D.C. in the first place. White people have learned to see themselves as individuals distinct from cultural movements, as people who just want walkable, diverse neighborhoods with beer gardens, instead of seeing themselves as the producers and proliferators of Black displacement.

In her book *Black in Place: The Spatial Aesthetics of Race in a Post-Chocolate City,* geographer Brandi Thompson Summers discusses this phenomenon as it plays out in D.C.'s H Street Corridor, not too far from Shaw. She describes how white newcomers and business owners justify their role in gentrification by referring to the "diverse" racial demographics in the distant nineteenth-century past of the neighborhood, before housing covenants and white flight in the twentieth century chopped the city into pieces. By connecting the neighborhood's racially diverse past with its socially segregated present, newcomers steep their own emplaced existence in nostalgia, obscuring the history of the recent Black-majority past of the neighborhood and the racial discrimination that Black residents of D.C. have always faced, even (and perhaps especially) in mixed-race living environments.

Though the consumerist and even emotional demands of white people may appear to direct many aspects of Black displacement, less acknowledged are the policies that make their roles as hungry gentrifiers possible: privatization of public spaces, unequal access to local and federal subsidy support for Black-owned businesses, the criminalization of Black movement in public space, decades of racist municipal and federal policies across the D.C. metropolitan area, and massive amounts of capital utilized by suburban communities to maintain white flight–era exclusionary tactics. Gentrification is not a simple closed-loop system of white appetite for diversity and correlative Black displacement that happens within one neighborhood; it is a regional ecosystem of intersecting policies, histories, and displacements across multiple communities.

Nevertheless, gentrification is experienced as a block-by-block phenomenon, where what makes a block or an alley distinct and place-specific is offered up to people who are willing to pay the high prices that a local sense of place demands in a national and, increasingly, global market. This situation is heightened by D.C.'s small-town feel, which further drives the demand for housing in certain neighborhoods that have been culturally designated as hyperlocal and community-oriented. It is one of many painful paradoxes of the city: As white gentrifiers move into Black neighborhoods, searching for a sense of place, many Black residents no longer belong on the blocks that were once their beloved communities.

Back at the restaurant, pickled ramp bulbs were on the menu, served with soft-shell crab and spring peas. It sounded exquisite, but we decided to skip this for a locally sourced meal of slow-roasted meat and corn bread with sorghum butter. As we ate facing the hearth, I thought of the late and onetime D.C.-based chef Edna Lewis. In her classic 1976 cookbook, *The Taste of Country Cooking,* Lewis describes in loving detail how in the Mid-Atlantic Black community of Freetown, Virginia, where she grew up, foraging was made possible by "the bounty yielded up by the woods, fields, and streams." At the restaurant on Blagden Alley where we ate dinner that evening, those same foraged, freely given ingredients from the woods and streams had been incorporated into a cuisine that white people could lift up as Mid-Atlantic *terroir* and charge almost two hundred dollars a person for it, prix fixe, exclusive of the wine pairing.

We may not have ordered the ramps, but by entering Blagden Alley we consumed that place as if we had. As I finished the last glug of a Virginia red, I thought that this was not at all unlike the way in which digging for ramps could gratify our hunger to belong while simultaneously destroying the community we sought to belong to. The food settled into my stomach like stones.

⚒

AFTER LEAVING THE RESTAURANT, we wandered. Too cheap to stop in anywhere for an after-dinner drink but too worked up to go home, we snaked through Shaw, went up Eleventh Street, then back down Thirteenth into Logan Circle. Past O Street, I realized we were on the same block that my grandfather had lived on in 1940, and we paused for a minute to stare up at what once had been a boardinghouse and was now an aging condominium complex.

Years ago, I had researched and mapped out where my grandfather Elmer lived during the ten years he spent in D.C., before he packed up and returned home to Nash County, North Carolina. Most of what I know about how Elmer spent his twenties he wrote on the back of a photograph of himself walking down some city street, his hat askew: "I left Washington DC May 1940 after being there since about 1930–31. I worked fast food, also Child's Restaurant which was a very nice place to eat—lousy place to work and then a chain of food service (all paid 10–12 cents per hour 12 hrs per day—6 days each week). Traveled 20 miles by st. car to work—same back home. I worked Life Ins. sales last few years. I had enough—I came back home."

Only during his last year in D.C. did Elmer make enough money to live in Logan Circle, what was then the inner part of the city. For most of his time here, he lived on the eastern outskirts of the District, first in Fort Lincoln and later in Kingman Park, neighborhoods that were small, sparsely populated, and rural. To live there was to live out in the country, an option that might have been more appealing—and certainly more affordable—to the southern newcomers pouring into the city in search of what was then called a "'GGJ,' a good government job." I would like to think that Elmer moved to these areas not just because they were inexpensive but also because they offered him some semblance of the small-town life he had left behind. He was always a farmer at heart; I can easily imagine him mounding sweet potatoes and planting beans in the corner of his landlord's lot off Benning Road.

When Elmer moved into these communities, he was poor and young, living primarily among working- and middle-class Black families, many of whom, like him, were from little hamlets—what are now called "one-stoplight towns"—across eastern North Carolina. I can't know how he felt about this—my grandfather is long gone. Segregation in rural areas was not as strictly enforced as it was in the inner city, and it may not have been unusual for a single working-class white man to rent out a room from a middle-class Black family, especially if they were from the same county back home.

Gentrification was not a word, nor even a concept, when my grandfather lived here. But from my view of twenty-first-century Thirteenth Street, I wonder if he ever understood himself to be a kind of interloper, not only as a white man living among Black neighbors but because he was conscious of the fact that D.C. would never be his home in the way it would become theirs. While I can envision Elmer planting collards, I cannot imagine him digging a hole for a fig tree, knowing he would not be there long enough to harvest the fruit.

Staring up at the condos, I thought of those last words on the back of Elmer's photograph, which I had long ago memorized: "I had enough—I came back home." Perhaps it was the poor pay or the long streetcar rides that made D.C. into a place where my grandfather never felt he belonged. Or was he frustrated by living in neighborhoods where some Black people had jobs that paid more than his own?

My grandfather had the privilege of going back home; most Black North Carolinians who moved to D.C. during the same time period never returned permanently. As a result, many Black neighborhoods—at least the ones not completely gentrified—still have a certain cultural slant toward the small towns of eastern North Carolina. Isabel Wilkerson, author of *The Warmth of Other Suns,* remembers that during her childhood in the 1950s in the Petworth neighborhood she was "surrounded by people who were from all parts of the South. It became essentially North Carolina and South Carolina in Washington, D.C." Census records from the 1920s and 1930s reflect this; for whole blocks of the city, particularly in Northeast and Southeast, the place of birth listed for every resident is North or South Carolina.

Heading north back to U Street, we passed a carryout spot I had been to once before, and I remembered, as the smell of oil hit us, the way they made their collards there with a kick of spice. It reminded me of the collards you might find at the kind of barbecue places that I had been going to my whole life while visiting family in Rocky Mount and Wilson, North Carolina. Food was one of the closest and perhaps only ways in which a white newcomer like myself might be able to access these traces of Black North Carolina that were all over the city. If we had wanted a taste of local *terroir,* we ought to have eaten here instead.

Black southerners came to D.C. not only for greater economic opportunity, as my own grandfather did, but to escape the violence that threatened them with an unsparing constancy. To live in the South was to "sleep over a volcano, which may erupt at any moment," a woman named Laura Arnold said weeks before she left North Carolina for D.C. in 1901. For many Black migrants, Washington represented a new form of freedom: the right to live free from white terrorism. Many hoped that in the capital, the place where equal treatment under the law had been enshrined in doctrine, they would find a safe and permanent home. Once in D.C., they found that the city provided only the pretense of safety; the menace of white violence and discrimination would never completely abate.

I am a white southerner, descended from ten or more generations of the same; I have long known that my ancestors include enslavers and Klansmen. And so it is likely, almost guaranteed, that my relatives are the reason so many Black North Carolinians left the only homes they had known for this strange city and the false promises of true freedom it held. White southerners' overt violence against their Black neighbors created the conditions for one kind of displacement, what we now call, perhaps too innocently, the Great Migration; but what of the kind of slow violence that was, and is, gentrification? What will we call this era marked by the mass exodus of Black residents from D.C.?

Perhaps my initial discomfort with D.C.'s small-town sense of place, then, had to do with how, in my desire to belong to this city, I had attempted to deflect my own feelings of accountability to this long and knotted history of white violence and Black displacement. If you want the place you live to be the place where you belong, you have to become accountable to it and to all of your neighbors. This is the core of reciprocity. But can we ever be accountable enough to one another to build a culture of belonging to this and every place together, or will our own desperate hunger to belong keep us apart and lead to our eventual destruction?

In midsummer, the ramps bloom, sending out a white inflorescence that looks like a sparkler. Each pearled flower opens to reveal a tiny black seed. Eventually, these seeds will drop or get carried away by the wind, and when they do make it into the soil, they sometimes rest for two years before germinating. The gift I give to the ramps is the gift I am still searching for myself: a place to belong. I wander around the plain, gathering seeds into my hand and carrying them to places along the trail where, after watching the river for so many seasons, I know there are no more ramps.

It's a modest act, wild-tending the stretch of the river I know best, and it will take many years to reveal whether my efforts have had an effect. But it is a way I show these plants my gratitude for the lesson they are still teaching me: Reciprocity builds accountability, accountability promotes care, care engenders community, and community can make a home. As I push these seeds into the soil, I imagine that I am not only planting ramps but creating a place of belonging.

Anacostia

I WAS FOUR MILES NORTH of the Capitol Building, but I might have been deep in a desert or out on an ice-caked sea. I heard no whip of cars on the highway, no metro rattle, no lilt of spring birdsong. There was no wind through the expanse of marshy grass, no squirrels scratching at the underbrush. Even the river I stood next to, the Anacostia, flowed south without a sound. But there was no peace threaded through the quiet, and I could not, at first, figure out why. Something about the way the Anacostia swept by me, so hushed that it was almost taciturn, was unnerving.

The Anacostia slushed along its concrete rim, the surface flecked with pollution. On the mudbank beside me, the silt had an iridescent, rainbow sheen, the colors garish against the ancient white-water river now running as tea-colored as black water. I willed myself closer to the water, but as I moved nearer, I began to sink in the mud. Everywhere along the Anacostia, the ground is fugitive.

Under the sun of a humid morning, a brackish odor rose in the air, like the seashore after a storm, all kelp rot and fish carcasses. It was not altogether unpleasant, but without wind and sound to muddle my senses, the smell was overwhelming. I kept walking along the bank, following the paved trail along the eastern edge of the river to the old Bladensburg port, now a city park. The place was swamped with seagulls, screeching and shitting. Terns flocked on the mudflats, and trash swept through drains and creeks to form islands of grimy plastic.

On mornings like this, after a few days' rain has carried litter into the river and sewage runoff has turned the water foul, it is easy to understand why this river is not known and loved by more D.C. residents. Despite its proximity to the Capitol and the Supreme Court, the Anacostia is perhaps the most disregarded waterway in and around the capital; I have lost count of how many D.C. residents—newcomers mostly, many of whom live in the Anacostia watershed—have asked me where the Anacostia is when I have brought it up. One reason for this is that the Anacostia is a narrow, shallow river you could wade across hip-high—that is, if it were not illegal to swim in the waters, and if you could make it across without sinking into the silt.

Flowing on the far east side of the fall line, the Anacostia marks the final shift from piedmont hills to coastal plain. It is the Potomac's largest tributary, so significant to the nation's river that it once had no name and was referred to only as the Potomac's Eastern Branch. Slicing through the District, the Anacostia is, by federal law, the only river within the boundaries of the nation's capital. (The Potomac technically belongs to Maryland.) As I walked, I wondered why the Anacostia is not the waterway celebrated as the Nation's River. If the measure of the epithet is how consequential a role in the nation's history a river has played, then the Anacostia comes as close as the Potomac in its right to claim the title.

I paused on a bench under the shade of a fruiting mulberry to rest, and there, I tried to imagine what the Anacostia had once been like: Forty feet deep and shaded with silver maples, its waters shone with herring as egrets and herons stalked them from the rocks. Perhaps the smell of rotting fruit and mud soured me, but I could only see the river as it was, choked with plastic jugs and toxic waste. The river wasn't just silent; it had been silenced.

✳

KNOLLS TRIM THE ANACOSTIA, a rise so slight that to see it, you need to find the high ground. From the top of certain buildings at the far edge of Capitol Hill, you can watch as the ridge oscillates down to the brink. It was here, in the foothills on its west bank, land now occupied by the Supreme Court, that the Nacotchtank people farmed squash, beans, and corn. In the floodplain forests, the Nacotchtank hunted elk, bear, bison, deer, wild turkey, wood duck, goose, and grouse. From the water, they pulled shad and eels, perch and oysters, crabs, rockfish, and sturgeon.

From their village at the confluence of the Anacostia and the Potomac, the Nacotchtank, a small but distinct tribe, earned a reputation as eminent traders among other Algonquin tribes and the nearby Susquehannock. Centered on the south shore, near the mouth of the Anacostia, the Nacotchtank were the caretakers of a landscape whose spiritual and geographical heart was the Potomac's tributary. Where the Potomac could be wild and perilous, choked with freshets in winter and gushing its banks by spring, the Anacostia was docile and modest but just as generous.

The first group of colonizers, led by John Smith in 1608, encountered a clear, deep Anacostia, with little soil erosion to cloud the waters. The clarity of the Potomac's rivers and creeks stunned the English, as did the epic trees on its banks. Lord De La Warr wrote home in 1611 of a "goodly River called Patomack, upon the border whereof there are growne the goodliest Trees for Masts, that may be found elsewhere in the World." Soon, English colonizers began to chop and saw along the Potomac and what they then called the Eastern Branch, which was only later given the Anglicized name Anacostia, after the Nacotchtank tribe. What remained was a deracinated landscape. When it rained, the tide ebbed, and a tidal river once churning white sloshed brown with soil.

Colonizers forced the Nacotchtank into an acquiescent trading relationship and relied on them for their expert knowledge of place; in return, they shared guns and disease. By 1670, colonizers and their pathogens had driven the Nacotchtank from their home ground along the Anacostia. For two decades, the Nacotchtank took refuge on the Potomac River's Anacostine Island, across from what is today Georgetown. After they were forced from this island, too, some remaining Nacotchtank joined the nearby Piscataway tribe, others left for the Susquehannocks, and still others were sold by the English into slavery in the Caribbean. According to experts at the National Museum of the American Indian, there are no living descendants of the Nacotchtank tribe.

Nevertheless, there are contemporary District residents who maintain an ancestral connection to the Nacotchtank. Within the Piscataway Indian Nation and related tribes, some members trace their lineage to the Indigenous peoples who once lived at the mouth of the Anacostia. For non-Native Americans, the existence of Indigenous peoples in and around the capital is often thought of as penumbral, a shadow of a prenational past. In fact, though, there are many residents who maintain the Nacotchtank legacy, ensuring that the Anacostia's Indigenous legacy will not recede with the tide.

❈

I WAS STILL SITTING ON A BENCH at the old Bladensburg port when a man walked past me, smoking a cigarette. The smoke curled through the air, and I breathed in the sharp nip of nicotine. The British colonies of both Maryland and Virginia made tobacco official legal tender in 1642: This plant was literally cash. How a society defines wealth is how it defines itself. To grow English wealth, tobacco had to grow, and to grow tobacco, English settlers sought a steady supply of labor stolen from another continent.

In 1619, the year that the first twenty Africans were brought to North America at Point Comfort, Virginia, the British colonies produced only twenty thousand pounds of tobacco; by the turn of the eighteenth century, the colonies were exporting nearly forty million pounds. As the production of tobacco proliferated, so did the number of enslaved people. By 1700, there were approximately 700,000 enslaved Africans and their descendants in the British colonies. The demand for tobacco in the British market was so great that within two decades of the installation of Africans into their economies, both Virginia and Maryland codified the conflation of lifelong enslavement with African ancestry, ensuring a permanent labor force for the crop's cultivation.

At first, tobacco flourished in the fields made from uprooted Anacostia forests. Tobacco agriculture extended up and down the Potomac and Anacostia by the turn of the eighteenth century as enslavers spread their landholdings and built their wealth. But colonizers did not yet understand or perhaps much care that tobacco depletes soil nutrients with astounding rapidity; as their annual crops grew weaker, enslavers moved west. In their wake, they left behind acres of emptied fields sweeping up the banks of the Anacostia, a waterway they had treated as a dump and sewer.

Standing on the wooden bridge that stretches high over the mudflats at Bladensburg, I tried to conjure the seafarers that once trawled up this river and docked here, depositing plundered people and collecting thousands of hogsheads of tobacco. Throughout the two centuries that the Anacostia served as a highway of dehumanization, wind blew across scoured fields, empty save for strip pine; then summer torrents lifted the ravaged earth into the river. By 1762, newspapers reported that the Bladensburg port was clogging up; by 1835, years before the slave trade ended in the capital, the last deep-bottomed ship slipped out into Chesapeake Bay. Now, during late-summer droughts, you can hardly slide a flat-bottomed canoe through the river at Bladensburg.

I staggered down the trail out of the port, back into the thick marshes along the bank. Death floated on the river like oil, though it was not quite right to say that the Anacostia was dead in the sense of being lifeless—quite the opposite. Because there are fewer human visitors using the trails along the Anacostia compared to the Potomac, its banks are among the best places in the District to observe the many animals with whom we share this city. I have encountered more wild turkeys along the Anacostia than I have anywhere along the Potomac, and in spring, the fields of Anacostia Park are an ideal spot for watching warblers curve through the air on their way north.

But the rupture of families and communities through the transatlantic slave trade is intimately bound to the destruction of land. Slavery, more than wind or rain, eroded floodplains and swept soil into the riverbed. Slavery choked fish and blinded otters, ordaining death to all who lived and worked on the banks of the Anacostia. Centuries after emancipation, death is still the current of this river because slavery made its bed.

⚼

BY THE END OF THE CIVIL WAR, the Anacostia was so choked with silt that the U.S. Army Corps of Engineers declared that the upper branches of the river were "not worthy of improvement" by the national government. But from Navy Yard up to Kenilworth—the area where the Anacostia runs through the District—the Corps began dredging and walling up the Anacostia for development. When they were done, they had, by their own admission, "destroyed some 2,600 acres of aquatic wetlands, 99,000 linear feet of aquatic habitat, and 700 acres of bottom hardwood trees in the forest buffer." The agency would later concede that it had delivered the greatest injury the Anacostia had sustained.

As industrialization expanded in areas north and east of the District, the Anacostia became contaminated with toxic dredge and incinerator waste. Robbed by the Corps of the tidal marshes that had mitigated flooding since the time of the Nacotchtank, the lower Anacostia was made ever more vulnerable to the onslaught of spring rains and pollution.

As the Corps gouged and filled, the mudflats swarmed with mosquitoes. Disease clouded the riverbanks, and white residents who could afford to do so escaped the fetor for the high terrain of Northwest. As a result of the white elite's abandonment of Southwest and Southeast, the land along the Anacostia was left largely to the working classes, though its individual neighborhoods were often as strictly segregated as those elsewhere in the city. In Anacostia, for example, white developers restricted the sale of buildings to persons of African or Irish descent until 1877, when Frederick Douglass broke the housing covenant by purchasing fifteen acres and a mansion in the neighborhood.

By the turn of the twentieth century, racist housing laws had chopped up the rest of the District, barring Black residents from many middle-class neighborhoods west of the Anacostia. When the city's Alley Dwelling Authority razed much of the city's working-class, Black-occupied housing in Northwest during the 1930s, thousands of Black residents were forcibly relocated east of the Anacostia. The remoteness of the area, due to topography and municipal neglect, fostered the development of a dynamic, self-reliant community of scholars, educators, religious leaders, and activists. By the 1950s, the few remaining white working-class residents of Anacostia and Fairlawn had fled west or south for the suburbs, creating the conditions for the area "east of the river," as people began to call it, to become the District's first Black-majority frontier, the original site of Chocolate City.

Washington expanded dramatically through the early twentieth century, its growth running parallel to the branching and ballooning of the federal government. With that increase in population came an increase in waste. As the city grew desperate for disposal options for the garbage piling up in the streets, the U.S. Army Corps of Engineers agreed to accept some of the city's trash for its Anacostia dredging projects. The Corps—now working together with the National Park Service, which supervised new parklands situated along the river's eastern border (today's Anacostia Park)—began adding incinerator ash and construction debris to their heaps of silt and sludge. The Park Service directed the trash-incineration process, monitoring the height of garbage mounds and unloading ash into tidy channels along the river, which the Corps then shaped into islands and banks.

By the beginning of World War II, the District's trash incinerators could no longer keep pace with the city's production of refuse. The Park Service allowed the city to temporarily dump trash along the river, near the Kenilworth neighborhood. Six days a week, Park Service employees monitored an open-air fire, burning a mound of broken Coke bottles, rusting bicycles and refrigerators, ink and dross and oil. Plumes of black smoke loomed over the Anacostia, and smog flowed through neighborhoods on both sides of the river, filling the lungs of children playing in nearby parks before settling as a fine powder on the dinner plates of residents.

The smoke followed the whimsy of the wind, often rising more conspicuously on the city skyline than the Washington Monument. At night, the fires from the dump glowed on the horizon like fallen planets. In aerial photographs of the city from the 1950s, you can see in the foreground the radiant marble, the graceful expanse of the Mall, and the lumbering blue Potomac. But behind all that and to the east, there is the black line of another river and a slim cloud, almost out of sight.

The Kenilworth dump was the worst source of air pollution in the District, a truth that residents east of the river carried in their bodies. Children developed asthma and adults died young from respiratory illness and strokes. For years, Black residents of the Mayfair and Kenilworth communities protested the racist waste policies that continued to bring the rest of the city's trash to their Black-majority neighborhood. In December 1966, twenty-five members of the Mayfair Parkside Civic Association used their bodies to block the entrance to the landfill, forcing dump trucks to idle while residents demanded the dump's closure. (Their actions later inspired a group of Black activists in Warren County, North Carolina, to lead a similar action in 1982, sparking what is now considered the modern environmental justice movement.) Through 1967, discussions about the future of the dump were stalled as local and federal government officials made halfhearted promises to end the fires and residents continued to fall ill and die from preventable pulmonary diseases.

For the children of Kenilworth, there was nowhere in their neighborhood as interesting as the trash heap they lived next to, which they called "Mystery Mountain." The trick to sneaking in was the timing of your arrival: after that day's deposits had been made, but before the fires began. On a gusty day in February 1968, four boys followed the length of the Watts Branch, a tributary of the Anacostia, to the dump, as they had likely done many times before. When the wind shifted, flames vaulted, capturing seven-year-old Kelvin Tyrone Mock and burning him alive. The coroner ruled Kelvin's death an accident.

Mayor-Commissioner Walter Washington ordered the fires stopped immediately after Kelvin's death, though trucks still rolled trash into Kenilworth for years. When the Park Service finally capped the landfill in the 1970s, covering the mounds of trash and char with dirt, they did not use water-impermeable soils, allowing pollution to seep out and into the ground. When it rains on the meadows of Kenilworth, today a beautiful but sinister stretch of land covered in blackberry canes, there is a rank smell as methane leaks out of the earth.

The underland is where we bury the histories we wish to forget in order to live in the flat terrain of the present. But the Anacostia knows better and remembers longer, carries silt and poison in its body to show us what we have hidden. Four miles northeast of the Capitol dome, there are sweeping fields of turf and sedge, lined with willows and maples, sinking thin roots into invisible trash and toxins.

⸙

FLUORESCENT ALGAL BLOOMS were standard sights on both the Potomac and Anacostia Rivers when President Johnson stood before Congress for his second State of the Union address. His administration, he promised, would work to make the Potomac "a model of beauty here in the capital." The Department of the Interior, along with the Interstate Commission on the Potomac

River Basin, immediately began work limiting pollution, restoring fisheries, and removing trash.

By the time Kelvin Mock was burned alive, the Potomac was already on the road to recovery, with a particular focus on cleaning upriver tributaries. While the white-majority environmental movement expanded through the 1970s, bringing conservationists, antinuclear activists, and deep ecologists to Washington to organize and lobby, the Anacostia, long ago coded in the minds of white residents as a Black space, was ignored.

Marion Barry, D.C.'s magnetic mayor for almost two decades, brought the Anacostia to the forefront of his campaigns, arguing that Black residents east of the river unjustly lived in poor, substandard housing and in a degraded environment. But even Barry's forceful rhetoric and efforts to improve the Anacostia's waterfront were not enough to remedy its problems. In 1972, the city completed construction on the Anacostia Freeway (now I-295), which cut a line through the public lands alongside the river and brought commuter traffic and air pollution to residents east of the river. Every weekday morning, commuters from the Maryland suburbs still make their way downtown along the river on an elevated highway, their vehicles spewing carbon monoxide into the air above Deanwood and River Terrace.

Building a highway through the neighborhoods with the highest percentage of Black residents was no accident. Urban renewal advocates in D.C. had strategically focused on Black neighborhoods for their improvement efforts, allowing the federal government to remove and resettle Black Washingtonians to undesirable locations. Moreover, eminent domain allowed the federal government to concentrate what was considered "necessary" pollution in one area of the city. The African American Environmental Association, a grassroots organization focused on environmental justice in D.C., wrote in their 2000 report that car exhaust fumes combined with the last four centuries of air and water pollution had turned the Anacostia into a "toxic soup" of PCBs, chlordane, mercury, and benzene. Exposure to these and other toxic substances gave residents east of the river some of the highest rates of cancer, lung disease, and asthma per capita in the District.

Raw sewage also remained a significant problem during the late twentieth century. During a downpour in, say, 1985, a United States senator who took a shit in the bathroom of his office on Capitol Hill would presumably flush the toilet to send his waste through thousands of feet of pipe and tube before it arrived at a sewage-treatment plan, inundated by reams of rainwater. The senator's feces (along with everyone else's in D.C.) would then be pumped into a sewage overflow system, which spewed into the Anacostia. Fecal coliform counts in the Anacostia rose so high during periods of rainy weather in the mid-1980s that an outbreak of cholera—a disease rarely seen in the United States in the late twentieth century, let alone in its capital—became a threat.

Meanwhile, the Potomac had evolved from a malodorous flood into a limpid river. Though it still was not safe enough to swim in or drink from, by the late 1980s the Potomac was cleaner than it had been in almost a century. The narrative circulating through the offices of Washington's environmentalists and legislators was that George Washington's river had been pulled from the brink of collapse, and that the federal government had been its savior.

But south of downtown office buildings and the Capitol grounds, the Anacostia, more contaminated than it had been in decades, still poured into the redeemed Potomac. Noting the discrepancies in care between the rivers, George Gurley, an environmental activist in River Terrace, explained that during the last decades of the twentieth century, "Georgetown on the

Potomac boomed while Anacostia communities suffered." Very few non-Black residents seemed interested in the fact that "the forgotten river," as the Anacostia was now being referred to by white journalists, emptied into "the river of presidents."

There are at least three reasons for this convenient amnesia. The first, geographical, is that the Anacostia is located south of Capitol Hill, beyond the sight, smell, and mouths of the city's white residents. The second, historical, is that the Anacostia had been, for over a century, considered a doomed and unsalvageable waterway, while the Potomac had risen as a cause célèbre in the world of restored watersheds. And third, the Anacostia served white residents as an expedient boundary—firmer even than Rock Creek Park—which contained Black residents and the associated racist ills of Blackness in a place of sickness and poison.

Compared to the Potomac, the Anacostia was considered the peripheral tributary of the past. Over four centuries, white Americans had made a river into a stream of Native massacre and Black death, placed the survivors of genocide and social death on the banks of that stream and held them there, called that place no place at all, left the refuse of their lives in that placeless place, burned a child alive, set their poisons wild and free into the air and the water, and then swore it never happened.

During the middle months of quarantine amidst the COVID-19 pandemic in 2020, I often biked from my apartment in Park View down to Hains Point at the far end of East Potomac Park. Leaning against my handlebars at the tip of the watersmeet, I would watch the Anacostia run muddy into the Potomac. I think I came to the Point as often as I did to remind myself of the time and expense spent by white Washingtonians to deny a geographical fact: The Anacostia is a tributary of the Potomac. The white-capped river of George Washington and his white nation is made, in part, by a river ciphered Black by racist policy. The waters of the rivers meet and fold, their interconnectedness impossible to deny as they mix into a cloudy brown.

One evening while I was at the Point, a storm curled in on a shelf cloud, a menacing, quick-moving ledge that left me stranded, with no time to seek shelter. As I waited for the deluge, the wind sent a line of oak leaves blowing across the water, on whose surface they landed. I silenced my breath to better hear the Anacostia and the Potomac, percussive and buoyant, in a dialogue they have held for millennia. Snatching a leaf from the air and holding it out, I caught a few drops and studied them, astonished that despite our sins against it and one another, water retains its circular capacity for repair.

⛭

WHEN I FIRST SAW THE ALABASTER FOOT in the shallows at Buzzard Point, my breath caught in my throat. Though the foot of an eastern lampmussel is no longer than half an inch, the soft opaline mass pouring from the shell was a bolt from the blue. More than the shock of pearly emergence from the animal's nacreous interior, I was shocked by just how many mussels there were in the water.

Centuries ago, in the Anacostia's former sandbanks, at least a dozen species of mussels trawled the shoals, sucking in and expelling water and filtering bacteria and sediment. In the centuries since colonization, the Anacostia's native mussel species have either gone extinct or suffered a significant decline. Considered an indicator species for the health of a waterway, just one freshwater mussel is capable of cleaning ten gallons of water a day. Every drop of water filtered clean is a reciprocal exchange of health between river and mussel.

The majority of this mound of elliptio, floater, and lance mussels was placed in the river over the last five years by members of the Anacostia Watershed Society (AWS), a nonprofit environmental organization founded in 1989. Though Black residents east of the river advocated for decades for increased environmental regulation without much response from local or federal governments, AWS, as (at least initially) a predominantly white organization, has used the political power of its membership in the three decades since its founding to block proposals for inappropriate development projects and sue companies responsible for polluting and illegal dumping.

In recent years, releasing freshwater mussels throughout the watershed has become one of the organization's most significant efforts. Thirty-five thousand freshwater mussels have been launched into the Anacostia, with tens of thousands more to be released over the next several years. As the number of mussels has increased alongside policies designed to decrease sewage and stormwater runoff, the Anacostia has begun to recover. Each year, AWS measures the river's health by assessing a variety of factors, including dissolved oxygen levels and water clarity; in 2021, the organization gave the Anacostia a D grade of 63 percent health, the best and only passing grade the river has ever received. The mass of mussels at Buzzard Point is a remarkable indication of the Anacostia's resilience, perhaps the sign used by AWS to show that even here, in the polluted waters of a forgotten river in the modern era of climate change, life finds a way.

Holding a mussel in my palm, a living creature the size, weight, and color of a skippable pebble, I was stunned that this animal, closed in a dark obscurity of its own creation, has become the symbol of the Anacostia's resilience. Environmental resilience describes the capacity of an ecosystem to bounce back and revive itself, despite the history of human harm enacted upon it. Increasingly, environmental organizations have adopted the term for use in urban contexts to herald the integrity of green or otherwise sustainable redevelopment projects that protect new construction against threats posed by climate change. To recognize the Anacostia's resilience, then, is to look toward its future, with only a cursory look back at its past to measure the distance between decay and resurrection.

As the guiding paradigm of the contemporary environmental movement, resilience has been applied to places and people as encouragement for further white amnesia. Tracie L. Washington, president of the Louisiana Justice Institute, explained this rhetorical tactic in a 2015 speech: "Stop calling me resilient. Because every time you say, 'Oh, they're resilient,' that means you can do something else to me." A focus on the resilience of people forced to live in degraded environments supports further degradation in its refusal to address the root cause of so many environmental problems. As the Anacostia heals and its centuries of resilience are recognized and even celebrated, there is a reflective fogginess settling in over the water, a forgetfulness that has more than rhetorical consequences.

Contemporary environmental resilience efforts east of the river include the demolition of the historic Barry Farms public housing complex to make space for a green-friendly mixed-development space, the construction of a seventy-acre park at Poplar Point, and the revamping of recreational spaces in Anacostia Park. The construction of the 11th Street Bridge Park, which connects the fully gentrified Navy Yard to a whitening but still Black-majority Anacostia, will be named Mussel Beach, in honor of the creatures currently at work healing the Anacostia.

These development projects levy critical questions about whom such projects are for, who will be able to afford to live in and near them, and who will benefit from their construction. When redevelopment is approached as an ahistorical, outsider-operated endeavor, it threatens communities east of the river by transforming Black spaces, once neglected by municipal authorities, into cultural commodities for consumption. Community organizations like the Douglass City Land Trust and Building Bridges Across the River are determined to see that redevelopment projects east of the river will not result in mass displacement of Black residents, many of whom have ancestors who were displaced to Southeast from other parts of the city; their work raising funds for housing has had a significant impact on the lives of many residents east of the river.

Nevertheless, there remain mounting concerns that celebrating the resilience of the river overlooks the history of the Black communities that formed along its banks. This outsized focus on the Anacostia's resilience is especially difficult to ignore when comparing the recent history of the Anacostia with that of the Potomac. Sixty years ago, both rivers flowed to the brink of ecological collapse, but with one river coded white and the other Black, the Potomac's recovery has been styled as the inevitable conclusion of a long, nationwide history of progress; the Anacostia's recovery, which has been slower and localized, has been severed from the river's long history of Black caretaking.

I scooped up a dead mussel, its valves hinged open and its body, once a pulpy nickel of flesh, dissolved into the mud. There was no clue, at least to my untrained eyes, how this creature met its death and finally opened itself up to the world. The shell's basins shone in the light, a kaleidoscopic luster hidden from human eyes until after the animal's death. Is this not the way that white Washingtonians have learned to think of the Anacostia? As a dark slit in the earth, with hidden lives of wonder that we would not recognize until we had choked and broken it? To love a river as it returns to itself requires nothing from us but our admiration, but to love a river as it flows toward its death is the most difficult love to give. The Anacostia needs more than a repudiation of resilience; it needs a replacement.

In late October 1991, the first National People of Color Environmental Leadership Summit took place in Washington, D.C. From a hotel in Capitol Hill, on the hills above the mouth of the Anacostia River, hundreds of people of color gathered to organize, draft, and adopt seventeen principles of environmental justice. The document they created more than thirty years ago remains a comprehensive and profound declaration of interdependence with the natural world and a demand for reparations for land and for people. The entire document is visionary, but the ninth principle in the list is especially moving: "Environmental Justice protects the right of victims of environmental injustice to receive full compensation and reparations for damages . . ." Reparation, in this sense, is the opposite of the white fantasy of forgetting; it looks backward in order to begin the difficult work of untying the direction of the future from that of the past.

In *Freedom Dreams,* scholar Robin D. G. Kelley describes reparations as a project focused on "reconstructing the internal life of black America, and eliminating institutional racism." It is less about the fixation on individual monetary payments, as reparations are often thought of and discussed, than it is about improving Black community life—which, east of the river, includes improving the life of the Anacostia. The moral impetus for reparations may be the past and present treatment of Black people and the land they live with, but the target of reparations is not necessarily debt repayment or redemption or even racial reconciliation; rather, reparations are a future-oriented project to build an equitable society. The location of the Anacostia, downhill, in the backyard of our democracy, thus gives it a particularly symbolic role in this national movement. But how do we learn to care for a place as an act of justice, as a way to create the kind of world in which we want to live?

I waded in, mussels glistening in the water around me. The Anacostia rose above my ankles, asking for life as it told me its story.

Honeysuckle

The MORNING OF THE SUMMER SOLSTICE, I was out the door before first light. By the time the sun fell over the horizon, I was gathering honeysuckle on a beach near the mouth of Piscataway Creek. The vines had grown together into plaited mesh as they descended from the bank into the swirl of the tide, and my fingertips were sticky with dew and dusted with pollen. I inhaled the aroma of blossoms and the salt of the air as I sipped on one nectar-filled flower after another. Standing there in the water, I felt a sublime sense of wholeness arise from this encounter with the Potomac.

Sweet and heady, with a cocktail of scent held in a slender tube, honeysuckle (specifically Japanese honeysuckle) runs riot over the shrub layer of the floodplain. More than almost any other plant, honeysuckle seems to contain a particular olfactory power over memories of an idealized past. Growing up in North Carolina, I learned that for my ancestors, the Scottish settlers who colonized the state's sandhills, planting common honeysuckle, which they called woodbine, represented a true love rooted in place, tightly bonded but not so rigid as to break.

Years later in college, when I met my partner, we took nighttime bike rides together along the greenways of our town, stopping to pick honeysuckle and kiss in the grass. As the semester hummed to its end and summer threatened, we picked a basket of the blooms along the fence that traced the bike path between his dorm and mine. In between sitting for our final exams, we made honeysuckle syrup, which we froze to make sorbet. I remember sharing that icy-cold dessert on the back steps of a paint-peeled house at an end-of-year party, looking into each other's eyes, realizing that we had fallen in love. Every spring since then, we have made honeysuckle syrup and sorbet, a ritual of our relationship, and a practice we continue to celebrate our love for each other.

I found it easy and pleasurable to revisit these memories, but it was also undeniable that this plant had come to bridge the places I had belonged in the past to the place I lived now. There was something about the loose curl of a honeysuckle vine that expressed an insouciant, almost self-possessed attitude, as if the plant was assured of its place in the world. I had never seen a honeysuckle vine that appeared not to belong wherever it grew.

A relative newcomer to this continent, Japanese honeysuckle arrived in the United States from eastern Asia in 1806, when it was first introduced on Long Island, New York, as a means of erosion control. New Yorkers were eager for botanical options to stem the clogging from erosion of the island's creeks and kills, which threatened their ability to ship goods through Long Island Sound. That the plant was also hardy and sweet-smelling was initially a bonus to the New Yorkers, and then to Floridians and Virginians, who planted it along the nation's roadsides and creek beds.

By the early 1900s, honeysuckle could be found throughout the whole of the eastern United States, making itself at home wherever it went. Everywhere it sprouted, honeysuckle embraced the world around it, entwining itself around every sapling it encountered—dry meadows were just as attractive as a dank cove, the sea spray of a coastline just as pleasant as a stripped riverbank. For the first century and a half after its introduction, honeysuckle was a celebrated species in America, commended for its ability to hold on to earth and provide browse for deer. But by the 1980s, honeysuckle was also viewed as a sinister killer, which throttled native trees as it sought out ever more sun, water, and space.

As punishment for its success, which appeared to come at the expense of native plants, Japanese honeysuckle was subsequently labeled an invasive species, a term the federal government has used since the 1990s for any "alien species whose introduction does or is likely to cause economic or environmental harm or harm to human health." In a handful of states, including Virginia, honeysuckle is legally categorized as a noxious weed, a term for any plant that is considered a threat to the state's crops, livestock, public health, or economy. In Illinois, Indiana, Connecticut, and New Hampshire, it is illegal to import, move, sell, purchase, transplant, or cultivate the plant, punishable with fines of up to one hundred dollars.

The invasive paradigm in ecology creates a harsh dichotomy between native and nonnative species. When a species has been labeled invasive, it can unleash a no-holds-barred situation, with any and all possible weapons deployed to stop its spread. From the widespread spraying of toxic herbicides to the introduction of other potentially invasive species as biotic barriers, the battle against invasives takes many different forms and occurs on many different fronts. The National Invasive Species Council, an organization whose very existence would suggest how high the stakes are, holds invasive species accountable for "unemployment, damaged goods and equipment, power failures, food and water shortages, environmental degradation, increased rates and severity of natural disasters, disease epidemics, and even lost lives."

I have never liked the term *invasive species* or many of the negative words associated with it. But looking around at the wash of yellow along the floodplain that day, it was impossible to deny that there was a lot of honeysuckle along the Potomac—perhaps too much. It seemed clear, from the notable lack of plant diversity in some sections of the floodplain, that other plants had disappeared to make way for it.

Perhaps the reason I was so drawn to a plant that didn't belong here was that perhaps I didn't belong here, either. This form of alienation was not only the familiar anxiety that D.C. would never be my home but also an even deeper fear, daunting and profound: As a descendent of settlers—an invader in much the same way that honeysuckle arguably is—this entire continent would never be my home.

✄

I MADE MY WAY DOWN THE TRAIL into the harsh sun of the open fields. To my left, there was a meadow filled with wildflowers and grasses, punctuated by cedar hedgerows and swarming with wineberries and honeysuckle. To my right, the riverbank descended into piles of rock, a human intervention against the erosive current. The Potomac is one mile wide here; objects on the other side are not, on the whole, discernible beyond their generalities as houses, boats, or parking lots. The one exception to this is an enormous white house with a bright red roof, ornamented with gables, a cupola, and a large portico.

George Washington's Mount Vernon occupies a scenic hill above the Potomac, and from the distant shore it does appear as if the house sits higher, even grander, than any structure above or below it on the Virginia side. On the other side of Little Hunting Creek, a few hundred yards upriver, the land lies flat and forested, with only a slight rise to the terrain. This view gave the impression of the house's wanting to appear imposing, even imperious, an aspiration that seemed only half met. There is an awkward quality to the way the hill had been cut to create the escarpment below. With its hard angle, the cliff seems unnatural, even discordant.

This bluff had not always appeared so harsh and artificial. At the conclusion of the Revolutionary War, Washington returned to the piazza of Mount Vernon, where he downed endless bottles of his favorite Madeira and looked out over the Potomac—or at least to what he could see of it through the tree line. Frustrated by the shrouded riverscape, Washington ordered the people he enslaved to hack down the trees and then chisel out portions of the bluff to make his home that much more impressive for visitors arriving by boat. After they had finished this grueling task, Washington proclaimed, "No estate in America is more pleasantly situated than this."

What you could see of the house was just as important to Washington as what you could see from it, and many visitors to Mount Vernon affirmed the importance of the two-way perspective. "The Maryland shore, on the opposite side, is beautifully diversified with hills, which are almost covered with woods . . . The scenery altogether is most delightful," wrote Isaac Weld. The Polish statesman Julian Niemcewicz claimed that the view from the portico was "perhaps the most beautiful view in the world . . . The opposite bank, the course of the river, the dense woods all combined to enhance the sweet illusion."

More than a century and a half after Washington was entombed on the grounds of his home, the idea that Mount Vernon should retain its lofty view over the Potomac prevailed. When commercial development threatened the land across from the house for the first time, in the 1950s, the Mount Vernon Ladies' Association, responsible for the preservation of the house since 1860, launched Operation Overview, a major effort to protect what they called the "viewshed" of Mount Vernon.

In large part through the efforts of the Ladies' Association, Republican congresswoman Frances Bolton, and the involvement of a local community and neighborhood group called the Moyaone Association, over four thousand acres across the river in Maryland were preserved in perpetuity. In 1968, Secretary of the Interior Stewart Udall (who was a Potomac River resident himself, living in a glass-clad modern house near Little Falls) presided over the ceremony that ushered this stretch of shoreline under the care of the National Park Service. Today, Piscataway Park retains the bizarre designation of being the only national park unit created for the scenic protection of a private property.

After climbing back up the embankment, I wandered down the trail, pausing to pick a handful of open daylily flowers and a small jar's worth of wineberries. Through a gap in the tree line, I looked out again to Mount Vernon, which seemed to me at once both incongruous and threatening, imposing a claim of ownership all the way across the river to the far shore and beyond.

The land opposite Washington's home, on the other side of the river, known as Moyaone, has been cared for by Indigenous peoples for over eleven thousand years. Flint and spear tips from the Archaic period have been excavated here, as well as hundreds of archaeological artifacts from 1300 to 1650 C.E., during which Moyaone was the central village for the Piscataway Conoy (the term they used for their confederation).

Centuries before the Washington family forced the people they enslaved to build their grand house on the hill, Piscataway people ferried back and forth here across the Potomac. At the mouth of what only later would become Little Hunting Creek, the Piscataway fished for sturgeon and gathered fruits, roots, and nuts from the hilltop forest, then paddled back across the river to tend the fields of corn, squash, and beans near their village. The Potomac was the center of their lives, and it gave them their name: Piscataway translates in the Algonquin dialect as "where the waters blend."

The seasonal demand to follow game, track the fish runs, and barter with other tribes meant that in the centuries before colonization, the Piscataway lived a seminomadic existence, traveling up and down the Potomac and the Anacostia, where they traded with the nearby Nacotchtank and fought with the Susquehannock. But because the Piscataway farmed crops and wild-tended the forests—planting pawpaw trees, pruning blackberries, and fertilizing hickories with wood ash—Moyaone remained the place to which they always returned.

Moyaone was not only a site for agriculture or gathering. It was also a sacred place, what we would now call a cemetery and what archaeologists call an ossuary. Underneath these fields are hundreds of human remains, some dating back a thousand years. One of the ossuary sites of Moyaone is marked by a large red cedar tree, its branches festooned with strips of colored fabric people have tied as symbols of their wishes and prayers. Buried beside the cedar is the man who planted it, Turkey Tayac, the former chief of the Piscataway Indian Nation.

By the time of Tayac's birth in 1895, almost three hundred years after John Smith first sailed up the Potomac, the Piscataway Conoy had been decimated by genocide. Though they had once been the largest tribe in what would become the state of Maryland, by the early twentieth century, many Piscataways had either left the state, taken refuge in small isolated groups, or married into non-Native families. Under the strict "one-drop rule" that dictated the racial social order in the South, many people with Piscataway ancestry were categorized by their states as "negro mongrels." Still others were forced to pass quietly over the color line into whiteness.

Tayac, born Philip Sheridan Proctor in nearby Charles County, Maryland, learned as a child about the land theft that had resulted in the dissolution of his tribe. Nevertheless, his family continued to tend the land near Piscataway Creek, where he learned to identify and gather plants, inspiring his later work as an herbalist and healer. In the 1930s, Alice and Henry Ferguson, white amateur archaeologists who owned a 139-acre weekend retreat and hobby farm that included the Moyaone site, began their first digs of the former village. Tayac began visiting Moyaone regularly to participate in the excavations, returning to the land that had once been cared for by his family.

According to the National Park Service's history of Piscataway Park, to honor his disinterred ancestors Tayac "performed ceremonial dances at the site to emphasize his own ancestral connections to the land," an act that was "generally dismissed by the white residents of the Moyaone as an amusing spectacle." That the Fergusons and their neighbors would have laughed off Tayac's presence is no surprise; to them, the Indigenous legacy of the Potomac was in pottery shards and skeletal remains, not in living people. At least in part because of his experience with the Moyaone excavations, Tayac became increasingly focused on what would become his lifelong work: to consolidate the living legacy of the Piscataway Conoy.

As part of the expanding American Indian Movement in the 1960s, Tayac was an important figure in the cultural revitalization efforts happening concurrently in other southeastern tribes, including the Nanticoke of Delaware and the Lumbee of North Carolina. These tribes, like the Piscataway, had spent centuries fending off racist accusations that they had become so assimilated they were no longer "real Indians." A critical part of dispelling this myth was asserting their cultural heritage and relationships to the land; Tayac often traveled to the stretch of riverbank between Piscataway and Accokeek Creeks to tend and gather herbs, as his ancestors had done for thousands of years, teaching whoever accompanied him.

Through the early 1960s, as various white interest groups sought to extend the boundaries of Mount Vernon's viewshed by preserving Moyaone, Tayac and other Piscataway descendants were excluded from communications between stakeholders. Although he was initially pessimistic about the National Park Service's taking control of the Moyaone site (not to mention the nearby development of a model homestead called the National Colonial Farm), Tayac eventually supported the creation of Piscataway Park on two conditions: that Indigenous peoples would always be free to access the land, and that he could be buried at Moyaone. Tayac and Stewart Udall shook on the deal in 1968.

Ten years later, Tayac died, but it would be another year and a legal battle before the National Park Service would permit his internment. On the morning of his funeral in November 1979, the road to the cedar tree, beside which Tayac wished to be buried, was blocked by local landowners. Tayac's family carried his coffin down the hill and across the fields to the riverbank instead, where he was buried with his ancestors.

Today, his grave is a pilgrimage site for Indigenous peoples of all tribes. Thousands travel to Moyaone every year to pay their respects to one of the southeastern leaders of the American Indian Movement, whose efforts to revitalize Piscataway heritage eventually led to the recognition of the Piscataway people by the state of Maryland in 2012. Visitors often leave mementos at Tayac's grave site. When I stood in front of it, it was covered in delicate pebbles, night-blue mussel shells, and a spray of osprey feathers.

Across the river, George Washington was entombed in white marble, surrounded by armed guards; Turkey Tayac was buried in the soil, surrounded by yarrow. It cost twenty-eight dollars to visit one grave, and nothing but a mile-long walk over beaver-dammed wetlands to visit another. Mount Vernon was exclusive and private, dedicated to the preservation of the slave-labor camp Washington had once owned; Piscataway Park was wide open and publicly accessible, its connection and significance to Piscataway history ancillary to the fact that the park was pleasing to look at from the far shore.

Moyaone translates in the Piscataway language as "home place." I wondered whether my own ancestors in North Carolina's sandhills had ever truly felt at home on this continent, even as they planted honeysuckle to root themselves in place. Along the banks of the Lumber River, my ancestors displaced the Lumbee people, with whom the Piscataway, centuries later, would forge a connection through Turkey Tayac.

Feeling the weight of my backpack, which was laden down with all of the plants I had foraged that morning—the jar of wineberries, the bag of daylily flowers, and another of honeysuckle—I was overcome with gratitude for these gifts from Moyaone. Dropping my pack beside the trail, I walked through the field, gathering another bouquet of daylilies, which I tied together with a knot of grass and left on Tayac's grave as my small offering to the Potomac and its people.

⚜

EVERY ONE OF THE PLANTS I harvested at Piscataway Park that day was, technically, an invasive species. The daylily, for example, was introduced to this continent in the early 1900s as a showy ornamental from Asia, cultivated for thousands of years as a versatile perennial vegetable. Now spread across the entire United States with the exception of the desert Southwest, the daylily is frequently accused of robbing soil from native meadow plants like yarrow. Similarly, wineberries were introduced to North America in the 1890s from Asia as breeding stock for fragile raspberry cultivars but soon escaped their confines. Wineberries produce, as their name suggests, some of the sweetest and mellowest summer berries but are nevertheless considered a significant threat to native blackberries.

Inasmuch as their original home is not this one, honeysuckle, daylilies, and wineberries could each be considered colonizers of a sort. Scholarship in biology rarely, if ever, uses the terms *colonizer* or *settler* for these species—which would remain a rhetorical issue, if, of course, these plants were not referred to instead as "aliens," "foreigners," and "immigrants," language that inculpates these plants in nationalist politics. When daylilies are said to rob soil from yarrow or when wineberries threaten blackberries, the verbiage used mirrors a xenophobic strain in politics in which immigrants are accused of stealing jobs and increasing crime.

It seemed to me that the blame assigned to these species had somehow been shifted over time from human settlers onto the plants themselves. A crucial part of the narrative of these plants—who had brought them to this continent, and why—was missing. The three invasive plants I had harvested that day were modern arrivals from Asia, brought to the United States by settlers to serve specific economic goals: honeysuckle for erosion control, daylilies for beautification, wineberries for breeding stock. Only once they failed at that task or escaped from it were they tagged as unwanted invaders.

In contrast, other invasive species from Europe were more likely brought to the United States in the first centuries of colonization, their trip across the ocean motivated either by sentimentality or chance. The presence of these species, including the familiar and common dandelion and plantain, is so long-standing and apparently nonthreatening on this continent that many Americans have forgotten that these species have been in the United States for only a few centuries. Though not by official decree, in general the majority of Asian-origin species are considered invasive, while European-origin species are considered "naturalized," the process by which a foreign species integrates into an ecosystem without harming native species.

Why are plants from Europe embraced as welcome settlers while species from Asia are demonized as sinister assailants? The answer lies in post–World War II England, where the term *invasive species* was first used and the new field of invasion biology, informed by the trauma and rhetoric of war, took root in the academy. The postwar notion that the Western world needed saving from wicked invaders emerged in the United States in the 1960s, through the first eradication campaigns aimed at "alien" and "aggressive" species.

During the same ten-year period in which Ronald Reagan signed the Immigration Control and Reform Act, making it unlawful for companies to knowingly hire "illegal aliens," the term *invasive species* left the academy and made its way into the public lexicon for the first time. In 1992, Bill Clinton signed the Alien Species Prevention and Enforcement Act, which prohibited the shipment or sale of certain species; this was followed by the National Invasive Species Act of 1996. During the same period, Clinton signed the Illegal Immigration Reform and Immigrant Responsibility Act, which significantly expanded the number of crimes for which an immigrant could be deported.

Though they might seem disparate, these political acts were related: The relationship between the nationalization of nature and how one becomes naturalized is rooted in the history of how white Americans have taken ownership of and control over land. In order for European settlers to make a moral claim that America belonged to them and that they were not invaders themselves, they created a fictional narrative of their new continent as a wild, untouched land, one in which Indigenous peoples never had a presence. Thus, nature, at least in a cultural sense, became a white place, pristine and pure. Any incursion by a species associated with the "non-white" necessarily threatened the perceived healthfulness of nature. Considering the racist ideology that underpins the antagonism for invasive species, it should come as no surprise that the American war on invasives is not designed to lead to a utopian paradise of restored ecosystems, but to a pyrrhic victory in which a purified version of nature triumphs.

❋

OUTSIDE MY KITCHEN WINDOW, tufts of dandelion had given way to white, and in the garden, where I'd yet to take on the task of early summer weeding, plantain popped out in wide mats. Both of these weeds are examples of nonnative species that have been here so long that they have become naturalized. Though some people might break out the Roundup when they see the first flowers sprouting across their lawns, very few would accuse these plants of threatening the health of natives.

For herbalists, these plants offer more than a neutral presence. They are critical, common medicine: The dandelion is a terrific diuretic, and nothing is better for a bee sting than a poultice of plantain. In their ability to provide sustenance and to live in commonality with native plants, the dandelion and the plantain model how to live ethically in places that are not our original homes.

That morning, I had stood on the bank, glaring at Mount

Vernon, hating it and its former owner for all the crimes of colonization it represented to me. But at the edge of Moyaone, I knew that there was no way to separate myself from the legacy that the house across the water carried. No matter how grateful I felt to the nonnative plants I had gathered there, Moyaone would never mean to me what it meant to the Piscataway. Instead of these being painful thoughts that separated me from the place, I found them liberating, even grounding.

I thought of other sections of Piscataway Park, profuse in pawpaws and ancient pignut hickories. The contemporary abundance of the landscape was the living legacy of Indigenous caretaking. What would the Potomac look like if we could do the same with nonnative plants, cultivating wineberries with the same care we might blackberries, monitoring the spread of honeysuckle while still using their flowers for food and medicine? In this way, we might create landscapes that are diverse and generous, reflective of the true history of the land and the people who live here now. This kind of radical land restoration would require that we all learn how best to enhance, diversify, and even reanimate ecosystems that support the lives of all living beings, not merely our own.

But without the presence of Indigenous peoples, restoration, even when conducted outside of the invasive paradigm and its dichotomies, does little to rectify the injustices created by colonization. Any effort to remove the settler presence from the land that occurs without a commensurate Indigenous presence is not a true act of justice, but a desire to restore innocence to white settlers by relieving their guilt. Sovereignty for Indigenous peoples demands the sovereignty of their land, which is inextricable from language, culture, and community—a fact that can feel impossible to reconcile with the white relationship to land, so often predicated on ownership and exclusive access.

The modern Land Back movement is an effort to rematriate land to Indigenous peoples. It is not merely a reparative real estate transaction; it is a way to ensure the sovereignty and self-determination of the land itself. Settlers are unaccustomed to thinking of the land, inert and malleable, as a living thing with its own sense of agency. It requires a new openness of spirit to believe the land would hear us if we asked how to take care of it.

Settlers can support the broader Land Back movement by paying a land tax to local Indigenous land trusts or by donating or returning land to Indigenous tribes instead of selling on the market. There is also precedent for municipal governments, including a line item for a Native land tax, with funds going directly to a local tribe, in their tax structure. Members of the three Piscataway groups maintain a donation fund for the Piscataway Land Trust, designed to raise funds for the purchase of Indigenous lands along the Potomac. One day, perhaps, the Piscataway will return Moyaone to their care.

***

THAT EVENING, AS WE CROSSED into the year's shorter, darker days, my partner and I sat in the dusk, watching the sky over the river melt from blush to inky blue. We were satiated by the meal we had just prepared: daylily salad, wineberry tarts, and, of course, honeysuckle sorbet. Bats squeaked overhead as birds sang their good-night songs, and our fire hissed as the last bit of light slipped from the western curve of the river. The Potomac softened into its banks in the dark, and we were quiet for a long time, both of us looking out at the river as the cicadas picked up. Eventually, my partner got up to walk the dog down the short lane, and I stayed by the fire, listening to the logs smolder.

They were gone for what felt like a long time, and at first

only the dog came back to me. She settled into the grass by my feet, as though she had grown impatient with my partner or had lost him somewhere down the road. When he came back to us through the grass, there was an energy rising off his body, as real as a mirage over a highway. "You have to come see this," he said, taking my hand, and the three of us walked together in the dark.

We turned the curve, and I saw them, felt them, an electric energy glittering above the meadow: tens of thousands of lightning bugs. They lit up the night in synchronization, incandescent flashes flying through the air like living stars. On the day of the year when half of the earth dives back into the dark, thousands of lives flared in the night, daring, in their desire for one another, to hold back that descent.

At some point, without my needing to ask, my partner took the dog back to the fire and left me to be alone. I have never experienced the luminescent joy of knowing that I was a part of the Potomac with the intensity that I did in the minutes I stood there, feeling the heat waves rise up from the pavement beneath my body, the cicadas screeching with want along the tree line, the light show of mating insects, the taste of honeysuckle still in my mouth.

Swimming

JULY SMOTHERED THE CITY, suffocating the prospect of any outdoor activity conducted between sunrise and sunset. Air conditioners hummed outside apartment windows like swarms of bees. It hadn't rained in over a month, and from up on the high Virginia slope, the mud-caked rocks riding the surface of the Potomac looked like dingy icebergs. Purple coneflowers withered to white, and yarrow dried into brown feathers. Summer chanterelles never flushed, and blackberries pruned into dark nubs.

When every day seems to die by noon, there is only one recourse for salvation: water. In the evenings, with our brains scrambled and limbs gone listless, my partner and I headed for the waterfalls of Dead Run. Edging carefully around lazing water snakes, we settled onto the sunbaked rocks and slid into the water. The chill shocked my broiling body. My attention drifted, and words wandered away. Our bodies dissolving into the deepest pool, we floated, together, in the quiet.

To enter a body of water is to cross a boundary. You slip beneath the surface and arrive in a different realm, aware of a certain loosening of the mind that follows a lightening of the body. Any emotion—hope or fear or anger—is diffused. During those evening swims, the only feeling I could keep hold of in the water was pleasure.

Surely there is no other act besides sex itself that is more sensual than swimming. It is not only the caress of water on skin but also the way that swimming requires you to reach across the surface, drawing yourself across a rolling tension. River swimming in particular requires a balance between submission to and dominance over the strength and will of the current. As water swirled around me, I found myself participating in a kind of somatic exchange of eroticism and affection with the place and person around me. Though we were not necessarily touching, sharing our bodies with a body of water joined me to my partner, and my partner and me to the river. Fingertips wrinkled like waves, and our hair swirled into eddies.

When I pulled my body out of the pool, my skin freckled and smooth, I sensed a piece of myself missing, as though the river had absorbed some part of me. It was obvious, wringing my hair out and toweling off, that I had also absorbed some part of it. A covalent bond formed between myself, my partner, and the river, three entities distinct but connected by a fluid exchange of desire.

I learned during that heat wave to interpret the river's current as the instrument of its more dangerous desires. On weekend afternoons, we crossed the river to slip into the water at the far edge of the Maryland islands, wading our way to a depth we could sink into. The closer we moved toward the center of the river, the quicker the current flowed against our legs. Around us, potholes and kettles, drilled into the rocks by millennia of churning waters, betrayed the covert violence of the surge just below the surface. On the riverbed, pocked with cracks, canyons, and sieves, the river can run at a rate of almost thirty-five knots, quick enough to pull you under, smash you against underwater outcroppings, and hold you down against the rocks.

I must admit here that it is currently illegal to swim in the Potomac River between Great Falls and National Harbor.

Although the 1971 law was once strictly enforced, it is no longer. On sweltering summer weekends, river swimmers can be found across the city. Boats and bathing suits dot the warm water north of Georgetown, children splash in the gentle rapids of Rock Creek, and something like a keg party assembles at the last waterfall of Scott's Run.

Still, it is true that an average of seven people drown in the Potomac Gorge each year, lulled in by the still and inviting surface. The river pulls them under when they dive from the tops of the high stone walls below Great Falls or hop onto the slick rocks above Chain Bridge. The speed of the current always kept me from full submersion, though I confess the illicit nature of Potomac swimming magnified the pleasure whenever I waded in. Each time I let the water rise up around my shoulders, it was as though I was flaunting my own life against a river that, under the right circumstances, seemed all too willing to draw me down.

One afternoon, my partner tied an old rope swing around my waist so that I could float in the Potomac without being pulled downstream. I lay back with the water around my ears, feeling the current drag my legs, my core relaxing, my senses adapting to the river realm. All sounds dampened, all smells went brackish, and my skin was fluid. For a sublime minutes-long sweep, I was the Potomac. This experience of being absorbed into the body of the river without drowning satisfied the part of me that wants to be swept up in something greater than myself and my body, and it explained why the yearning pull of the slipstream carries pleasure as well as peril.

Later that month, it finally rained. The river came up and the current quickened; for days, it was too dangerous to swim. Stuck on the shore, it occurred to me that while swimming in the river, I had willed myself into incorporation. On the bluff, I looked down at the Potomac like a lost limb, and when the rain swell came down and it was once again safe enough to wade in, I felt, as soon as the lap of the water hit my ankles, the thrill of restored connection. River swimming had cultivated an erotic bond I could not have soldered on the bank. Each dip was the ultimate act of emplacement, each watery encounter a consummation of real love.

As we returned home at sunset to throw our sodden towels over the porch railing, the joy of sincere connection with the river could seem fanciful and immoderately romantic. My partner would go in to make dinner, and I would sit out on our porch in the last light, pinching my puckered fingertips, trying to write down what that ephemeral awareness felt like when my body turned into the Potomac. My words sank as I scribbled equivocations on the river's "natural beauty" and my own inner shifts toward "a certain seasonal warmth." There was an unnameable absence that permeated my incipient memories of swimming. When it became too dark to write anymore, I would go inside, spotty with mosquito bites, chagrined by my failure to express what I am now able to say plainly was love.

※

THE INADEQUACIES OF MY WRITTEN DESCRIPTIONS of love for the Potomac are what, in part, compelled me to take up another mode of documentation. I no longer retain in my memory the image of my partner waist-deep in the current, but I can recall the photograph I took of him: Standing with arms outstretched next to a pillar of speckled rocks, he appears, by comparison, to be as immovable as the sycamores in the background. The water around him is dark, almost indigo, and his skin beams against it. I can only suspect that I took this photograph because I thought he was beautiful there in the water, and in that moment of desire for him and the river I wanted to remember that feeling forever.

"Photographs can abet desire in the most direct, utilitarian way," Susan Sontag explains in *On Photography*. When I look at this photograph, I remember that feeling of want—for my partner and for the river, but also for the memory of those carefree summer swims. In my most nostalgic moments, these photographs can even reduplicate a shadow desire. I am pricked by a stray wistfulness as the bands of blue images scroll by on my phone screen. In total, there are hundreds of images of us that first summer of river swimming: frolicking, smiling, looking at the camera or looking away, while the Potomac, reflecting the sky, fills in the background.

Even though I might have said I felt more alive than ever during these evening swims, my sense of aliveness was predicated on the slow flow of death around me, manifested in the threat of being caught in the current. "All photographs are memento mori," Sontag explains. "To take a photograph is to participate in another person's (or thing's) mortality, vulnerability, mutability." Death, and our yearning for it, Sontag argues, hovers in the corners of photographs like smudgy fingertips.

Perhaps this explains why, beginning that summer, I became obsessed with taking photographs of plants I encountered while out hiking along the Potomac. If I didn't take a photograph of the plant right then and there, it might not be around long enough for me to walk by it again and take its image home with me. During these evening swims, which brought us out to islands usually unreachable, I became acquainted with plants I now consider close companions. This was the season I first encountered the royal gauze of water willow flowers and the emerald beads of unripe spicebush, which popped like peppercorns in my mouth. I remember learning how to distinguish boneset from snakeroot, two plants I met on Plummers Island later that summer.

Photography became for me a way to observe and recognize the life around me, expanding the web of relationships between plants, animals, fungi, the river, and myself. Snapping a photograph transformed the riverbank from a heavy wash of summer greens, dotted with a few familiar plants, into a whole interconnected community of living things with names and histories. Photography was a tool not merely for documentation but for observation and even integration.

Sitting on a rock in the middle of the river with my legs low in the water, I took a photograph of a night heron as it emerged from a knot of ironweed, and I felt myself so deeply there. Swimming in the river and taking photographs of plants and animals living along it had woven me into the material reality of that place in an unalterable fashion.

But while the material fact of that connection to the river remained, what waned in the years since was the pleasure that first accompanied my expanding consciousness of that fact. Some unexamined attraction beckoned me back to the shore each subsequent summer, hazy-eyed and hungry for a connection that I struggled to identify. Was it simply a desire for the river, or was it something else? All I had left with which to interrogate the nature of this desire were my own faint memories and a thousand photographs.

※

AT SOME POINT AFTER THAT FIRST SUMMER, I stumbled onto an online treasure trove of archival photographs of Potomac River swimming. I had been searching for panoramic shots of the river, eager to compare images of the same wide vistas in the past with those I had taken myself, but the vast majority of these images are not of the unattended landscape, but of people occupying the foreground—just like the photographs I had taken of my partner. I trawled through this collection of bathers, waders, boaters, and divers, delighted by the many mustachioed men in rubber caps, windblown women in woolen bloomers, muddy-faced boys in fishing dinghies, and, in one particularly mesmerizing photograph, a posse of teenage girls cuddling a stuffed alligator on the shore.

There are hundreds of these images, dating from the 1910s to the 1940s, many from the same two collections donated to the Library of Congress. The photographs range in style from formal family photos of bathing-costumed cousins to candid shots of flappers with their lanky dates to hazy aerials of the river with hundreds of bobbing heads and limbs in the water. A few are even paparazzi shots, capturing the swimming adventures of such minor celebrities as Kay Laurell, a Ziegfeld Follies star who made her name on the Washington vaudeville stage, and Miss Dorothy Parker, better known as Miss Washington, 1938.

In a hundred different photos, anonymous men in tank suits pose proudly with a medley of relevant river accessories, including canoes, rowing oars, racing trophies, ukuleles, and strung-up shad. Disheveled children with faces coated in sand splash on the beaches and dive from makeshift boards into the canal. Bashful teenage girls in knee-high bathing stockings grin self-consciously up at the camera, betraying their adolescent satisfaction at having been seen, in all the vast crowds, through the lens.

What is it about pleasure that demands documentation? Compared to most historic photographs where subjects are captured looking ambivalent at best and dour at worst, the people depicted in these photographs appear jubilant, giving the impression that there is no greater pleasure on Earth than to don your bathing slippers and bonnet and ride a mule along the Arlington bank of the Potomac River. The sheer number of these century-old photographs, as well as their archival longevity, highlights a certain fundamental goal of all photography, then and now—to capture joy in its rawest, rarest, and most ephemeral forms. I am not sure I have ever seen a person quite as ebullient as the curly-haired preteen winner of the 1921 Tidal Basin Bathing Beach Pie-Eating Contest, eyes crinkled with glee and mouth smeared with blackberry filling.

Most of these photographs were taken at four locations along the Potomac: Arlington Beach, Glen Echo Amusement Park, the vagabond summer canoe camps housed on various islands between Georgetown and Cabin John, and the Tidal Basin Bathing Beach. Located where today's Jefferson Memorial perches on the outer rim of the Tidal Basin, the bathing beach there opened in August 1918, primarily through the efforts of the sweaty and agitated Nebraska senator George Norris, who found, upon his arrival in the nation's capital, "one of the most trying climates in the United States and inadequate bathing conditions." The beach itself was a short man-made stretch of sand, though the park around it eventually included attractive bathhouses, as well as umbrellas, lounge chairs, vending stands, and a full-time chloro-boat, which dumped chlorine into the Basin to sanitize the water. The city's public health service also installed four liquid-chlorine dispensers along the arches of the Inlet Bridge, determined to keep the water clean enough not just for swimming but also bathing.

Throughout the early 1920s, the Tidal Basin Bathing Beach was one of Washington's premier social centers, a place for young and old to see and be seen. In view of the Bureau of Engraving and Printing, Washingtonians took swimming lessons, dived off a multiplatform, twenty-foot-tall dock, played a game called pushball (which featured a beach ball at least six feet in diameter), and participated in numerous beauty contests, diving competitions, canoe-tilting tournaments, tug-of-war battles, and boys' drag pageants (though they were not necessarily called that).

Operating in the days before air-conditioning, the beach was one of the only places in the city where residents could seek respite from the heat. In July 1919, the line to access the beach extended more than three blocks. On one particularly scorching day in July the following year, over twenty thousand people flocked to the beach for relief in the cool water flowing into the Basin from the Potomac. The subjects of the hundreds of photographs taken here underscore the broad popularity of the Tidal Basin Bathing Beach. There are old men lounging in the sand, licking ice-cream cones; married couples dozing in each other's arms; and toddlers, hardly old enough to stand, cooing with delight as the water laps at their tiny feet.

For Virginia residents across the river, there was Arlington Beach and Amusement Park, located near the present-day Pentagon Building, adjacent to the airport. Crowds of up to twelve thousand people packed the beach and bathhouses in the summer, drawn to the park's numerous nonaquatic amusements, including a merry-go-round, a Ferris wheel, aerial swings, a roller coaster called the Whip, and a ride called the Dodgem. After dancing for hours in the park's pavilion to music provided by the Washington Jazz Orchestra, people cooled off by going night swimming in the Potomac, the dark water lit by strands of twinkling lights. The glow of the Washington Monument and Lincoln Memorial pooled across the river.

For those less interested in river swimming but still in need of a cool breeze offered by Potomac proximity, there was

Glen Echo Amusement Park, located on a scenic ridge above the river two miles from the District line. Accessible from the city by trolley, Glen Echo was one of the most popular weekend recreational spots in and around the city during the first half of the twentieth century, and the park continued to adapt to its changing audience as Washington sprawled into suburbs over the decades. Eventually, its amusements included over a dozen attractions, including a bumper car pavilion, a hippodrome, a menagerie carousel, two roller coasters (the Hydraulic Dive for the less adventurous rider and the Dip for the daring), a marine toboggan water race, modernist whirligig rides called the Satellite Jet, the Paratrooper, and Comet Jr., an elaborate Art Deco ballroom, and a giant Ferris wheel perilously positioned over the Potomac.

As for its swimming attractions, Glen Echo featured the enormously popular Crystal Pool. Built in 1931 at a cost of $200,000 (equivalent to $3.8 million today), the pool could accommodate over three thousand swimmers and included a ten-thousand-square-foot sand beach, high and low diving platforms, a water slide, a refreshment stand, and a first-aid building (which was, apparently, much needed). In the water itself, there was an electric fountain with nighttime rainbow lighting, blue-white floodlights, and a complex filtration system that cleaned the 500,000-gallon pool every eight hours. On summer weekends during World War II, mobs of off-duty soldiers and government workers came to twirl their dates around the ballroom to the music of Tommy Dorsey and Glenn Miller, before jumping into the kaleidoscopic depths of the Crystal Pool.

If you weren't in the mood for the crowds at Glen Echo, you could hike down the ridge and catch a boat ride over to one of the canoe camps located on the islands between the canal and the river. Every summer, middle-class Washington families moved from their inland row houses to makeshift cabins and canvas pole tents on the Potomac islands and shore, where they established impromptu summer camps for adults and children alike. Though some camps were restricted to solely male membership, *The Evening Star* reported in 1908 on the growing popularity of these rustic summer outposts for families, explaining that "every available island, as well as the Maryland and Virginia shores, is lined with shacks, each surrounded with ground enough to provide for the utmost seclusion and privacy."

Rarely leaving their island refuges except to work, adults spent their summers gossiping in lounge chairs, making and drinking whiskey, swimming in the river, and generally ignoring their children, who roved about the islands like tiny pirates, starting small wars with the children of other camps. Members of the canoe clubs also gathered and trained accomplished athletes, young men who displayed their rowing prowess during regularly scheduled regatta events. At night, the members of the various camps at Fernwood, Sycamore Island, High Island, and others sang and played music, drank and told fireside stories, and generally indulged in what one article headlined as "The Thousand and One Sources of Pleasure for the Camper" to be found on the Potomac canoe club scene. At the end of every season, members of each canoe club gathered together for a group photo, posing for the camera in their white suits, their faces tanned.

Having studied every one of these photographs a dozen times, when I look into the smiling faces of these long-deceased strangers, I experience an uncanny sense of unreality. The settings of these photographs are intimately familiar to me—I can recognize by the slope of the distant shore or the sight of a marbled monument where the photograph was taken, and my recognition of that place supplies a sense of reality to the photograph.

But the subjects of these photographs—a young woman cuddling her pet possum by the Tidal Basin or a rangy man in summer whites strumming a mandolin on High Island—are so contradictory to my modern understanding of how people relate to the river that I find these people of the past so fantastic as to be almost imaginary. It's as if these photographs have imprisoned their reality, and once in my possession, I imagine that I, too, can possess the past. But the more I look at these photographs, drawing myself away from their settings to their human subjects, the less I feel that I possess them than they possess me, a frightening, almost narcotic feeling.

By documenting a culture of recreation that no longer exists in D.C., these photographs have the remarkable power to induce a nostalgic desire on my part to enter them. I would very much like to be able to walk my pet possum down to the bank of the Potomac while my partner in a boater hat strums a guitar and feeds me a slice of lemon meringue pie. Who, indeed, would not like to enter this scene? Still, I find myself struggling against that desire, however silly it may be, for reasons that Sontag explains when she writes that "a photograph is both a pseudo-presence and a token of absence. Like a wood fire in a room, photographs—especially those of people, of distant landscapes and faraway cities, of the vanished past—are incitements to reverie."

It's the "pseudo-presence" of these foregone Potomac people's delight that elicits a longing on my part to enter their past. But as Sontag explains, in every photograph there is also an absence, an invisible exclusion that undercuts the wild pleasure that these photographs appear to document. Simply put, the exclusion is this: They contain almost no nonwhite faces.

Within these archival collections, there are only a handful of images that include Black people. In one photograph, two Black boys, fully dressed in overalls and newsboy caps, splash in Rock Creek, accompanied by two white boys, all of whom look no older than six years old, too young to have learned the social conventions of Jim Crow. In several poignant snapshots taken in 1938 by Farm Security Administration photographer Marion Post Wolcott, white tourists throw pennies into the Union Station fountain, where Black boys are shown diving into the water to retrieve the coins; as compensation for their willingness to delight these white visitors, the boys presumably received consent to keep the money.

Archival photographs from the early twentieth century—that is, photographs deemed worthy enough to be preserved by major American research institutions—do not, on the whole, document equivalent subjects of Black joy. In the Library of Congress archives, images of Black Washingtonians participating in recreation or leisure activities are few and far between. Of the existing archived images that depict Black residents of D.C. swimming, fishing, and generally enjoying themselves, the photographer responsible is most likely Joseph Owens Curtis, Addison Scurlock, or Gordon Parks, three of the nation's most renowned Black photographers of the early twentieth century. Their work remains some of the most evocative of everyday life in D.C., providing critical documentation of Black joy from within the city's Black communities. The images created by Curtis, Scurlock, and Parks provide an essential counter to those of white photographers in D.C., in which Black residents are commonly found positioned in the foreground of images of potential slum and alley clearance; through the lens of white photographers, Black Washingtonians are less subjects of pleasure than objects tagged for removal.

Returning to these images of white swimmers and bathers, it's not merely the absence of Black people from these images that makes their reevaluation as such so striking. Rather, it is in the consideration of how the absence of Black people creates the conditions for so much white joy. The obverse, then, is also true: The presence of Black people, even the threat of their potential presence, creates the conditions for white anguish, and it's that fact—that white joy cannot permit its Black counterpart—that occupies every one of these otherwise delightful photographs, disguising white supremacy with the glimmer of sentimental desire.

❊

ASK MOST D.C. RESIDENTS TODAY whether they might consider swimming in the Potomac, and you'll likely receive a sneer, scoff, or slap in the face. Many Washingtonians believe that swimming in the sewage-stocked, parasite-choked Potomac is an invitation to contract gastroenteritis. Longtime residents in particular are repelled by the prospect of river swimming; memories of the stench of effluent keep many people from even wading in. The city's enduring river-swimming ban, first instituted by local authorities in the 1930s and extended by the EPA in the 1970s, supplies further reinforcement to the argument that only a fool would enter the pathogenic Potomac.

The apparent filth of the Potomac has long been used as a scapegoat to keep certain people out of the river while forcing others into it. When the Tidal Basin Bathing Beach closed in 1925 after only seven years, despite having been exceptionally popular among the city's white residents, Congress cited as the primary reasons for its closure the increasing dirtiness of the Potomac and the expense of keeping the Basin chlorinated. While it is true that, by the 1920s, the Potomac had begun to suffer from increased upstream pollution, the principal reason the beach was closed had little to do with sewage runoff; it was, instead, a matter of who was permitted to enter the water.

Even before the Tidal Basin Beach's official opening in 1918, Black residents had lobbied Congress for funds for a "colored beach," to be located on the west side of the Basin (approximately where today's Martin Luther King, Jr. Memorial is located). Black advocates for a segregated beach sought not just separate-but-equal facilities but also a way to establish formal protection for Black children who already sought relief from the heat by sneaking into the Basin to swim—a seemingly harmless act that had, nevertheless, infuriated white swimmers. White anxieties about integrated swimming were largely twofold: Racist preconceptions about Black people's predilection to spread communicable diseases heightened fears of what might be transmitted through the water, and myths of Black male hypersexuality saturated white imaginations, creating a panic over the potential for interracial sex that might be engendered by the intimate public space of a beach.

The threat of white mob violence against Black residents ran particularly high following the opening of the white beach. During the hot summer of 1919, the potential for white riots in the capital swelled as the "Red Summer" of white supremacist violence raged across the country. The necessity of a Black beach on the far, opposite side of the Basin was bolstered by events in Chicago in late July, in which a Black teenager was stoned to death while swimming, having crossed the invisible line in the water demarcating that city's adjacent white and Black beaches. In D.C. that same week, Black Washingtonians were forced to arm themselves against a spate of white vigilante violence in the city's Black neighborhoods, a "race war" that left thirty-nine people dead. Black-majority neighborhoods in Southwest, adjacent to the Tidal Basin, were a particular locus for white mobs storming through the city.

In 1924, the House finally approved a fifty-thousand-dollar

line-item appropriation for the creation of a Black beach, but several white supremacist senators stonewalled the funding. Under intense pressure from Black city leaders to respond, Congress declared it illegal to swim in the Tidal Basin, solving the issue of how to create separate-but-equal swimming facilities by removing all swimming facilities. The buildings on the white beach were demolished, and various sand-tolerant shrubs were planted to discourage swimmers from returning. Newspapers circulated the convenient fiction that the Tidal Basin Bathing Beach had been closed for reasons related to hygiene, not white supremacy.

Across the river, Arlington Beach, also strictly segregated, shuttered in 1929 due to the ostensible dirtiness of the river, as well as the danger posed to swimmers from increased air traffic from the adjacent airfield. But because the beach had been located near the Black neighborhoods of East Arlington and Queen City, it is also likely that the threat of integration played a role in its closure—and the subsequent establishment of Arlington's nominally public, segregated swimming pools. Black children growing up in Arlington would not gain access to a community swimming pool until the 1960s, and for decades they were relegated to swimming at a spot off Four Mile Run they called "Blue Man Junction," today's Bluemont Park.

After the closure of the two public Potomac beaches, white people abandoned the shores of the river for swimming. Several great floods in the 1930s, as well as the increasing accumulation of acid mine drainage, also put an end to the annual canoe regattas and minstrel shows that had been so popular among the middle- and upper-class white membership of the Kolumbia Kanoe Klub and the Klassy Kanoe Klub, both of which claimed the terrifying acronym KKK. By 1940, whatever white culture of river swimming that had existed on the Potomac had been disbanded, and today it has been largely forgotten, the banks of the river long ago replaced by a cerulean-studded constellation of suburban swimming pools.

※

FOLLOWING THE CLOSURE OF THE RIVER BEACHES, white working-class swimmers retreated to the small whites-only municipal pools near the Washington Monument before those pools, too, were demolished in 1935. Afterward, more well-to-do whites, perhaps eager to abandon the memory of the Tidal Basin battle, endorsed the building of separate-but-equal public pool facilities to be built across the city, following a trend emerging across the country. The economist Heather McGhee describes this era of civic-minded public pool construction in her book *The Sum of Us,* explaining that city "officials envisioned the distinctly American phenomenon of the grand public resort pools as 'social melting pots.' Like free public grade schools, public pools were part of an 'Americanizing' project intended to overcome ethnic divisions and cohere a common identity."

Of course, that common identity extended only to white residents. By the late 1930s, white Washingtonians of any social class could visit six outdoor public swimming pools—Anacostia, Rosedale, East Potomac Park, McKinley, Takoma, and Georgetown—while Black residents could visit only two—Francis in West End and Banneker in Pleasant Plains. Francis and Banneker immediately became critical social spaces for the city's Black residents, fostering a distinctive Black swimming and diving community, rare in southern cities in the years before the passage of the Civil Rights Act. Though each of the eight pools was ostensibly open to all residents, in line with the Department of the Interior's nondiscrimination policies, de facto segregation and citizen-policing efforts kept some pools as all-white and others all-Black, even as neighborhood demographics began to shift during the era of white flight.

Despite their popularity for Black swimmers, Francis and, to a lesser extent, Banneker were not conveniently located for the majority of the city's Black residents. Anacostia and Rosedale, two whites-only pools located in Black-majority neighborhoods, became two of the city's most volatile sites throughout the 1940s as white swimmers refused access to Black children who sometimes lived next door. For Black children growing up outside of Northwest, options for cooling off on hot days were limited: You could slog upward of forty blocks to Banneker, take a long, sweaty, and segregated streetcar ride all the way to Francis, or you could find your way to the bank of your neighborhood creek or river. Many took the latter option.

By the mid-1940s, the Anacostia and Potomac Rivers were as dirty as they had ever been. The Anacostia, long the capital's riparian sewer, was now also the site of its public landfill, and the Potomac had seen its first bacterial-born fish kills. It had been over a decade since the first formal restrictions on river swimming between Georgetown and Fort Washington were instituted—less a racist social pretense than an actual concern for swimmers' intestinal safety.

But for the Black children who sought a place to play away from the routine torment of segregation, the rivers and creeks they lived along were cool and inviting. The Watts Branch of the Anacostia, the outflow of Oxon Creek into the Potomac, and the Virginia shore north of Alexandria were all local swimming spots where Black children living in and around D.C. created their own worlds of recreation and leisure, distinct spaces of pleasure and resistance that were not captured in archival photographs. The rivers, with all their associated stench and pollution, were certainly not desirable spaces for swimming by any means, but along their banks Black children found spaces of refuge in a segregated city.

The pleasures offered by the rivers came with their own risks. Even for the strongest swimmers, the currents of the Potomac and Anacostia, particularly south of the city, can be quick. Between one eddy and the next, the countercurrent is mercurial, capable of pulling swimmers below the surface. Unlike the city's white children who'd had access to public swimming lessons at least since 1918—not to mention the security offered by lifeguards at swimming pools—Black children were less likely to have learned how to swim, precisely because they had been barred from formal swimming spaces. From 1931 to 1951, at least nine Black children drowned in the Potomac, including two sets of brothers, Theodore Exzell and Benjamin Watkins in 1948 and Lonnie Richard and Morris Leroy Johnson in 1951.

The Watkins brothers, aged nine and eleven, had gone to the mouth of Hunting Creek in Alexandria to play with surplus army gas masks that they hoped would allow them to breathe underwater. Exzell was pulled under by the current of the creek, and when he did not resurface, his older brother Benjamin jumped in after him. "Neither could swim," reported *The Evening Star*. The deaths of the Watkins brothers sparked an agonized outrage among Black residents, already frustrated with the socially codified segregation that kept their children from accessing pools and playgrounds in their own neighborhoods, particularly in Southeast D.C. Under duress from Black organizers who threatened to picket the pools until they were integrated, in 1949 the Department of the Interior, which oversaw the operations of the city's federal pools, announced it would formally desegregate Anacostia Pool later that summer.

Anacostia Pool was one of the city's finest park facilities, an example of the federal government's civic (albeit paternalistic) investment in the white residents of the capital. When Black children arrived on the morning of June 23 to swim, they were surrounded and driven off by white teenagers and their parents. Similar confrontations over the next few days led to a final melee on June 29, in which a crowd of five hundred people gathered to witness bloody brawls between white and Black swimmers. Mounted park police officers arrived to break up the crowd and made several arrests, some for the distribution of antisegregation flyers. In response to the fracas, the Interior Department announced the closure of Anacostia Pool for the rest of the summer. As with the Tidal Basin Bathing Beach, the issue of integrated swimming was solved by closing off access to the water entirely. When Anacostia Pool reopened the next year on a desegregated basis, there was one important change to its membership: There were no more white people.

The horrific pattern of a Black child drowning, followed by anguish, outrage, and protest, continued across the city over the next few years. After the tragic drowning of the Johnson brothers in the Potomac in 1951, Black residents of Alexandria pressed their city government for a Black pool, which opened the following year, named in honor of the Johnsons. Soon after, the city also began running weekend bus service for Black Alexandrians from Old Town all the way to D.C.'s Banneker Pool.

In 1952, a Black teenager seeking relief on a particularly hot night drowned in the Rosedale Pool after scaling the fence, resulting in intensified demonstrations against the segregated pool and surrounding park. After the park was closed to all visitors following white attacks against Black picketers, one hundred Black children climbed the fence during an impromptu protest, leading to the final desegregation and subsequent white abandonment of the Rosedale facilities. Later in the 1960s, protests called "swim-ins," held in the Union Station fountain, would pressure the city to dedicate resources to maintaining the supposedly integrated public pools of the city, which had, over the course of only five years, largely become all-Black recreational spaces that the city had let fall into disrepair.

As they fled from the city, white Washingtonians established no less than 125 private whites-only pools and country clubs across Northwest D.C., northern Virginia, and the Maryland suburbs, which remain all-white or mostly so to this day. White self-segregation was and remains as critical a social factor in maintaining segregated swimming spaces as any federal law. The majority of the region's most exclusive and celebrated swim teams and country clubs can trace their origins to the white abandonment of the city's public pools during the era of mandated integration.

For the working- and middle-class whites who could not afford to join the lavish country clubs but would not deign to swim in the city's integrated pools, there was always Glen Echo's Crystal Pool, which maintained a whites-only policy and was easy to access via car, bus, or trolley. But the segregated amusement park paradise that Glen Echo had dutifully maintained for the prior six decades came to an end in the summer of 1960. Inspired by that spring's successful sit-ins in Greensboro, North Carolina, a group of students, many from Howard University, arrived at Glen Echo in the evening of June 30 to protest the park's discriminatory policies. After they were turned away from the park's entrance, the students rushed to the carousel—long the park's favorite showpiece—where they were confronted by a security guard and arrested.

The Nonviolent Action Group (NAG), an affiliate of the Student Nonviolent Coordinating Committee, returned to Glen Echo Park to picket for the remainder of the summer, holding signs that read GLEN ECHO SHOULD ECHO DEMOCRACY and

BIGOTRY IS NO FUN. The American Nazi Party soon arrived at Glen Echo to counterprotest, attacking Black activists and carrying signs with racial slurs. Jewish residents in the nearby neighborhood of Bannockburn joined the picket line, and President Kennedy's future secretary of commerce, a resident of Bannockburn, reportedly played a significant role in putting pressure on park management to change their policies.

The following spring, Glen Echo Park opened for the first time as an integrated facility, though it remained a white-majority affair. Black patrons, while allowed, were not made to feel welcome, particularly in the Crystal Pool. After an incident in 1966, in which a roller coaster was allegedly damaged due to a cigarette thrown from a coaster car by a Black teenager, park administrators abruptly decided to close the park for the day. Dubious reports of vandalism by Black teenagers returning to D.C. via bus prompted the city transit authority to cease bus service to Glen Echo, leaving hundreds of people stranded in the suburbs, furious and frightened. Attendance fell as rumors spread that Black teenage gangs frequented Glen Echo. Within two years, the park closed. The rides were broken down and sold off, and the Crystal Pool filled in with concrete.

Across the country, from 1940 to 1970, hundreds of public swimming pools were closed, drained, filled in, or otherwise abandoned by white citizens and municipal authorities as the threat of legally mandated integration advanced. The Tidal Basin Bathing Beach, Arlington Beach, D.C.'s public pools, and Glen Echo's Crystal Pool are only a handful of the swimming spaces across the nation that white Americans demolished or deserted rather than desegregate. Rather than allow Black people to share in the pleasures offered by public parks and pools, white Americans willingly destroyed the spaces that had created the conditions for so much of their own joy.

Heather McGhee calls this zero-sum mentality "drained-pool politics," a useful metaphor to describe the ways white supremacy hurts not just people of color but whites, as well. "Today, we don't even notice the absence of the grand resort pools in our communities; where grass grows over former sites, there are no plaques to tell the story of how racism drained the pools," she writes.

But the issue today is less about a lack of public swimming pools than it is that the principles that drained these public services live on, now in a subtler design. White Americans believe deeply that another's gain is our loss, and our cleaved, embittered political system is largely the result of this kind of thinking. In this way, American society has become a macrocosm of the drained pool, and white abandonment of public services and spaces for costly private options emerges almost everywhere in our politics, from education to health care to housing. Americans of all races live without these basic guarantees of the social contract because, as McGhee's metaphor goes, white people will not share their swimming pools.

※

To say I was sweaty as I reached the Tidal Basin would be polite. I was drenched after walking just two miles down to the Basin from dinner with a friend in Chinatown in ninety-five-degree heat. It had poured two days before, causing the river to rise, and the evening had the kind of torrid, swampy feeling that prompts people to repeat the old adage that if you ever want to know what hell feels like, come to Washington, D.C., in July. If there was ever a day to go swimming, this was it. A half-dozen plastic bottles bobbed in the water, and the sun sank below the cherry trees on the far side of the Basin, spilling color across the surface. Despite the trash, the colorful reflection and promise offered by cool water subsumed me with an urgent need to jump in.

To hell with whatever social mores prevented my entering the water. I lay facedown on the brink of the Basin, avoiding eye contact with the people around me, and extended my left arm up to my elbow in the water—it was cold, bracing even, and my fingers swirled in the slight current as I let my arm relax into a pliant sort of absorption. If not for my own self-conscious awareness that tourists were watching a grown woman dangle over the edge of the Basin, I could have comfortably fallen asleep there.

"I wish I was brave enough to do that!" a woman walking by said, and I smiled shyly at her. I wanted to say she didn't need to be brave, that the river was not only safe enough to touch but also to swim in . . . well, most of the time—in certain places, and certainly with precautions taken. While dropping a limb into the Tidal Basin doesn't currently pose much of a risk, river swimming in the District remains a somewhat precarious undertaking, the ban on swimming notwithstanding.

But that precarity is fast disappearing. As the city updates its sewer system, sewage is being diverted from the rivers at rates unheard of in many urban areas. In 2023, D.C. Water finished construction on a massive tunnel that promises to prevent over 98 percent of sewage outflow from entering the Anacostia; similar promised upgrades are in store for the Potomac by 2030, when construction on another set of sewer tunnels is set to be completed. In the meantime, researchers have found that in some locations along the river, including the Tidal Basin and the Washington Channel, bacterial counts are low enough that the water is safe to swim in over 97 percent of the time.

As for the dangers posed by the current, it is prudent to avoid the water for at least two days after a downpour, and there are certain coves along the river where the flow is slower than in its center channels. The installation of partitions between the shore and deep channel could also keep swimmers safe from the current, as would the construction of floating docks around established river pools, a design popular in many European cities.

Under the right circumstances and along the right stretch of shore, swimming in the Potomac can be one of the most pleasurable summer experiences that D.C. offers, as evidenced by the hundreds of people who already take to the water every summer. But this number of lawless river swimmers is quite small compared to the city's population, some of whom have simply never thought to swim in the Potomac. Perhaps especially for newcomers, the prospect of swimming in the Potomac is not so repulsive or risky as it is simply unimaginable. Cut off from public access to the shore, many residents encounter the river to the south of the city less as a body of water than as an obstacle that creates traffic jams.

Our inability to even imagine what a riparian culture of recreation in D.C. might look like in the twenty-first century stems from the white abandonment of the river as a space of recreation. It has now been almost one hundred years since white Washingtonians flocked en masse to the river to swim. White residents continue to self-segregate in private swimming clubs, while nonwhite swimmers are relegated to the city's public pools, which are well maintained, albeit crowded, an indication that there is a greater demand for public swimming spaces than is currently being met.

White residents, it seems, have forgotten—perhaps intentionally—that they lost both shores of the Potomac not just to pollution but to drained-pool thinking. For Black residents, the loss of access to the city's rivers is not an issue of memory. On the contrary, many residents retain both the bitter memory of the drownings of Black children as well as the secret pleasures of illicit river swimming. For Black Washingtonians, then, the shores of the Potomac and Anacostia are sites of both sorrow and bliss.

My forays into river swimming had certainly connected me to the river, to its plants, and to my partner, but I had never experienced while swimming in the Potomac the kind of wild joy that a shared day at the beach can engender. Further, my predilection for photography that accompanied the delights of river swimming necessarily exposed a certain absence in my own photographs. My connection with the natural world that was established by swimming was powerful, but it was, nevertheless, undercut by the depravations of human connection that should have constituted swimming in a space as open and free as the shores of the Potomac River. The dull ache of desire I felt when swimming in the river was, at its wellspring, a wish to share the river with others, to experience the Potomac as the integrated space of coalescing pleasures it should always have been.

The ambivalence and fear of the river that D.C. residents maintain is, I think, less a legacy of its dangers or dirtiness than it is uncertainty of the kind of democratic convergence that swimming in the nation's river would inevitably produce. The river belongs to all of us, yet both the racist impulse to forget and the understandable hurt of remembering keep all residents from its shores.

I thought then that I might produce my phone and take a picture of the sunset washing the surface of the Basin into a blur of roses and reds, to remember the joy of imagining a Potomac where all could swim freely, but I thought better of it and watched the pink dissolve into blue, listening to the river lap at the edge, calling me and all of the city back into the water.

Pawpaws

THERE ARE A STRING OF DAYS IN LATE AUGUST when the air cools, a false touch of fall that hangs around the Potomac like an invisible film. The light shifts slightly, and a sick yellow quality clings to the floodplain as the first waves of goldenrod bloom and the first sycamore leaves drop. Then, just as soon as these days have arrived, the heat returns.

In the early morning of one of these dim days, I headed down the trail toward a pawpaw patch above the Little Falls dam. Orb weavers, those quarter-size spiders that work gossamer into massive wheeled webs, were emerging. Born in spring no bigger than pinheads, they had spent the summer eating and growing, building webs too precious to notice. Now, close to full size, they knit fine cross-cut circles the size of bicycle tires between spicebush branches and silver maple suckers. As the sun crested over the east ridge, the spiders revealed their nighttime work: hundreds of webs, flecked with dew, glittering among the trees.

The way the webs seized the sun didn't stop me from walking face-first into some dozen. Though I regretted ruining such painstaking work, coming into contact with these spiders increased my awareness of other potential animals around me. I looked up, combing the trees for a songbird flare, then down to the water for a flash of fish in the eddies, but I saw nothing. I watched sunlight filter through the canopy, flickering on the surface of the stream. Then, in an eerie way, the light appeared to sink, settling into the stretch of silt at the confluence. It was quiet this morning, quieter than it had been since winter.

Down the trail, I saw the imprint of deer hooves in the rust-colored clay and the furry links of fox scat. Farther still, I found the site of a jaybird massacre, dozens of sapphire-streaked feathers splayed across the bloodstained earth, where a hawk had found its next meal. Each of these traces appeared as a palimpsest, evidence of these animals' existence that underscored their absence. A walk at daybreak would usually reveal, at the very least, a few squirrels or sparrows, but I saw nothing and no one.

I could smell the pawpaw grove before I entered it. Spongy, cloying, saccharine, and soft, there is no one right word to describe the pawpaw. North America's largest native fruit (and, by some opinions, the tastiest), pawpaws ripen along the Potomac in the very last days of August. The oblong green fruit, between two and six inches long, had already begun to ripen, fall, and rot on the ground. Once dropped or snatched from between the leaves, pawpaws turn to mush within days. They are notoriously difficult to ship or preserve, edible for a day or two, and only truly delectable for a fleeting twelve-hour period. In a week, the ground of this grove would be spattered in moldering fruit.

Under their speckled skin, which darkens when ripened to perfect sweetness, pawpaw pulp is a pale yellow custard, dotted with dark emetic seeds. Every year I returned here to gather pounds of the fruit; at home, I skinned each one and removed its seeds, mashed it all into a creamy pulp, made cakes and breads, canned preserves, and froze the remaining puree to use all year round.

Most folks describe the taste as a cross between a banana and a mango, with touches of pineapple, vanilla, and citrus. But there is also a hint of something rotten in their flesh, even when the fruit is not. Sugary and strange, a bite of pawpaw leaves the lightest wash of putrefaction on the tongue. For some, that slight tang is enough to put them off this fruit for good. It is undeniably a peculiar flavor, as exquisite as it is repellent. Nothing tastes of the falling away of summer like a pawpaw.

Though it was still early in the season, this patch was already putrid. The aroma overwhelmed my senses as I shook each thin trunk to drop the ripened fruit to the earth. I waded through spoilage and swarming flies, bending over to gather salvageable pawpaws into my bag. When I stood up, suddenly hot and dizzy, the bizarre quality of the light caught my attention again. Gazing up at the canopy spotted with the plump unripened fruit, I found it difficult to square the smell of decay with the appearance of such lushness.

What is it about fecundity that so attracts and revolts? Perhaps it is that the ability to produce abundant life is equally marked by a mean excess; the perverse proliferation of nature heralds an untold number of deaths. Through the paradox of fecundity, all that we are drawn to observe and care for in nature can simultaneously cause us to recoil in horror.

I made the mistake then of taking a small bite from a ripe pawpaw. When I swallowed, an acid rot slithered down my throat. All around me, in places unseen and unknown, mycelium bloated into mushrooms, moths mated and swelled with eggs, ragweed caked stream tops with pollen, maggots chomped through corpses and flies laid eggs in flesh, fish spawned and gobbled fish spawn, and somewhere inside me, cells cleaved and died, bacteria swarmed, and microbes multiplied. I was blood and tissue and bile, a body that, given the chance, would rot as quickly as the black mash of pawpaw.

I felt sick. I longed to scoop out the insides of my mouth,

but there was nothing to remove. My stomach turned and I sat down and threw my head between my legs to keep from retching. After a moment, still feeling queasy, I stood up and pushed through a crowd of tattered wood nettles down to the shore. I knelt in the mud, my pants already plastered with pawpaw, and lowered my head to the surface, sticking my face in the water. Cold and velvety, the water relaxed me. When I pulled my head back up to breathe, I felt less nauseous, just terribly alone.

I had never considered just how much the presence of other animals on the trail made me feel not simply safe or at ease but alive. The sight of a copperhead could have comforted me then, any reassurance that I was not just another solitary body on the cusp of decomposition. I scanned the wide surface above the dam, a plane often flecked with herons and gulls. There was nothing but the thrum of the dam and the suffocating, smoggy chill. I gagged and threw up into the Potomac.

It was the hideous contradiction that undid me, I reckoned later, curled up in bed with my dog at my feet, a trash can at the ready beside me. That, and dehydration. There was the yellow light dripping through the abundant green, the feculent smell of pawpaw, and the hole these false fall days pierced through the gauze of summer. They all added up to the prick of some unknowable loss as summer, light, life slipped away.

❊

"The world has signed a pact with the devil; it had to. It is the covenant to which every thing, even every hydrogen atom, is bound. The terms are clear: if you want to live, you have to die," Annie Dillard wrote in 1974. I wonder now if this is still true. Don't humans these days have a greater hand in choosing what lives or dies than, say, the devil?

Current scholarship suggests that one species slides into

nonexistence every five minutes. In a recent comprehensive report from the United Nations, scientists estimated that one million plant and animal species will become extinct in the next decades. By the year 2100, over one half of the Earth's life-forms, untold billions of organisms, could be extinct. Even as the exact data surrounding extinction forecasts inevitably fluctuates, the sum of all these alternating figures is apocalyptic.

I confess I have little sense of what these speculative losses mean. I can hardly imagine the loss of one familiar species, never mind the unknown one billion across the world. As the numbers of lost species mount, we often struggle to quantify them, let alone qualify them. The chances are high that in the minutes you have spent reading these last several pages, the species that went extinct had never been known or named by humans. Endlings—the last individuals of a species—that we do know are often given a human name, as in the case of Lonely George, the last *Achatinella apexfulva,* a species of Hawaiian tree snail, who died in January 2019. Lonely George was a doleful name for a mollusk, a name with a certain predetermined inevitability. Looking at a photo of the snail, the modest stripes across its shell, I understand that our gift of human (also gendered, European-origin) names like George to these endlings is a desperate attempt to extend our own all-important humanity, a stab at undeserved repentance, like tossing out a life preserver after you've thrown someone overboard.

Names are how humans build relationships with the living world, the words we reach for first in our quest to make meaning. The need to recognize other living beings by their names is perhaps especially important when we know they will otherwise die. Humanity will not act to protect what we do not know, and we will not know what we do not name. "I'm trying to imagine what it would be like going through life not knowing the names of plants and animals around you," Robin Wall Kimmerer writes. "Given who I am and what I do, I can't know what that's like, but I think it would be a little scary and disorienting—like being lost in a foreign city where you can't read the street signs." This state of isolation and disconnection is called "species loneliness," a profound grief rooted in our loss of relationship to other creatures and our alienation from the natural world. As the number of species extinctions rises, our loneliness expands.

Back in bed, recovering from my bout of nausea, I wondered whether I had been struck by a bizarre form of species loneliness. I had felt myself in the midst of such an acute isolation that morning, though I had not felt estranged, exactly, from the world around me. If anything, the overpowering abundance of the pawpaw patch had thrown me into the world a bit too far. Sickness had almost been a kind of retreat from these feelings of overwhelm, a cure from the sensory saturation of fecundity.

Perhaps at the root of ecological grief and its subsequent silences is the fact that not only do we not know whom we stand to lose in the future; we do not know whom we have already lost. Where to even begin looking for the words that could explain how one life links to and lights so many others? Where were the stories that could illuminate the darkness that falls when that one life ends and all other lights flicker out?

⛭

THERE IS A BROAD OUTCROPPING along the south bank of the river, not a quarter mile downslope from the headquarters of the Central Intelligence Agency. On a better-hydrated visit to the pawpaw patch a few days later, I paused at this pile of rocks to look out over the river. As macabre as it may be, I was out looking for death as much as I was looking for pawpaws, trying to find some thread to the story of how extinction had already altered my home by the Potomac.

Rains earlier that week had caused the water to rise and quickened the current. Thousands of gallons of water thundered against stones and silt and still more water in an endless roll of sound. Loud as it was, the current created a kind of flatness, like the base note to a major chord. When I suddenly heard a massive thwack, it was like the first note of a song.

I had seen a beaver in the Potomac just once before, treading through algae in the canal in Georgetown. Massive and lone, that beaver had seemed disoriented, paddling in circles, incongruous with her surroundings. The idea that a beaver could be out of place anywhere across North America is a wholly modern one. Prior to colonization, the beaver population across the continent was estimated at 400 million, with some areas along the East Coast housing over a hundred beavers in a single square mile. Whether the first colonizers stepped onto land that would become New York, Virginia, or Massachusetts under their dominion, they walked onto a soggy continent made watery and lush by hordes of beavers.

Beaver fever blazed across seventeenth-century Europe, where beaver pelts were in high demand for use in fashioning felted hats, and lured settlers across the ocean. Later, enterprising traders would peddle castoreum, the musky secretion of a beaver's anal glands, as a panacea and perfume. While the commodity most closely associated with the colonization of Piscataway and Nacotchtank land is certainly tobacco, beavers also played an early and critical role in the invasion of lands upriver.

When Henry Fleet, a young English colonizer, first sailed up the Potomac in 1621 to seek his fortune, he wasn't looking for gold, nor even land quite yet. He sought the real treasure of his wet new world: a large waterproof mammal. "I conceived all my hopes and future fortunes depended upon the trade and traffic that was to be had out of this river," he wrote. The sites of an impending beaver boom, every creek and tributary of the Potomac brimmed with beaver; since their conspicuous dams and lodges advertise their presence, they made for easy slaughter.

Fleet was an extraordinarily unscrupulous trader, cheating Virginians, Nacotchtanks, and Piscataways with comparable contempt, all while writing the most complete record of the Potomac beaver trade that exists. His journals sag under the weight of dead beavers: "beaver skins to the value of 40,000 gold crowns"; "1500 weight of beaver and cleared 14 towns"; "114 skins at Potowomek and 80 more at Natchochank."

As trappers like Fleet pressed westward, they butchered beavers on a frenzied and barbaric timeline. By the time the steel trap had been invented in 1823, some states and territories were almost totally devoid of beavers, and the need to find and kill more accelerated the national movement west. By 1900, in sixteen states along the East Coast, including Virginia and Maryland, trapping and deforestation had functionally extirpated the American beaver.

The story of the beaver contradicts a critical fallacy in our modern understanding of extinction, which is that species rarely seem to disappear in North America. In modern American discussions of ecosystem collapse and climate change, it can often seem that the extinction of native species always takes place somewhere "exotic." Lonely George, the previously mentioned Hawaiian tree snail (d. 2019), and Lonesome George, the last Pinta Island tortoise of the Galapagos, in Ecuador (d. 2012), were two of the last widely publicized extinctions. Both endlings were grieved over by the American public, most of whom had never visited the far-flung Pacific island chains. Far less widely mourned than the two Georges were the last dusky

seaside sparrow of Florida (d. 1987), the last Bachman's warbler in Louisiana (d. 1988), the last Smith Island cottontail of
Virginia (d. 1987), or, indeed, the American beaver of the early
twentieth century.

Beavers are a keystone species, one of the rare and remarkable organisms whose activities support an entire ecological
community. Building their dams from the limbs and muck of
streamside forests, beavers create and maintain wetland habitats for an untold number of species. Hundreds of fish species
depend on the slow, warm current of beaver ponds to spawn.
Crawdads, salamanders, and turtles all feed and breed in the
unsilted water that filters through dams. Dozens of songbird
species build their nests in the branches of willows, coppiced
by the gnawing beaver. Thousands of creatures, some as small
as zooplankton and others as massive as moose, all depend on
the beaver's instinct to masticate and construct, and so whole
habitats disintegrated as settlers slaughtered the beaver.

One of the tragedies of the debeavering of the continent
is that we will never know exactly what our homes were like
before their massacre. It was undoubtedly a waterier world, a
morass of swamps and ponds, mire and marsh. Beavers once
submerged approximately 234,000 square miles of wetlands
across the continent, an area approximately the combined size
of Virginia, Maryland, Washington, D.C., West Virginia, Delaware, Pennsylvania, and New Jersey. As beavers perished, their
engineered waterways evaporated, leaving behind rich loam
made from centuries of decomposing organic matter. Massive
swaths of American farmland were settled in no small measure
because of the fertile soil made from desiccated beaver ponds.

America's rivers were utterly transformed by the extirpation of the beaver. Instead of the tidy channels that many rivers now funnel into, America's rivers were broad, fluctuating

flows under the beaver's domain. Floodplains were inextricable from the current, together one wide, multithreaded river. Prior to colonization, wetlands comprised 220 million acres of the continent; by 1980, that number was 100 million—over half of the waterlogged continent had dried up and been pastured, paddocked, or planted. Entire American cities, including the nation's capital, were built on the once wet ground of a landscape made by beavers. Once, there was not a distinction between what was land and what was water; the land we live on now was all fluid, unsettled ground.

Trapping restrictions and recovery efforts imposed in the twentieth century led to a gradual increase in the beaver population. The once exterminated creature now lives in forty-nine states, plus the District, and numbers between ten to fifteen million critters. The beaver I had seen from that outcropping was likely the descendant of a beaver formerly native to Alaska or Canada, trapped in the mid-1910s and dropped off, perhaps with a companion or two, in the foreign waters of the Potomac. Indeed, almost all the beavers now living on the East Coast count among their ancestors an emigrant from the west. Although nowhere near their numbers from the precolonization era, the recovery of the beaver has been an encouraging story, one often repeated by scientists and activists eager to stem the tide of extinction.

However, it is impossible to recover the communities that existed before. While it is a futile project born of guilt to attempt to perfectly restore our precolonization landscapes, we do need to measure our losses. What makes this prospect unfeasible is that it is unknown how many other species were annihilated during the beaver boom, and how their absence has created the world we inhabit now. There is a piercing pain to the loss of a specific creature, but the loss of an entire ecological community is a hurt made intolerable by the fact that we will never know the extent of who was lost. Past extinctions, known or not, are the countercurrent of modern life, millions of small deaths reminding us this land has never been ours alone.

⋈

SURE THAT THE BEAVER WOULD NOT RETURN, I made my way down the trail, noticing now the animal's traces: wood shavings at the base of silver maples, gnawed-off suckers, and, around a familiar sycamore snag in the current, a thatch of leafy limbs, perhaps placed to protect a beaver clan in a covert bankside den.

Trudging past a tangle of vines, I approached four white-tailed deer nibbling the greenbrier. After my lonely hike earlier that week, I was especially pleased to see them. They lifted their slender heads at my approach, swiveling their ears to measure the threat of my presence. I must not have been judged much of a danger, because the deer did not prance off until I was perhaps fifteen feet away, and even then they took mincing steps, impatient to return to their dinner table.

White-tailed deer are so numerous along the Potomac, it's more common to encounter a herd while out on the trail than not. Massive and muscular, adult male white-tailed deer can weigh almost three hundred pounds, a heft they carry with ease as they bound across the plain. As I approached, the deer leapt away so effortlessly, they appeared to bounce.

With plenty of access to woodlands and grassy fields and no current nonhuman predators, the white-tailed deer of the Potomac live la dolce vita. The profuse flora of the floodplain and well-landscaped suburbs result in well-fed does becoming pregnant twice a year, often giving birth annually to a minimum of four fawns. Reproducing that speedily without correlative predation, the deer population across the entire United States is enormous. Today, there are an estimated thirty million white-tailed deer frolicking across the country, more than at any other time in history.

Prior to colonization, the Nacotchtank and Piscataway peoples regularly burned the forest to improve the understory browse for deer, making hunting an easy sport and restricting the growth of fields. At least half a dozen carnivorous species, including black bears, wolves, cougars, bobcats, coyotes, and foxes, also lived in the open forests and kept the white-tailed deer population in check. The abundance of carnivorous predators, a landscape cultivated to benefit human hunters, and limited meadows for grazing kept the deer population at a number five times smaller than at present.

Though small by our modern standards, the deer herds encountered by the first colonizers were astonishing compared with those in herbivore-depleted England. Henry Fleet, recalling a Nacotchtank campsite close to what is now Little Falls, wrote enthusiastically that "as for deers, buffaloes, bears, turkeys, the woods do swarm with them." Colonizers did not recognize the forests they occupied as the skillfully crafted hunting grounds of the continent's Indigenous peoples. They were instead a vast and terrifying wilderness, seething with horrible beasts. For men like Fleet and the trappers, planters, and enslavers who followed him, it would not do to have their new land swarming with such fearsome creatures as bears, wolves, and bobcats.

The destruction of certain species to make way for others was not undertaken as an indiscriminate, individual pursuit. Many colonies codified and incentivized the dispatch of specific animals seen by the colonists as undesirable or dangerous. In *Notes on the State of Virginia,* Thomas Jefferson explained that in his colony, "the laws have also descended to the preservation and improvement of the races of useful animals, such as horses, cattle, deer; to the extirpation of those which are noxious, as wolves, squirrels, crows, blackbirds." By 1700, what remained of black bears, wolves, and cougars of the Potomac had been driven to the outer fringe of the Appalachians. The population of smaller, peskier predators—bobcats, coyotes, and foxes—while still present, had been decimated.

The extinction of a species from a certain ecological community but not necessarily from the face of the planet is known as defaunation. The term is most often used to describe the depletion of large vertebrate animals from an ecosystem, as well as a decline in the abundance of biodiversity that stems from the loss of such large animals. The defaunation of the Potomac, which followed a pattern of colonizer-led massacres up and down the East Coast, had a profound effect on the ecological community of the river. As white settlers butchered the region's predators, the population of animals that were once prey increased.

Deer numbers, already high from forest cutting and farming, rose even higher with the disappearance of predators, though this momentary respite did not last long. Soon, deer population numbers were on the decline as settlers usurped the role of predators from wolves and bears. By 1890, the U.S. Biological Survey estimated there were only 300,000 white-tailed deer in the entire United States.

The premiere of Walt Disney's *Bambi* in 1942 did much to augment a growing cultural awareness that deer were in danger of extirpation. New hunting laws, coupled with the postwar suburban boom that turned dense forests into leafy suburbs, were the springboard for a rebounding white-tailed deer population. Like the beaver, once white-tailed deer were protected from overhunting, they multiplied rapidly.

Today, each of the 1.5 to 2 million deer currently living in the Potomac River Basin eats ten to twelve pounds of food every day, which measures out to somewhere between 7,500 to 10,000 tons of mushrooms, nuts, flowers, foliage, and fruit. Across the near fifteen thousand square miles of the basin, this seems like a small number. But in areas where the population exceeds the carrying capacity of fifteen to twenty deer per square mile, the effects of all that nibbled-down greenery amount to a far browner and less biodiverse landscape.

In Rock Creek Park, for example, from 1990 to 2010, an enormous population of approximately seventy-seven deer per square mile regularly decimated oak tree seedlings, leaving beech saplings to take root. The deers' preference for oak has already shifted the mesic hardwood forest, formerly comprised of a canopy of mixed oak and beech trees, toward a beech-dense future. Without a sufficient community of white and northern red oaks, it is possible that the wild turkeys, possums, and raccoons that rely on fat-dense acorns could find themselves starved out of Rock Creek Park in the coming decades.

At the understory level, the Potomac landscape already reflects the consequence of outsize deer populations. In addition to oak seedlings, deer also enjoy munching on spicebush, beautyberry, sumac, and the majority of other native shrubs, with one notable exception. Pawpaw leaves and twigs have a distinctive petroleum-distillate odor, rendering them unpalatable to deer. Chowing down on other saplings, deer have cleared the way for the reign of the pawpaw. Ecologists for the National Capital Region Network have found that pawpaws now comprise about one-fourth of all saplings in the parks the organization oversees. While pawpaws show almost no signs of deer browse, other native species preferred by deer are disappearing.

Almost every state and municipal wildlife division maintains some kind of euphemistic "deer-management program" of monitored hunting in the name of ecological maintenance.

In many regions, including within the District, the outcome of unchecked deer browsing is already the reality. We hardly recognize our world as less green and less diverse than the same lands were even fifty years ago, let alone four hundred, when humans were not the only hunters stalking through the forest.

If the snowballing deer population had been accompanied by a parallel return of predators, their story might be spun, like that of the beaver, into a heartening one of human ingenuity. But the defaunation of the Potomac is likely to be a permanent condition; it is doubtful the public would support the release of wolves or bears in so-called "recolonization" efforts to naturally diminish the population of herbivores. (Eastern cougars are no longer a potential option for predator recolonization; the U.S. Fish and Wildlife Service officially deemed them extinct in 2018.)

The results of an increased deer population over the twentieth century have been catastrophic. But somehow worse than that, those results have become increasingly difficult for humans to notice and make sense of. Very few of us can look out at the silvery stands of beech and draw connections between their omnipresence and then the extinction of the eastern cougar. Nor do we recognize our modern dried-up landscape to be one that is simply less vital, with fewer—and fewer kinds of—living creatures. The failure of settlers to think ecologically with the whole community in mind is, it can seem, absolute.

⋈

I TURNED AROUND TO CATCH THE DEER HERD gamboling back to their meal, white tails up and twitching as they sensed my gaze again. There was a grace and guiltlessness in the lines of sinew beneath their skin, which quivered in the sunlight. Perhaps this was just psychic transference, but I sensed their innocence pivot, as if on a fulcrum, throwing a shadow of responsibility onto me. Shamefaced, I turned away.

In the few days I had been away from this pawpaw patch, the ground had acquired a fresh carpet of putrid fruit. The whole stretch stank of rot. A few years ago, these trees had been four-leafed saplings trembling a foot above the earth, but now they rose a foot or more above my head, dumping their clutches of fruit onto the plain. I considered that at least part of the reason this particular stand was so lush was that the prolific white-tailed deer population had chewed to death these pawpaws' shrubby neighbors. I walked under their shadows, wondering what the landscape would have looked like if not for the massacres of the animals and people who once lived here. What was the Potomac like before settler-led extinction?

It's not just hard to answer this question because my ecological knowledge is limited or that the records don't exist. I find this question difficult to answer in the fullness it demands because, as a descendant of white settlers, I live in the landscape of annihilation made by my ancestors. It is, in a visceral sense, painful to me to imagine the Potomac in the times before the massacres, because it requires me to acknowledge that I, too, am responsible for hurtling this world toward its end.

Ecologist Aldo Leopold wrote in *The Sand County Almanac,* "One of the penalties of an ecological education is that one lives alone in a world of wounds. Much of the damage inflicted on land is quite invisible to laymen." For such a statement to be true, the laymen, I think, must be white, for to be white in the United States is to live steeped in an innocence that renders as ignorance. I live in a world of wounds, but the idea that I might live there alone is a fantasy bred of shame.

As I stood under the pawpaws, awash in their putrefying perfume, I thought about fecundity and the stream of near-invisible deaths that ran through the profusion of life here, and I forced myself to imagine the land that is now Washington, D.C., as it once was. The sprawl occupied by the CIA, located between two runs on the flat bluff above where I stood, would have been a saturated sump. Under the reign of the beaver, with both streams dammed, water yawned across the plain, and waterfalls trickled down in gauzy, drizzling streams to the river. Rock Creek, Tiber Creek, and the Anacostia River dribbled into one another as their boundaries expanded over what is now the District. Over that ooze, ancient oaks, stands of laurel, and piles of purple beautyberry grew in abundance. The creeks ran so clear, you could see to the bottom, silt caught in the crosshatch of beaver dams. Ponds speckled the future suburbs of Arlington and Bethesda. Willows lined the runs, where bears and elk and wolves came to drink.

Taking a pawpaw the size of my palm out of my bag, I washed the fruit in the river, then brought it to my lips. Tropical and warm, with that familiar slight taint, the pulp dripped from the sides of my mouth. Delicious, disgusting. I took another bite. Perhaps the reason I am both drawn to and repulsed by this tree is that it reminds me of the shattered landscape of extinctions that settlers have made. I return to this grove in a ritual, not of penance, but of accountability: Pawpaws remind me what it is to inherit a legacy of death.

Drought

THE FIRST WEEK OF OCTOBER, I slipped off the trail behind my house and onto another planet. An alien terrain stretched out before me: Millions of pebbles and clay-caked stones formed a vast sweep of scree. Logjam mountains punctuated the odd vista, followed by heaps of trash, clamshells, plastic debris, and tumbleweeds of seedy asters. A month without real rain and two straight weeks with a temperature gauge flirting with 100°F had shriveled the Potomac to a threadlike streak. At night, dark clouds spit out half a dozen drops before passing on, giving way to another dusty morning and a river growing thinner and more desperate by the day.

Earlier that afternoon I had sat with my landlady on her back porch, situated on the south ridge across from High Island, which was swiftly ceding its status as an island. As we drank from crystal glasses filled with her signature orange-mint iced tea, we stared down not at a rushing river, but at an anemic stream. Lazy water drained through a labyrinth of newly emerged snags and sandbars. Even from the height of the porch I could see the outline of every pebble resting underwater, a clarity I found thrilling. After another week or two of this weather, I expected there would no longer be a Potomac River so much as there would be a sunbaked ravine of gravel, spotted with a few boggy puddles.

"It looks sick," my landlady announced. The surface of

the river was pitted with rocks as if by scars or pox. Along its edges, the dregs of its covert underworld had erupted as bulbous mounds of marooned whiskey barrels, flotillas of plastic soda bottles, and long-ago disposed furniture.

"It's just awful," she said then, referring, I think, to both the emaciated condition of the river and the filth cropping up along the banks. I said I agreed, though I was not sure I did. There was something compelling, if not quite appealing, about the dissipating river. I felt a perverse need to imagine the desert chasm that a desiccated Potomac would reveal. I envisioned the river gone, fish swept to sea, trees turned to parched toothpicks. A curious, almost compulsive desire for things to get worse overtook me, as if I could not help but prefer the most sensational outcome for this bit of bad weather.

Perhaps this fantasy was shameful, but it was one I shared with many others. Most of the Potomac region was then under the conditions of what the National Weather Service calls a "flash drought," or the rapid onset of warm surface temperatures and low soil moisture. All that week, the city was preoccupied with the spectacle of the weather and a shared fascination with this decidedly modern phenomenon. How much worse do you think it will get? we asked one another. Even politics had taken a backseat to conversations about the heat, though perhaps that is not altogether true: No one had to say "climate change" as we all shook our heads in self-serious concern.

The obsession with the flash drought was sourced from the sort of surreality that accompanies belief that the slice of time you occupy is, in some sense, extraordinary, and that your memory of an exceptional event—and by extension, you, yourself—might one day become history. Disaster, even if it is the prolonged type, as most droughts are, has the capacity to thrill us. We like to look at disaster as long as we don't have to participate. Eventually, I knew, it would rain, and one day I would be the old woman on the porch remembering the great October drought that almost drained the river.

I thanked my landlady for the tea and conversation, went home, pulled on my grippy boots, and headed off down the ridge. I arrived at the edge of the water, stumbling over rocks so dusted with red clay, they looked Martian. Down on the bank, the river seemed healthier than from above, still running, still blue, but drained and dull. The water didn't seem deeper than two or three feet, even as my eyes followed a trail of rocks out toward the center of the river and over to the other side.

I did something impulsive and dangerous then: I crossed the Potomac.

At first, it was rather like walking a garden path, each stone placed in front of the other as if by persuasion. Rock-hopping my way from slab to stone, I stepped from one boulder to the next, never once slipping into the water, which was translucent and bright blue, almost Caribbean in color. The shade and sedate pace of the river was calming, even lulling. In the middle of the river, silt-crusted rocks rose like sawtooth ridges out of the water. These mounds jutted out of the current, slicing the span for fifteen or twenty feet before breaking off, which only required me to step onto the next ridge. In this way, my path across the river felt rather like climbing a mountain, traversing a serrated range toward some peak or destination.

When I reached the Maryland shore, I looked back at the path I had crossed. My heart, previously beating slow and steady, began to pound. Staring across this flat perspective, it seemed that I had traveled a great and terrifying distance. My home, which had seemed so close, only a thousand or so feet away, now appeared to be on the other side of an abyss. Nothing about the current, shape, or speed of the river had changed—only my perception of it. The power I had felt vanished, and my stomach curdled at the thought of a return trip.

From up on the bluff, the Potomac had appeared to me almost as a diorama, a mere depiction of the river in drought. The Potomac had, of course, been there in front of me, but my sense of the river, unmoored from its banks and displaced from its bed, was that it existed somewhere else. Under the conditions of the drought, the Potomac had ceased to me to be a real, coursing, threatening thing. As I crossed, though, the river regained its materiality, and by the time I had reached the far edge, the Potomac was again as wild, tangible, and terrifying as it had ever been.

Hyperobjects are things so vastly distributed across the universe and our perception of it that they transcend spatio-temporal specificity. Styrofoam is classified as a hyperobject; so are pandemics and black holes. Climate change is the most enduring example of a hyperobject: It is everywhere, happening all the time, and is in constant relation with real, concrete objects. And yet, because its effects are so massive and diffuse, we struggle to comprehend its existential components—that is, the things that make it real.

Both droughts and floods support our recognition of climate change as a real phenomenon. But natural disasters might also be thought of as hyperobjects in themselves. Disasters often happen on a spatiotemporal scale that makes them difficult to understand. Droughts, even ones termed flash droughts, appear gradually, and their effects are always dispersed across a certain locality. Floods, on the other hand, are usually a sudden phenomenon tied to the immediacy of the present, even as the prospect of sea-level rise involves a certain future inevitability. Floods might also be considered hyperlocal, at least in urban environments; one block is inundated, the next one spared, the scope of crisis appallingly intimate.

Severed from the usual context that directs our experience of reality, such disasters can seem—at least to those with the privilege to exempt themselves from their effects—like things of either the past or the future. Even as we might indulge in imagining the worst-case scenario, disasters remain problems that happen to other people in other places.

In retrospect, this is the moment that climate change became real to me. Prior to crossing the Potomac, the catastrophe of climate change lacked a context and a scale that I could comprehend, let alone feel in my body. By crossing the river, I had moved through what theorist Eve Kosofsky Sedgwick described as "the gap between knowing something—even knowing something to be true—and realizing it, taking it as real." Knowing is rational, instant, and fact-based; realizing is a process and a long one, an affective journey you take to and from a place of deep awareness as you encounter again what you think you already know. Navigating the gap between acknowledging epistemological fact and the process wherein truth becomes lived reality is difficult, if not nearly impossible. This is particularly true when it comes to climate change, which we often treat as an object of science, an entity made of knowable facts and figures.

Having crossed through the gap into the realm of realizing, I was gripped by a new exigency that accompanied the arrival of my own personal climate disaster. There was a difference, I now realized, a chasm really, between knowing the facts about climate change and feeling those facts rush through your veins, your fingertips pulsing with terror.

When disaster is something that happens only in the distant past or the far-off future, what do we do with our catastrophic present? How do we move beyond mere acknowledgment of climate change as fact without succumbing to the realized horror of doom and disaster? How do we learn to occupy Sedgwick's gap between knowing and realizing? How do we—figuratively, of course—cross the river between them?

I do not think it will spoil the metaphor to report that eventually I did rally the courage to begin the return trip, which I accomplished in half the time, leaping across the water like an upstream trout, my body screaming flight, flight, flight as I vaulted over the rocks and collapsed on the shore. When I turned back around to face the river, elbows on my knees and head in my hands, I was startled to once again see a sad little stream. The vantage had changed again. I collected my things and walked back home, probably cooked dinner, watched television, and fell asleep.

My sense of peace was short-lived. I dreamed of landscapes of dust-covered stones and red river tidal waves crashing through my bedroom window. I would wake sweaty and scared, stuck in the threshold between sleep and wakefulness. Visions of scorched forests and drowned towns woke me hours before sunrise, when I would leave the house to wander to the top of the ridge and stare down at the dried bones of the river. My body felt drained in these early hours as I tried in vain to retrieve the urgency and gravity I had felt after crossing. For as frightening as it had been in the moment, I recognized that some part of me wanted to return to the terrain of realizing. Though I struggled in my waking hours to access my own memories of what disaster had truly felt like, weeks later, it finally occurred to me that perhaps instead, I could access the river's memory.

JUST SOUTH OF BRUNSWICK, MARYLAND, a small town forty-five miles upriver from D.C., the Potomac runs low and rocky past the confluence with the Shenandoah River. It is a perfect spot for fishing, lined by heavy sycamores that cast shadows over the shallows. The Massowomeck and Manahoac peoples built dozens of structures across the river here. Called weirs, these are V-shaped traps made of thick rock walls, which funnel fish into certain areas and trap them against the stones, making them easy targets to hook, spear, or catch in wooden cages.

Toni Morrison wrote that "all water has a perfect memory." I thought of her words when I pictured these weirs, the perfect markers of the river's memory, material evidence against which to measure the scale of droughts and floods.

Colonizers also built and rebuilt weirs up and down this low stretch of the river. By the mid-nineteenth century, Brunswick had become known across the region as "Eeltown," an appellation it owed to the millions of pounds of fish pulled from the river with help from the weirs. By 1936, overfishing had nearly exterminated Potomac fish populations. To protect what fish remained, federal law demanded the abandonment of the weirs. Almost all weirs in the river—of which there are some thirty-six between Harpers Ferry and Point of Rocks alone, a distance of only thirteen miles—have gone unused for over a century, though they remain in place on the riverbed. Eels, on the other hand, have been almost entirely extirpated from the upper Potomac.

By the time I reached the boat ramp at Brunswick, I was sweating in the shade, the mid-October morning practically broiling. I slipped my feet into the freakish warmth of the water, and though I wanted to wade into the river and walk out onto the weir, the second the water touched my ankles, my adrenaline rushed. An eerie feeling trickled through me as I realized that my body remembered fear far better than my mind.

I watched the current run around the weir's colossal striated rocks, though it wasn't until I climbed up onto the bridge that I understood how large this structure was. A wedge that formed a dart across half of the river, the weir cut a distance of several hundred feet. Talking later to a fisherman casting off under the bridge, I learned that while in summer it is normal to see the outline of these underwater weirs as the current carries their shape on the surface, it is unusual to see the weirs themselves, let alone the entirety of the boulder foundations.

Perhaps *normal* or *unusual* have become meaningless words to use in this context; they adhere to a temporal pattern that climate change has snipped in half. In October 1930, during the very worst drought on record, the Potomac above Bruns- wick disappeared. In D.C., it rained just one and a half inches between July and November. Between July 19 and August 10, the temperature shot over 100°F for thirteen days, while it was over 90°F for the remainder. Thousands of residents slept in Rock Creek Park and along the National Mall to gain respite from their hotbox apartments. A former congressman from Minne- sota died of heatstroke after venturing outside. Baptisms were suspended due to lack of water, and then, like a sign from God to nonbelievers, 300,000 acres of forest combusted and burned across northern Virginia.

The upper Potomac was reduced to a chain of fetid pud- dles, reeking from dead fish, algae, and animal droppings, creating a miasma of disease. The National Fish and Wildlife Service reported that hundreds of wild ducks died after con- suming novel parasites, and large herds of cattle also died, likely from the same source. The blow to agriculture was enormous. Orchards went under as thousands of fruit trees died. Livestock starved and were prematurely slaughtered. In Loudoun and Fauquier Counties, which provided a good portion of produce consumed by residents of the District, an expected corn crop of

1.5 million bushels shrank to just 5,000. The state of Virginia alone paid an adjusted total of one billion dollars in damages to farmers.

Brunswick residents took brief advantage of the vanished river by laying wooden boards over the rocks of the weir to drive their cars across to Virginia without paying the bridge toll. Some traveled to West Virginia to access the few high mountain streams that were still running. (The fact that Brunswick residents had gas for their cars but lacked water to drink is ironic in light of what we now know about the relationship between the use of fossil fuels and climate change–induced drought.)

Though there have been only three major droughts in the Potomac River Basin since 1930, two of those have occurred in the last twenty-five years—1999 and 2002. The years 2007, 2012, and 2019 also saw a combination of rainfall deficit and high temperatures that resulted in short-lived drought conditions. Regardless of their perceived intensity, five occurrences of what the state of Maryland calls "severe drought" in the last twenty-five years is not an encouraging statistic. And yet, with the exception of 1930, drought conditions in the region generally did not affect the everyday lives of D.C. residents, who draw almost all of their water from the river; city dwellers on the East Coast are largely sheltered from the consequences of drought by an industrial, globalized food system and a matrix of municipal water agreements.

For D.C. residents, then, the heat that precipitates drought conditions is a considerably more urgent problem than drought itself. Extreme heat kills more people every year than any other weather event, and in urban areas, heat is never distributed equitably. Heat islands occur in urban neighborhoods where there are fewer trees and park spaces to provide shade and cooler temperatures. Multiple studies have demonstrated that formerly redlined neighborhoods, often populated by working-class people of color, are more likely to lack canopy cover and contain paved surfaces, which absorb and radiate heat. The temperature in these neighborhoods is often dramatically higher than those in leafy, lawned, and usually white-majority neighborhoods. On one day in August 2015, while the recorded temperature in D.C. overall was an uncomfortable 93°F, in the Ward 5 neighborhood of Trinidad, the temperature was a sweltering 102°F, and in the Rock Creek Park–adjacent neighborhood of Colonial Woods, it was a balmy 76°F, the difference between a heatstroke and a picnic.

The health risks to D.C. residents from higher temperatures are not limited to the singular threat of heat exhaustion. In neighborhoods with long histories of fighting against environmental racism, such as Mayfair and River Terrace, centuries of industrial development and chemical contamination have lacerated the landscape. Residents of these Anacostia River–adjacent neighborhoods now face extreme health hazards as a result of little more than living in neighborhoods where pollution and racial discrimination have combined to contaminate the soil, water, and air. Children living in Ward 8 are hospitalized for asthma at a rate ten times higher than those in the wealthy white enclave of Ward 3, a fact doctors attribute to air pollution and mold-studded public housing. Today, Black Washingtonians are now two to three times more likely to suffer from heart failure, stroke, and asthma than their white counterparts, in part a result of the environments in which they have been forced to live.

Current projections from D.C.'s Department of Energy & Environment (DOEE) state that the number of "heat emergency" days with a heat index over 95°F will double or triple over the next fifty years. For some Washingtonians east of the river, climate change will exacerbate the health conditions they already live with as a result of their neighborhoods' histories as the city's landfill and waste dumps. For those with good health and housing, with ancient trees sprawled above their heads, drought and heat are conditions not just to weather but to gab about. But for the children of Fairlawn who live with the legacy of environmental racism in their lungs, droughts and the heat waves that accelerate them are a direct threat to their ability to breathe.

Back in Brunswick, I stared out over the wavy, watery mirage of the river and the hard angle of the weir, pointing downstream to the city. Maybe the heat was getting to me—the sun poured down not in streaks but as a thick curtain, smothering the paved bridge I stood on in light so bright, it was blinding. The fisherman had told me the fish weren't biting—but of course they weren't: It was too hot and there weren't enough of them left. The past had already come and taken what it wanted from the present.

⁂

CROSSING THE BRIDGE TO TAKE THE JAGGED ROUTE through suburban Virginia toward Great Falls, I drove past idyllic rolling farmland, slave-labor camps refashioned as horse farms, crumbling liquor stores, strip-mall sprawls, and whopping Amazon data-storage centers. It was a deeply incongruous landscape, a mélange of modernity and decay.

I slowed to take in a massive wolf tree that darkened the lawn of some newfangled farmhouse. Older than their neighbors by a hundred years or more, wolf trees (some also call them mother trees) are the most striking markers of the memory of any landscape. Several wolf trees located in the Potomac's floodplain are almost four hundred years old, and the history of the river's floods can be read from their rings. At Great Falls, I planned to visit a particularly wolfish silver maple, which, in my memory, was enormous, maybe three hundred years old, rough with shaggy bark, and in fall, a riot of bright yellow leaves.

When I arrived at the park, I walked south toward the third observation point. Set back at least twenty-five feet from that overlook, which itself is perched on the brink of Mather Gorge, seventy-five feet or more above the water, there was a ten-foot pole. It was notched with engravings that signified the high-water mark for each of the river's great floods, marked with the years in which they happened: 1936, 1937, 1942, 1972, 1985, 1996. With my eyes level to the 1972 marker, I could hardly imagine how much water would have to rise to reach the lines on this pole.

Skepticism about the name and frequency of these so-called one-hundred-year floods is, I think, a rational reaction to learning that in the last century there have been six of them. Add to that the twenty-eight major Potomac floods, or so-called fifty-year-floods, that have wreaked havoc during the last two centuries. This is not to mention the spring freshets and ice jams that occur when the frozen river buckles under the pressure of the ice, sending chunky floes downstream. Nor does it account for the tidal surges and flash flooding that regularly inundate Old Town Alexandria, the Tidal Basin, Navy Yard, Georgetown, and Kenilworth.

Of course, attaching the designation one-hundred-year or fifty-year to a flood event does not necessarily represent the likelihood of a great flood happening within a certain span of time. These designations, while originally implemented to measure recurrence intervals of flow, are constantly updated as flooding occurs. Climate change has accelerated their obsolescence. In 2019, D.C.'s DOEE reported that the kind of precipitation event that could lead to a one-hundred-year flood would more likely become a one-in-twenty-five-year event by mid-century and a one-in-fifteen-year event by 2080.

Past the pole at the overlook, Great Falls in drought was still an awesome sight. The water cascaded through a welter of stone chutes and slots, descending over seventy-five feet between jagged scarps. As I walked south down the rim of the gorge toward the wolf tree, the river below shimmered with the last gold light from behind the tree.

As I stared down the fatal drop of the cliff, I imagined the river rising, rushing and tumbling toward the brink of the gorge and beyond. On the morning after Saint Patrick's Day in 1936, the water gauge at the mouth of the gorge registered the height of the river already at eighteen feet above normal and rising at the rate of three feet per hour. A dozen heavy snows fell that winter, and the ice pack in the mountains was substantial. The Potomac froze, and when warm weather arrived with the advent of March, it began to melt and rise. Then it began to rain, and the combination of melting ice, snow, and rain created a stampede of water.

The 1936 flood killed two hundred people up and down the Potomac, a number thought to be relatively low considering the damages to land and property, which in D.C. alone rose to an adjusted twenty million dollars. In the mountains, the flood washed farms off hillsides, and many farmers abandoned their lands. Brunswick, Hancock, Harpers Ferry, and several other towns along the C&O Canal were decimated and never regained a semblance of the prosperity they had enjoyed before the waters rose. After 1936, the canal was in such a state of disrepair that the federal government took ownership over the so-called Grand Old Ditch. Many of the old stone hearths that can be found in the woods along the canal are the last vestiges of homes destroyed by the 1936 flood; rather than attempt to rebuild, many residents who lived on the river moved away. Those few who remained were bought out by the federal government under eminent domain when the canal was finally transformed into a public park in 1971.

In Washington, Black workers from the Civilian Conservation Corps (CCC) labored overnight to stack sandbags as a levee against rising waters, sparing the city from the worst-case scenario—an inundated White House, Congress, and Supreme Court. Meanwhile, President Franklin D. Roosevelt rode to the home of Herbert Hoover's former secretary of labor, located on the Virginia bluff at Little Falls. There he joined a crowd of spectators who had gathered to watch the collapse of Chain Bridge, which surprised them all by holding on, though the river crested over it, and entire houses, swept from upriver, smashed into the deck and cables.

Richard Stanton, the future superintendent of the C&O Canal National Park, remembered watching "the turbulent brown water hissing past the Lincoln Memorial, carrying pieces of houses and bridges in its grip. The Lincoln Memorial was eerily resting on what resembled an island, surrounded by water. A freight schooner was stranded near the Washington Monument." Both East and West Potomac Park were inundated. The tops of trees at Hains Point were the only visible remnants of land. Newsreel footage taken after the waters subsided depicted residents piling their drenched belongings on the sidewalk: three grand pianos lined up on their sides, barbershop chairs blooming with mold, a cash register soaked with useless dollar bills.

After the water receded, the CCC installed a permanent levee along the Tidal Basin and Seventeenth Street to protect against future floods. In the decades since, the U.S. Army Corps of Engineers and the National Park Service have expanded and raised the levees. Today, glossy granite walls that often confuse tourists in search of the Vietnam Veterans Memorial protect over fourteen billion dollars of property in the Federal Triangle, seemingly the last visible trace of the impact of a flood almost a century past.

But the 1936 flood—and later, the 1937 and 1942 floods— had a far more lasting and pernicious effect on the city than the building of levees. These disasters devastated the once tight-knit Black waterfront communities of Southwest. Even before the floods, white Washingtonians considered this segment of the city to be an impoverished "shantytown," located very literally in the shadow of the Capitol. The contrast in postwar photographs was stark and embarrassing for a nation now engaged in the expansion of self-modeled international democracy.

And so, in the early 1950s, the federal government declared eminent domain over all land south of the National Mall and north of the Potomac. They evicted almost all residents and businesses, destroyed all streets and buildings, and started over from scratch. This was the nation's first effort at what became known as urban renewal. Within two decades, the federal government demolished an entire quadrant of the capital and destroyed a community. Southwest became a model for dozens of other American cities seeking moral justification for the removal of Black residents.

The original 4,500 families of Southwest D.C. were forced to find housing elsewhere, with a two-hundred-dollar housing voucher provided by the federal government. Many of them moved across the Anacostia River into Southeast, where they faced the same familiar threats from floods, in addition to those of pollution and poor housing. White supremacy became the very foundation of the redevelopment of the capital's Southwest waterfront. In this way, the legacy of disasters a hundred years past still influences and even dictates the segregation of the city and disparate health risks among residents.

Cutting uphill from the trail, I headed away from the gorge and onto one of the old carriage roads, on which horses and buggies once carried white tourists up from the city to see the falls. The leaves of the wolf tree were such a brilliant yellow that they shone through the forest like a beacon. When I reached it, I sat down and closed my eyes.

Fissures of bark scratched into the space between my shoulder blades, pressing insistently, as if the tree had a point to make. Why had I felt the need to plumb the depths of history and memory that day, when it was obvious that disaster was not an object of the past or future, but the present? I had not needed to travel at all; the whole landscape of D.C., the matrix that connected and divided its neighborhoods, was an augury of disaster in itself.

※

THE DAY BEFORE IT FINALLY RAINED, ending the drought, a friend invited me on a walk with her and her dog around the National Mall. From her apartment in Capitol Hill, we walked west toward the Mall, sweat speckling our backs and necks. Humidity clung to our bodies like coats. We talked about little else but the weather as the dog panted and slobbered ahead of us, until it was clear he could no longer continue. On an elm-shaded bench by the National Gallery, we sat to rest and people-watch.

"Do you ever think about what climate change will be like here?" she asked almost out of the blue. I heard the slightest bit of hesitation in her voice, the kind of tone that carries preemptive shame. I was reluctant to give a wholehearted yes, afraid, I suppose, of what that might imply about my proclivity toward a performance of progressive piety. "Sometimes," I replied.

"You know, in a hundred years, where we are sitting will all be underwater." I looked across at the wide, flush fields, filled with dog walkers and sightseers and adult kickball leagues. I was silent, unsure of what to say. "We can talk about something else," she said kindly, and reached down to pet the dog, who lay spread out in the gravel, heaving for breath.

If global temperatures rise 3°C or higher, the Lincoln Memorial will be an island in the Potomac River in eighty years. The White House will be accessible by boat. The Capitol Building, located as it is on a hill, will look out over a pond that used to be the National Mall. Military personnel will be able to commute by canoe to the front doors of the Pentagon. The National Archives and almost every Smithsonian museum—flooded. The Vietnam War Memorial, the Kennedy Center, the Federal Bureau of Investigation, and the Departments of the Interior, Justice, and Education—all underwater.

If global temperatures increase only 1.5°C, the capital will lose the Tidal Basin, the Jefferson Memorial, the majority of West Potomac Park, the entirety of East Potomac Park, and half of Reagan National Airport. Several entire neighborhoods—the Wharf, Navy Yard, Old Town Alexandria, and Mayfair—and portions of others—Georgetown and Foggy Bottom in the District, Colmar Manor, Edmonston, and Bladensburg in Maryland, and Potomac Yard, Belle View, and South Alexandria in Virginia will also be forfeited to the river.

The following week, the hunter's moon and the last dregs of a tropical storm swept up the tide line. Foamy crests licked the edges of the Tidal Basin, and water slipped up King Street and through front doors in Alexandria. The flash drought had ended with a flash flood. After the storm, I biked down to the

Wharf, a redeveloped strip of the Southwest waterfront that forms one side of the Washington Channel across from East Potomac Park. I crossed the Mall as I cycled through the city, and I thought of the conversation, or really the lack of one, I'd had with my friend.

I should have told her yes, I think about what climate change will look like. I think about what it already looks like. Although I think about disaster, I still don't really know—I haven't realized—what disaster will be like. Privilege always obscures our view of reality. And yet there remains an undeniable utility in imagining the worst-case scenario, either by narrating the future inundation of the nation's capital or conjuring the ghosts of past crises. We might even call these imaginings a necessity; how can we understand climate change except from our own place, time, and body? But while imagining disaster may aid our personal recognition of climate change, it can also sensationalize disaster, making it ever more unreal.

Across the Channel from the trendy backdrop of the Wharf, benches along the edge of East Potomac Park were partly underwater. I watched car after car lightly hydroplane as they drove south toward Hains Point. Salt water pooled around a few cherry trees, leafless and bare. I wondered if the drought had stripped them or whether they had been dead already.

I stopped at the dock closest to the old fish market, the smell of oysters and black drum on ice familiar and strong. Tiny yachts packed the marina, and behind me, first-floor bars and restaurants brimmed with people enjoying a Saturday afternoon out. Apartment buildings and hotels loomed a dozen or more stories above the riverwalk. Forty-five hundred families had called this neighborhood their home one hundred years ago. Disaster swept through again and again, flood and federal government, the catastrophe of a community stolen by the river and racism all too real.

I got back on my bike, headed for Hains Point, pedaling slowly toward Fourteenth Street and Ohio Drive. Somewhere on the pedestrian bridge, the Tidal Basin to one side and the Washington Channel on the other, my muscles softened, the churn of my legs steadying into the pattern of movement the bike required. As I spun, I thought again of Sedgwick's gap between knowing and realizing. Months before she wrote the essay, Sedgwick learned she had terminal breast cancer. The prospect of death made "inescapably vivid in repeated mental shuttle passes the considerable distance between knowing that one will die and realizing it."

To live in this gap is to acknowledge the difference between what you know and what you know you do not. I cannot know, not really, what families in Southwest felt when the river took their homes and the federal government pushed them out. I cannot know, not in the detail and depth required, what it must feel like to live in the place where the ground is poisoned and the air thick with heat because of who your ancestors were. I cannot know, even as the water rises up to my knees, what kind of future climate change will bring.

Halfway across the Washington Channel, I felt the gap collapse and meld. We live in the aftermath of disaster, as we always have, but we live in the before times, too. When I reached the other side, I hung a left. The flood tide rose around my tires as my bike plowed through the puddles. By the time I had circled Hains Point, I was soaked in sweat and salt water.

Tiber

Tiber Creek rises on the other side of the street from the jukebox dive bar and the barbecue spot that serves sweet corn bread. Only when it rains is the creek visible: Water sweeps down the back alleyway behind the bar and sloshes through a channel of mossy bricks. For most of the year, all that is left of the run that once drained almost half of Washington, D.C., is that empty green-furred culvert and a hundred oscillating hills.

My legs learned the slopes and drops of Tiber-made terrain long before I ever learned where its headwaters sprang. Every Tuesday, I biked from my apartment in Park View to a house in northeast Petworth, where I picked up a box of vegetables delivered from a local farm. As I climbed Rock Creek Church Road and coasted back down New Hampshire Avenue, I felt the dips and surges of the landscape in the burn of my quads, aware, only in the smallest sense, that these hills had been cut by a creek I could no longer see.

Then, on one of those pickup days, there was a downpour. Rills rushed the causeway that was usually Sherman Avenue, and the current carried away dirt from front yards along Park Place. Wiping off the mud at home, it occurred to me that the next Tuesday, I ought to try to follow from head to mouth the creek that was clearly here but somehow hidden.

The next Tuesday turned out to be frosty, and I shivered as I rolled my bike up to the high wrought-iron fence that separates the three hundred meadowed acres of the Old Soldiers' Home from the rest of Petworth and Park View. Sticking my face against the cold bars, I stared down at the spring source of what had once been the second-largest stream in the District, one rivaled in size only by Rock Creek. A thin rusting pipe fell out into an empty gully. Washed-up chip bags rimming the channel were the only evidence of water. Bean trees sheltered the stretch, and in the shadows, privet and ivy choked the space between their trunks. I supposed the headwaters of every stream must seem piddling compared to their mouths, but that morning, the beginnings of the Tiber struck me as particularly pathetic.

Following a historic city map I had downloaded to my phone, I pedaled downslope, my eyes on the glorified drainage ditch on the other side of this ten-foot-tall fence. Within a month of my moving to Park View the previous year, my next-door neighbor had taken it upon herself to teach me one of the essential truths of the neighborhood: This fence was not just a fence, but a long-standing affront. The vast grounds surrounding the Old Soldiers' Home, established in the 1850s as a federal retirement home for veterans, had once been open to the public. For a full century, the grounds of the Soldiers' Home served as D.C.'s version of Central Park, complete with pedestrian paths, expansive gardens, and streamside fishing holes. But in the mid-twentieth century, as the neighborhood around the Soldiers' Home changed from all-white to mostly Black, the federal government closed the park to the public. After the 1968 uprisings, coiled loops of barbed wire—and later, chain link—went up, along with four additional feet of spiked palings. For those who live on the sidewalk side of this enclosure, the Old Soldiers' Home's fence remains painfully paradigmatic of the divide between the racist, federal power of Washington and the residents of D.C.

At the next curve in the road, the creek turned toward a distant pair of ponds, one with a dinky fountain, the other occupied by a family of mallards. I stopped to look at the archival map on my phone, then thumbed over to Google Maps, frowning. If I was reading street names and contour lines correctly, then these outlying ponds were the last aboveground vestiges of the Tiber. For the rest of my ride down to its mouth, the creek would not be visible.

As I stared out at these paltry ponds, I thought of the previous week's rain and the turbid puddles it left behind on Quincy Street, where there is a triangle-shaped pocket park. Underneath it and the surrounding row homes were surely miles of piped-up streams. In the late 1800s, real estate developers channeled and buried hundreds of creeks across the city to make more land available for construction. Washington was expanding dramatically then, and city planners insisted that every inch of ground was needed for their new gridded suburbs. Rather than building around seeps and streams, even ones as large as the Tiber, developers paved over them, believing, I suppose, that water will stay where you order it to.

What had happened when the Tiber was severed from the land it carved? Wherever streams are channeled into concrete tubes and mixed with sewage, the transport of water is, surely, considerably slowed. A substantial amount of sediment must be building in those pipes, too, further obstructing the movement of water. Where did groundwater flow when it stormed and sewage overflow systems could not hold the deluge? No wonder parts of Park View and Petworth flooded every time it rained. This entire city was built on the bones of buried creeks.

Looking back at the line of renovated row homes behind me, their terraced yards fronted by election signs, I considered the ecological consequences of snatching streams from the sun: Cattails cannot grow in paved-over drains, and shad cannot swim up concrete pipes. I did not want to mourn for some imaginary preurban idyll, but as I thought about the constant waterlogging of my neighborhood, I doubted that burying these streams and then building homes over them had been the right idea. Staring out at the old path of the Tiber as it cut across the fields, it occurred to me that this lone aboveground stretch of the creek had likely been saved from interment precisely because it had once been part of a public park, a waterway visited and beloved by D.C. residents who lived along it.

As I watched the ducks circle the near-frozen ponds through the iron bars, I felt unusually and profoundly alienated from my own neighborhood. It was as though that fence and the interring of the Tiber had placed me beyond the boundaries of a place that I otherwise knew myself to be a part of: Every morning I walked my dog to the community garden across the street; I knew which neighbors still sat out on their porches and who actually wanted to talk; that dive bar was my dive bar; the barbecue spot was where I picked up ribs most Thursdays; that pocket park was where I inevitably gave in to the dog's whining and fed her one on the walk home.

I lived here; I carried the curves and fells of this city in my body. And still, I sensed that my neighbors and I were cut off from something we should belong to.

FROM THE SOUTHERN BOUNDARY of the Old Soldiers' Home, the Tiber had flowed southeast, meandering across the basin of what is now the McMillan Reservoir. Since I could not ride directly through a lake, I followed the route as best I could, up Fifth Street as it turned into Fourth. Cruising down the far side of the Howard hilltop, I slowed at every stop sign, giving the right-of-way to students hurrying to class under banners reminding them to vote, and vote early.

Election season is, perhaps counterintuitively, a quiet time in D.C. Incumbents depart for their home districts, followed by crowds of nonprofiteers and journalists. In their wake, the city goes still. No one comes to D.C. to canvas, and why would they? D.C. has only three votes in the electoral college, no senators, and no voting representatives. More to the point, public acknowledgment of Washington as part of "real America" now edges you closer to political suicide than a sex scandal might. To be electable, politicians on both sides of the aisle have learned to describe themselves in opposition to the city, à la Bernie Sanders, who is not an "inside-the-Beltway kind of guy," and Donald Trump, who pledged ad nauseam to drain the Washington swamp.

Most Washingtonians are aware that the city wasn't actually built on a swamp, but on streambeds, though few people living outside D.C. care to make the distinction. All that matters for the metaphor to work is the idea that Washington occupies a mucky landscape, where moisture befouls politics and breeds corruption. As I hung a left onto O Street, I wondered whether anyone who still uses the expression, either in support of this message or against it, has any sense that the "swamp" of the metaphor refers to the lower reaches of Tiber Creek.

I cycled into a shady alleyway lined with burnweed and paused to look around. Here, somewhere between the din of North Capitol Street and New York Avenue, tucked back behind a Tex-Mex place and a homeless shelter, the two main branches of the Tiber had met and merged. If it wasn't a swampy landscape, it was certainly a marshy one, where reeds lined the wide banks and beavers dammed the rills.

I examined the scene for any trace of the place where kids

had cannonballed into a ten-foot-wide Tiber. A few blocks south of here, near Union Station, there were swimming holes with such evocative names as the Piggory and the Blue Cork, cool, deep ponds that disappeared when developers bricked up the lower Tiber into tunnels and pipes beginning in the 1870s. As I exited again into the sun of the main street, I rolled over a manhole cover, the only clue that this alley had once been a blue pool—or, perhaps, if you were looking at it from far away, a stinking swamp.

I hadn't made it a half block west before a man with a clipboard flagged me down. Was I registered to vote in Washington, D.C., he wanted to know, and had I already voted? Yes and yes, I reported, feeling dutiful. The man praised me for voting by mail the week prior, and then, pointing down the block in the direction of Dunbar High School, asked if I could promise to bring five friends later that day to vote. "It's an incredibly important election," he said seriously when I told him that I would try.

The line to vote at Dunbar stretched out the door. To be denied the most basic right of American citizenship—the right to full enfranchisement—could understandably turn District residents cynical regarding the democratic process. And yet here was this line of people, gathered together in the atrium of a public high school—the nation's first public high school for Black students, no less—to participate in this essential act of democracy.

The first seeds of District disenfranchisement were sown over two centuries ago, before there was even an idea of a place called the District of Columbia. In June 1783, Continental army veterans marched on the Pennsylvania State House, in Philadelphia, where, at the time, the Confederation Congress also met. Four hundred veterans, largely farmers and other working-class men from the rural reaches of Pennsylvania, occupied the State

House, demanding the back pay they were still owed by state leaders. Alexander Hamilton, as a prominent delegate to Congress, demanded that the ragtag gang disperse at his order; they did, but again requested to meet with the Pennsylvania Executive Council, an appeal that left Hamilton fuming.

Hamilton reasoned that when the country had an official capital, it would be critical for Congress to have complete power over that capital's residents to prevent future insurrections. Although historians have confirmed the Philadelphia Mutiny was more a protest march than a riot, Hamilton's anxieties over the possibility of a working-class rebellion influenced the writing of Article I of the Constitution, which mandated that the federal government reside in a ten-square-mile "District" over which Congress would exercise "exclusive legislation."

Other congressional members pointed out the tension between the imperial need for "exclusive legislation" and the revolutionary imperative of "no taxation without representation." Commissioner of the Treasury Samuel Osgood wrote to Samuel Adams in 1783, explaining his concerns about the electoral future of the District:

> It has cost me many a Sleepless Night to find out the most obnoxious Part of the proposed Plan.—And I have finally fixed upon the exclusive Legislation in the Ten Miles Square.—This space is capable of holding two Millions of People . . . shall there be in the Bowels of the United States such a Number of People, brot up under the Hands of Despotism, without one Privilege of Humanity, that they can claim . . .

Following the ratification of the Constitution, Congress stalled on the question of whether to amend or even implement the "exclusive legislation" clause. And so, for over a decade after the creation of the District, all land-owning white men living on the south shore of the river were allowed to cast their ballots in Virginia, and on the north shore they did so in Maryland.

But in 1801, Congress finally decided to enforce the clause. The city's three developed areas—Washington City, Georgetown, and Alexandria—were placed under the exclusive control of Congress, and while Georgetown and Alexandria were permitted to keep their preexisting town governments, the law made no provisions for the formation of a Washington City government. Nor did the law address how people living in the capital would be represented in Congress, nor whether they would participate in presidential elections. What was clear was that District residents were no longer citizens, but subjects of the federal government.

White elites in Washington City immediately sought to establish a small-scale system of local government, which Congress permitted could consist of a presidentially appointed mayor and elected council. In Virginia, Alexandrians' desire to regain their voting rights fueled the movement for Virginia retrocession—along with the need to protect the slave trade as an essential part of their economy. When Congress returned the portion of the District on the south shore of the Potomac to Virginia in 1846, white male residents regained their full voting rights as American citizens.

After emancipation, thousands of formerly enslaved people moved into Washington City. In January 1867, the Radical Republican–led Congress passed a bill that allowed Black men to vote in the city's municipal elections, and that June, Black voters helped give Republicans a majority of seats on the city council, now locally elected. In 1869, Black men from each of the city's seven wards won election to the now biracial council, which passed significant antidiscrimination and education legislation later that year.

The speed at which civil rights had advanced in the capital and the liberal reach of new municipal laws terrified white congressmen; many imagined that Black residents in their home districts might be inspired by the political activities of Black Washingtonians. To curtail Black electoral power, Congress established in 1871 a "territorial government" for Washington City. The new system did away with the city council and consisted instead of a presidentially appointed governor, a Legislative Assembly, and a Board of Public Works. Though residents could still vote in some smaller local elections, almost all political power now lay with the Board of Public Works.

Under the leadership of charismatic businessman Alexander "Boss" Shepherd, the board spearheaded a colossal public works project across the District. Muddy streets were paved, parks were established, and residential development expanded. Dozens of creeks were buried to make room for new buildings. Engineer Adolf Cluss, also a member of the board, oversaw one of the most ambitious projects of the Shepherd era: the construction of an enormous tunnel for Tiber Creek, "wide enough for a bus," extending from the Capitol to the Potomac.

Shepherd was a productive but unscrupulous leader; in less than three years, he drove the city into a spiral of debt and corruption. A congressional committee mandated to investigate his contracts found fault with his profligate spending, but it saved its harshest criticism for voters, lambasting them for their support of his prodigal behavior, though residents had little to no control over Shepherd or the board. Drawing on racist stereotypes of Black people as children and irresponsible spendthrifts, the committee suggested that what the District needed was a federal overseer. In 1874, Congress accepted the committee's recommendations and scrapped the territorial government. In its place, a board of three presidentially appointed commissioners would manage the entire city.

The scope of this disenfranchisement was hard to understate. "Under this bill," the *Nation* reported, "not a vestige is left of popular municipal government: aldermen, common councilmen, mayors, boards of works, school boards, police boards, primaries, conventions, all are swept away, and the entire government is handed over to three men, appointed by a foreign authority, responsible not to their fellow citizens, but to the President and Senate." All District men had lost their right to vote, but for Black Washingtonians, the loss of suffrage was particularly devastating. City commissioners—who were all white men until 1961, when President Kennedy appointed the first Black commissioner—routinely ignored Black voters, who now had the memory of holding political power but no recourse to regain it.

District residents did not accept their fate without complaint, and through the early twentieth century the topic of reinstating some form of suffrage occasionally surfaced in congressional committees. In response, southern congressmen routinely resurrected the specter of Reconstruction-era Black power. In one particularly vile speech, Alabama senator John Morgan described the Black-led biracial government of the late 1860s as so "abominable and disgraceful" that Congress "found it necessary to disfranchise every man in the District of Columbia," an act that was akin "to burn[ing] down the barn to get rid of the rats ... the rats being the negro population and the barn being the government of the District of Columbia."

White fear of "negro domination" kept all residents of the

city disenfranchised for the next century. Though "the present form of alien government is about as bad as can be devised," *The Washington Post* explained, "a system which gives the control of the District to ignorant and depraved negroes is still worse." This logic prevailed for decades among white residents; many seemed to solve the problem by fleeing the city for the expanding suburbs of Maryland and Virginia, where they regained their full voting rights.

But by the late 1950s, two important changes had taken place. As a result of white flight, D.C. had become the nation's first Black-majority city, and by 1957 almost all public institutions in the District had been desegregated with the passage of early civil rights legislation. With the ferment of the civil rights movement in the air throughout the emergent Chocolate City, Black residents began organizing toward a new political strategy of "home rule"—self-government by means of a locally elected mayor and council.

Early efforts to pass home rule legislation were almost immediately blocked by white supremacist congressmen. Senator Robert Byrd of West Virginia and Representative John McMillan of South Carolina were the greatest obstacles; for decades, the two men dedicated themselves to the task of reworking the city's budget, gutting education and housing programs while funneling pork-barrel funds into the city's police force.

The overt antagonism directed at the District from congressmen eventually inspired political activism among both white and Black residents. In 1956, an upper-class cadre of white Washingtonians began organizing through a group called Citizens for a Presidential Vote for the District of Columbia. Largely relying on their own personal political connections, organizers lobbied for District residents to have a say in who is elected president. In 1961, the Twenty-third Amendment to the Constitution was ratified, which gave the District the same number of electoral votes as the smallest state. Three years later, Washingtonians voted for Lyndon Johnson, the first president they had been allowed to vote for since Thomas Jefferson.

President Johnson supported home rule, as had Kennedy and Eisenhower before him; indeed, by the mid-1960s, home rule had largely become a bipartisan issue due to significant lobbying efforts from District residents. Despite lingering opposition from select members of Congress, by 1970, support for home rule was so substantial that Congress was able to approve several bills aimed toward the eventuality of full home rule, including the creation of a locally elected school board and the approval of a nonvoting delegate to the House of Representatives.

Walter Fauntroy, a long-time civil rights activist, was the District's first delegate to the House, and he took on the fight for home rule as the central plank in his platform. The greatest obstruction to past bills had been the chairman of the committee on the District of Columbia, John McMillan, who remains infamous in D.C. for having once sent Fauntroy a truck of watermelons. Fauntroy arranged for dozens of organizers to rally Black voters in McMillan's district, and in 1972 Black South Carolinians ousted the longtime white supremacist from public office. With McMillan removed, home rule sailed out of committee and was signed into law by President Nixon in 1973.

The Home Rule Act created the foundation for the current form of D.C.'s local government; it allowed for a locally elected mayor, thirteen-member city council, and the formation of the city's Advisory Neighborhood Commissions. But the Home Rule Act did not give total control of the city's affairs to its residents, as many organizers had expected it would. To this day, all legislation passed by the council, including the city's twenty-billion-dollar budget, remains subject to veto by Congress, and local judges are still appointed by the president instead of being elected by residents, as they are in other states and major cities. Because the federal government oversees the District's courts, it also oversees its prison system; as a result, residents convicted of felonies are shipped to federal prisons, which can be located a half dozen states or more away from their families.

Included in the law are also a number of exceptions to self-government that range from the bizarre to the outright damaging: The District cannot make changes to the Height of Buildings Act of 1910; it cannot change the composition of local courts; it is not allowed any additional authority over the Washington Aqueduct, which supplies the city with its water, nor the D.C. National Guard, which is overseen by the president, in contrast to states where governors serve as commanders in chief.

Home rule gave District residents more control over the civic institutions that governed their lives than they had had in almost two centuries. But because that control was limited, it also gave new power to citizens who did not live in the District. It is still possible for voters in, say, Vermont, to elect a representative to the House Committee on Oversight and Reform, which oversees the District's municipal legislation; that representative may not approve of a newly passed District law and compel the rest of the committee to veto it. It does not matter that District residents may support this law or that more people live in the District than live in Vermont (or Wyoming). American citizens living anywhere from Maine to Hawaii have the final say over how the District governs itself.

This is not a theoretical exercise in the structures of democracy. Over the last three decades, Congress has challenged District efforts at gun-violence legislation, blocked queer couples' ability to register as domestic partners, prevented the creation of a clean needle exchange program designed to limit the spread of HIV/AIDS, and barred public spending designed to offset abortion costs for low-income residents. Contrary to all democratic sense, the District is still controlled by people who live anywhere else but here.

Washingtonians rarely say out loud that we live under federal colonization. It sounds histrionic and ahistorical—even ungrateful; we live, after all, in the nation's capital, the beating heart of American democracy. But *colony* is the only word that correctly describes the political condition of our city. What other term should we use to describe being forced to surrender our sovereignty to people from distant places, who occupy our home for two to six years, depending on how an election turns out? Is there another word that describes a place where a white-majority nation maintains a stranglehold of power over a Black-plurality city? In what other place but a colony would residents be reminded to be thankful for their proximity to political power, while simultaneously being told that they cannot hold it themselves?

Sometimes I forget where I live—and then I remember that because I live in Washington, D.C., I am not a citizen, but a colonized subject. To live in this city is to have your citizenship stolen by other Americans, who believe that your home exists only in service to theirs. To become conscious of this fact and then to hold it in your mind and in your body is to burn blue like the hottest flame.

⊹⊹⊹

BIKING SOUTH DOWN CAPITOL STREET, I headed past Union Station, where the Tiber once took a hard turn to the west, pouring out nearly one hundred feet wide across what is now the National Mall. By the time I hit Constitution Avenue, traffic had picked up and tour buses clogged the bike lanes, making me feel so ill at ease on the road that I stopped on the sidewalk in front of the Capitol Reflecting Pool and stared out across the Mall. Pierre L'Enfant, the city's original architect, intended for waterfalls to cascade from the base of the Capitol in a system of waterworks fed by the Tiber. Squinting across the vista, I struggled to envision the grottoes and canals that were supposed to flow from tidal streams.

Turning around to face the white-stoned Capitol, the building struck me as so forbidding and grandiose, I found it impossible to imagine it at the helm of an island surrounded by a free-flowing Tiber and the Potomac. It wasn't just that my powers of imagination were faulty; I was preoccupied, as I had become almost every time I visited this section of the city, with memories of the Capitol insurrection.

I spent the morning of January 6, 2021, on the Valley Trail in Rock Creek Park. By noon, I was walking home down Irving Street; I remember thinking that the Columbia Heights metro corner seemed unusually quiet, but I chalked it up to the near-freezing weather. It wasn't until I was home and settled into my study that I checked my phone. A barrage of text messages filled the screen, most requests from family and friends that I call back and confirm I was okay. All afternoon, I kept listening for an explosion or the pop of gunfire, but all I heard beyond the blare of television news were helicopters overhead.

The next morning I had a dentist appointment at an office on K Street. With the pandemic still raging, it seemed foolish to take a bus, and it was far too cold to ride my bike, so I walked the three miles through Park View, across Columbia Heights, past U Street, and down Sixteenth. I had never seen the city so still. No one, save an occasional dog walker, was out on the street.

As I made my way into downtown, I began to see a few more people on the sidewalk. These were tourists, I thought at first, judging by their roller bags and the awkward, impatient glances they took from the phones in their hands out to the street as they waited for Ubers to arrive and carry them to the airport. More and more of these groups of men appeared on the street in front of their hotels, for they were almost all men, and almost all of them white. Still, it wasn't until a man in a MAGA hat out on a coffee run nodded in my direction as we passed each other that I realized that these men were not only tourists but terrorists.

When I arrived at the dentist, there was no one there; when I called, I learned the office had been closed for safety concerns. I sat in the empty waiting room for a half hour, waiting for my heart rate to return to normal, working up the courage to walk home. When I did leave, I cut west and took a long, out-of-the-way route away from downtown over to Twenty-second Street, then up through Kalorama, Adams Morgan, and Columbia Heights. As I walked, I passed the old Quaker Meeting House, and then my favorite Ethiopian restaurant, the site of a dozen happy dinners. I touched the stonework around Malcolm X Park and grinned at a psychedelic spinning Christmas tree still up in the front window of a row house. The Florida Avenue Grill wasn't open, but even the sight of the sign made my mouth water and heart ache. Then I climbed the Cardozo hill toward home, as I had a hundred times before.

Back on the Mall, in front of the Capitol, I tried to remember why I had taken such a roundabout route home that day. It wasn't just that I was afraid of white supremacists on the street; the man in the MAGA hat who had nodded to acknowledge my presence had reminded me that my whiteness and gender were, in fact, a kind of shield. Less than twenty-four hours after the attempted coup, I hadn't yet learned that these citizen-terrorists had attacked District residents on the street, or that the federal government took three hours to approve the D.C. mayor's request to call up the D.C. National Guard to protect the city. I didn't know that a barbed-wire fence would soon go up around the Capitol, or that bombs had been placed around residential sections of Capitol Hill.

I observed a young family taking photographs of one another on the Capitol steps, their smiles and easy posture in such contrast to the blood and broken glass of January 6. "Say Washington, D.C.!" the woman told the children, who obeyed, cheesing for the camera. This perfectly normal family of tourists had something in common with the rioters of January 6: Both understood Washington, D.C., to be a place typified by the structure and functions of the Capitol. Both encountered Washington, D.C., as more of a scene or a stage than an actual city. For this family perhaps, D.C. was a backdrop for their photographs and family memories; for others, it was a necessary setting against which to mount an insurrection. I wondered, watching the father adjust his ball cap, which carried the name of some midwestern college, if he understood that Washington, D.C., is as real a place as wherever his family had traveled from, the kind of place where people have Thursday-morning dentist appointments or dogs that need to be taken out for a walk.

For most Americans, the conflation of the city and the government is not merely rhetorical, as it is for politicians who boo and bash "Washington" and complain about "the swamp." Rather, this conflation and the concomitant erasure of D.C. in the American psyche suffuse the city with a potent sense of placelessness, which underscores and even substantiates its political vulnerability as a colony. Severed from the democracy it houses, D.C. appears to outsiders as *terra nullius,* belonging to no one but the nation. And because it belongs to no one, it can be claimed by all.

The sense of entitlement that American citizens extend over Washington, D.C., is made all the more compelling by the fact that D.C. remains a very Black city and is therefore understood to be a subject that not only can be but should be possessed and controlled.

A block from home on January 7, I paused in front of a familiar house on Eleventh Street with no less than a dozen signs staked in its yard that read STATEHOOD FOR THE PEOPLE OF D.C. Statehood emerged as a political strategy after decades of failed attempts to gain congressional representation by other means. Having won the limited right to home rule in 1973, the District forwarded a proposal for congressional representation in the form of two senators and one voting representative. Self-determination for D.C. still had widespread bipartisan support, and the D.C. Voting Rights Amendment (DCVRA) easily passed through the House and the Senate in 1978. But by the 1980s, New Right activists, riding the Reagan-led wave of power into Washington, had successfully labeled the DCVRA as an "affirmative action" program; only sixteen states ratified the amendment before the 1985 deadline.

In the wake of the failed ratification of the DCVRA, the movement for D.C. statehood blossomed. In 1980, 60 percent of D.C. voters supported a referendum for statehood as their preferred route toward self-autonomy, and in 2016, 86 percent of D.C. voters did the same. In April 2021, the House passed for the first time H.R. 51, the bill that would create a new state from the District called the Douglass Commonwealth, though it has yet to pass the Senate.

With partisan power teetering on a knife's edge in the upper chamber, arguments against statehood have become increasingly preposterous: D.C. is too small to be a state; D.C. is too partisan to be a state; D.C. does not have car dealerships (it does). Other arguments rest on the bad-faith conflation of the city and the government: Washington, D.C., is the federal government and its residents are all lobbyists and aides. These people do not need statehood, because they already represent other states.

Still other arguments are blatantly racist: D.C. is too crime-ridden to be a state, as if the city holds a monopoly on urban crime or that low crime statistics justify suffrage. The subtext to this argument is the falsity that Blackness and crime are linked; a place too crime-ridden to be a state is understood to be a place too Black to be a state. But perhaps the long-lasting and most destructive argument against D.C. sovereignty is that its leaders are not capable enough to take on the responsibilities of full enfranchisement. This line of reasoning is rooted in centuries of congressional paternalism directed at Black residents, going back at least as far as 1874, when Congress stripped all District voters of their rights to suffrage in order to stifle Black political power.

But the origin of this logic goes further back and deeper even than this. Washington, D.C., is the nation's last internal colony, the last jurisdiction in America where white people may still legally control Black ones.

When Americans think of Washington, D.C., they think of the White House and they think of the Capitol. But as I stared up at it, I saw only the racist power that maintains the District as its personal colony. Situated on the hill, looking out over the city, the structure looked to me less like the home of democracy and more like a plantation house.

How few Americans know the kind of quiet violence of disenfranchisement that District residents live with daily! This, I realized, is because American citizens do not think of us at all, and so they cannot know the kind of anger and loneliness that builds like water behind a dam when your home is denied a place to belong within the nation.

WITH ANOTHER MILE STILL TO GO, I rode down Constitution Avenue, past the Smithsonian museums and the Sculpture Garden, the National Archives and the Washington Monument. At Seventeenth Street, I hung a left and passed through the high gates of the levee. This granite wall is designed to hold back the Potomac as it reaches for the Tiber, but it can't stop the creek from reaching back out to the river. Occasionally, the Tiber still floods the basements of the Internal Revenue Service, the Department of Justice, and the Environmental Protection Agency.

The cherry trees along the Tidal Basin burned red against the gray water and sky ahead. Because the Basin had been constructed around and over the mouth of the Tiber, I no longer had an obvious destination. The Tiber had ended somewhere past what is now Independence Avenue, between the World War II Memorial and the paddle boat marina. There was no marker that commemorated the Tiber's end, but as I passed the Jefferson Memorial, mud from the last high tide splashed against my ankles.

After crossing Ohio Drive, I got off my bike and walked down to the edge of the river. The Potomac glittered in the cold sun, so that the wind seemed to lift the light right off the surface. Traffic thundered on the bridge ahead and on the parkway across the water. Standing there amid the light and noise, I waited to feel some sweep of affection for the river or at least a sense of accomplishment at having finished my ride. Instead, I felt drained.

How many times have I stood on the banks of this river, reflecting on that essential truth of all rivers: that all flows to them, that in their bodies are all of our own? The Tiber showed me, as I followed its path to the river, that to live in D.C. is to be forever severed from that to which you already belong.

I can forget, at times, how enraging, even painful it can be to reflect on all the histories that have been buried in the District, all the ways in which white Americans have struggled to keep the racist legacy of District disenfranchisement underground. And yet, if we do not bring these histories to the surface and try to repair that which has been broken off from the whole for centuries, we risk not only physical floods but political ones, torrents that come in the form of violence and rage and riots. District residents are already citizens—other Americans need only to accept this truth to account for that which has been hidden.

I wondered what it might be like to bring the Tiber back to the surface and to reconnect it to the Potomac. At the headwaters, up in Petworth, the daylighting of the Tiber was easy to imagine: Remove the high fence, dig up the brick channel, and rebuild the creek side. Farther south, it would undoubtedly be a harder sell to dig up roads and train tracks to reinstall a free-flowing creek across H Street. Still, I couldn't help but picture a great blue heron perched on the clock tower of Founders Library and muskrats playing in the pools of Le Droit Park. From the base of the Capitol, the Tiber could flow into the Potomac as it once did in a braided system of streams and chutes, mitigating the threat of flooding to the Federal Triangle. As absurd as it may seem, I imagined the Mall replaced by a stream.

But as I looked out over the Potomac, its epithet—the

Nation's River—came to mind. For some, it was perhaps as equally impossible to imagine what D.C. statehood might look like. For over two hundred years, the residents of this city have lived estranged from the rest of the nation. To restore the Tiber to its river would be as daunting a task as restoring citizenship to the people of Washington, D.C.; both undertakings would require that we exhume that which we would not wish to reencounter.

For the thousandth time, I stood on the bank of the Potomac and watched it flow out to the bay. Somewhere on the bed, in the rocks, or in the water itself, the Tiber coursed within the Potomac. You could not remove it from the whole, not by force of will or law or might.

Bones

Streetlight leaked through the room where I awoke and readied. Driving south through the city, the lights were all green and the sidewalks were white, dusted with the slightest snow. Past Georgetown, a column of fog covered the river and hovered along the cliffs. I parked and stumbled down the bluff in the blackness, feeling my way over familiar rocks. Ice cracked underfoot as I traced the trail across the plain to the tip of a long shoaly spit. And there, in the middle of the Potomac, I sat down and waited for the shortest day of the year to begin.

Seven years now in D.C., and it has become my custom to spend every solstice and equinox with the Potomac, a ritual intended to direct attention to each season as we—the river and I—cross its threshold together. I keep this practice to keep track of time. The longer I live in this city, the more uncertain and recurved the concept becomes.

On those four days, I'm out the door before sunrise with a bag filled with tea, bread, and foraging supplies, and I do not return home until the sun falls under the furrow of the south ridge. During these hours, I walk with the river and even talk to it, alone or with any friends I might have been able to cajole into accompanying me. As we wander, we gather whatever edibles we come across—greens and fruits and nuts; the day often ends with a meal cooked over a fire, crackling in the sand of the riverbank.

These high days have become a sacrament to me, and I take their purpose seriously. As I look for signs of the new season, I can sense myself settling into the soil, as if I am landing back on home ground after lighting off for some time. Or rather, this is what I hope for. With every year, I find I need this ritual more than I did the last.

The fog was so heavy, I couldn't tell when the sun first lifted over the city. In one moment, I could not see what was in front of me, and in the next, I could: Mist rolled downriver, steady and slow, as if each particulate in the air was bound to a molecule of water. Sun seeped through the haze but hadn't yet split the ridge. Leaning and lonely, the snow-crusted sycamores out on the small islands began to appear as the air warmed.

And then all the light was in the tops of the trees. Tall oaks glowed, as if lit from within. Another minute now and the peaks of both ridges were on fire. Bright heat filtered down branches and boles, so unhurried that I hardly recognized the light line was moving toward the water. In winter, especially in the snow, the sunrise does not turn the landscape gold or yellow, but sharper and silvery. The ripples between the rocks turned white at their crest, then softened. The river was blue—so blue—as the mist dissolved.

I watched for another ten minutes as the river turned a bold and bright color, a blue beyond all blues, until it reached some maximal hue. I closed my eyes and could still feel it on the other side of my eyelids: a shade I dreamed of enveloping myself in, as if under a heavy quilt or close in someone's arms. Then, in an instant, the sunrise was over and the morning was on; the water returned to its usual pearl gray.

There are times when my love for the Potomac catches up with me, and I am shocked that I could have forgotten, even for a breath, that every minute by this river is a revelation. I do not know of a greater gift from a lover than that of a good surprise, a flick of something new that draws curiosity and sparks wonder. That the river grants me these moments of astonishment every day, if only I can will myself to go out and discover them, is a generosity I never dared to dream of before I moved to D.C.

By the time I finally rose, I was almost frozen to the rock. The far side of the river was a hill painted white, threaded with dark trees. Though I had seen this ridge a dozen times in snow, I had never noticed the depth of the rifts in this incline. There is no better way to see a place fresh than under a scattering of snow. When the ground is no longer green or dark, but white, marvels emerge: the lemon feather of a long-gone warbler, the purple shock of the last aster. These things hide in a mottled landscape, but against the snow, they flare. Off-white, ivory things especially seem to materialize out of nowhere, set off darker than their surroundings for a change.

Since there is not much in the way of wild edibles to forage come the winter solstice, I planned to spend the day in search of these not quite white things: I was going bone hunting. It's a term I used tongue in cheek; I wasn't going to kill anything, just go out looking for where animals had died, only skeletons left behind. Sometimes I took the bones I found home, laid a skull on the bookshelf, and stared at it while eating soup, but more often, I left the bones where I'd discovered them. Animals die by human means along highways and by other animals along the vulnerable expanse of the riverbank. The boundary between the parkway and water is a graveyard, if you know how to look.

To hunt for bones, you cast your eyes about the ground for a white that is gray, even a bit yellow. You must move slowly— there are false starts and many impostors. Quickly, you learn how to distinguish the white of a bone from that of a knuckle of quartz or rain-bleached beech leaf. You must imagine that you are the animal that knows it will soon die: The deer collapses in a clearing, just off a worn trail; the fox curls up in a tree burrow to breathe its last; the turtle finds rest in the safety of a rock scramble. Sometimes, you find only the shams of bones: the vomit of river otters, fleecy owl pellets, shards of shad coughed up by a heron. With practice, your eye develops.

As I made my way downriver, inspecting the textures and colors of the duff, I saw a dirty white thing poking out from under a scrim of snow. I trudged over. It was a plastic bag. A bit farther, a hunk of Styrofoam led me astray again.

But past Wood Duck Run, I found a single sharp tooth, poking out from the humus where some other critter had already scratched up the litter. Many animals engage in osteophagy, or the chewing of bones, in order to supplement their diets with calcium and phosphorus. Maybe a squirrel or fox had found this skeleton and tossed about the bones, gnawing their edges. I scanned the clutter of snow and sticks for what was missing, and there it was: a jawbone, a hole where the tooth, now in my pocket, should have been. I picked it up and kept looking. Here was a small vertebra, and another, and another. Here, a scattering of ribs. And then, there was the skull, round as a moon, sockets like craters.

I picked it up and held it in my palm, considering the raccoon brain that once had been inside. The mornings it must have seen on the river: the violet haze on the ridge, the ice-melt green of winter floods, the firestorm of fall pawpaw leaves. The things it must have eaten! Soft persimmons, succulent mussels, frog legs, and trash, straight from the can.

Pocketing the skull, I thought how peculiar it was to be preoccupied by thoughts of this animal's existence while holding in my hand the stuff of its demise. But this, of course, was the paradox and pleasure of bone hunting. To fish and ferret and grub about for these objects made me feel more animal-like myself, conscious that I was alive and kicking.

Even with the morning sun streaming in, the clefts in the ridge took on a blue tone from the snow. The pale branches of the sycamores looked bruised. It seemed that the mist had not so much burned off the water as blown back into the forest. It had the effect of every tree and rock turning dark in outlines against the murk, as if everything were a piece apart. The skull in my pocket now felt as heavy as a stone, and a sudden wave of isolation cracked through the air around me.

I'm not sure why it happens this way, how I can feel, within the span of a few minutes, a love for this place so deep that I want to drown in it, and then an alienation so acute that it feels as though my skin is being threshed. There are moments with this river that feel close to madness, when I think what foolishness it is to be in love with something that by its nature only seeks to leave you.

This, I think, is the reason I like walking upriver more than I like walking down. I can imagine the water pressing against me that way, depositing silt or something else that I might always carry. To walk the other way, with the water, I am reminded that we are separate bodies, that as much as I would like to become part of this place in a way as indelible as the river itself, I cannot, not fully. And so I turned around, moving back against the current, willing myself to remember that I live here and that I love it, and that I, along with everything else here, belong.

❊

I STOPPED FOR A LATE BREAKFAST along a slim run lined with naked berry canes. Last year, a flood chewed off a section of the trail ahead, forcing hikers to wend their way around on top of the ridge before descending again to the plain. I took a last sip of tea, plotting my route. Then I crossed the run and began to climb, moving slowly over the melting snow.

When I reached the top, the view over the river was glorious. But there at the precipice, something else stole my attention: an intact deer skeleton. No animal had yet scuttled its bones. The deer, a young buck with two-point antlers, lay in place exactly as it had died, sans organs and skin. The skeleton appeared to be almost in movement, as though the animal could, in one shake and huff, rise and bound away.

Kneeling, I looked down at the skeleton, just one in a litany of wonders the Potomac had shown me. Even in the past month there had been spectacles beyond accounting: an enormous sycamore leaf nearly twenty inches wide; a club of hooded mergansers visiting for the first time that season; that morning's fog lifting like a veil off the cliffs. These sightings struck me then and now as so sublime, I'm inclined to call them miracles, but that would suggest these things are rare, when, in fact, they are anything but. The river is profuse in the gift of its visions.

For every moment when I still feel the stab of isolation, there is another when a familiar buttonbush or certain slab of schist reminds me that it is impossible to give your attention and care to a place and not, in some way, become a part of it. This sense of situated incorporation is accompanied by an equally dynamic sense of responsibility, a feeling stronger than belief that my fate is bound to this place.

The problem is, this feeling of belonging doesn't last, and I can return, with such ease, to the time in which the Potomac was to me only a border, separating a Black city from a white one, with no room for shades between. On every walk it seemed that the Potomac revealed another layer of the nation's history of fracture and violence. Even now, perched high above the water, these stories came back to me like breakers: George

Washington's slaves being forced to hack into the bluff below Mount Vernon; centuries of poison trickling into the Anacostia; the floods that moved shorelines and people around against their will; even the fact of D.C.'s being located here, in this spot, on this river, in order to extend the reach of slavery.

I still frequently pictured the city as an overstuffed memory palace with hundreds of rooms crammed with tales and articles of national history. In D.C., it seemed there was a double layer to the James Baldwin adage that "people are trapped in history, and history is trapped in them." What other American city is forced to bear the burden not only of its own past but that of the rest of the nation? This fact of the capital is what makes the character of this city so evasive, resistant not just to categorization but even to description.

Thumbing the grooves of the deer skull, I wondered, after all this time walking and writing about the river, whether I had ever been able to make sense of both the marvels and horrors of the city. Part of me still believes that I might strike the right balance between a love for all this city is and a furious contempt for the histories that have made it. The musician Gil Scott-Heron called D.C. "a ball of contradictions" and "a mess of ironies," and sometimes I think this is all that can be said about the city: that it refuses clarity, that it thrives on paradox. Other times I think that if I can just get out on the river one more time, that will do the trick, that the city will become whole to me, and those histories of division and displacement will slip away.

I know by now it's folly, the idea you can get free of the past by rooting yourself in the present. There's no escaping D.C.'s strange union of liminality and centrality. D.C.'s location in a regional borderland, its status as the capital, and its long cultural associations with Blackness have meant that it has been pulled among alternative identities for centuries;

had I not spent years now trying to tease them all out? Is it a northern city or a southern one? Is it a small town or a global metropolis? Is it a city for political insiders or social outsiders, between, as Scott-Heron sang, "the folks who come and go and the ones who've got to stay?" Is it more Washington, or is it D.C., or is it both? And of course, whom does it belong to—all Americans by virtue of their citizenship, or those of us who live here and care for it?

Torn between various, conflicting identities, D.C. has never been permitted to assert itself as a real and present place or to map political possibilities for its future. And this is what makes this city's relationship to the past different: It has never been allowed to exist on its own terms. No wonder when I first moved here and began to recognize the persistent sense of placelessness that shuffled about the alleyways, I sought out the most real thing I could find: the river.

To say I love this river because it is real may seem superfluous. But when the place around it has been robbed of its sense of place, it is the truest thing I can say about my relationship to the Potomac. It's not merely the exchange of love between the river and myself that makes me feel so certain, at times, that I am a part of this place. It is that the Potomac is an antidote to the enforced ubiquity of the past in D.C., flowing, as all rivers are said to do, between then and now. In this way, the river provides a sense of temporal abundance, a transubstantiated folding of time such that I am conscious all at once of the mess of the past, the beauty of the present, and the strangeness of the future.

When I think about whatever future I might share with this city, whether I will live here forever or fly off for another town, I think about the Potomac. How, in my desire to become a part of the river, I came to care for it as deeply as a lover. How all forms of care involve an open relationship to futurity. That to care is to attend to the consequences of the past, to attempt to mitigate the suffering of the present, and to do what you can to preclude future pain and sustain future life. These moments of temporal abundance flash by in an instant, but repeating as they do, they have left imprints on my body. It's impossible, then, to get stuck forever in those cold moments that I have described as isolation or alienation, division or loneliness, when what I really mean is the fear that I will never be able to belong here.

This Potomac River! How many times must it show me that I belong on its banks before I believe it? I slid down the hill en route to the trail, using saplings like ski poles. I left the deer skeleton where I had found it, though I was tempted to take home the skull. Of the thousand things this river has taught me, here is one: You cannot claim anything to be yours except by attention and care.

※

DOWN ON THE FLOODPLAIN, the snow was all slush. I passed the mammoth sycamore, still the largest I had ever seen along the Potomac, and paused to rest my hand on its scales. Then I walked beyond the pawpaw grove, over the skunk cabbage sump, and on to the crust of shore where I had seen bald eagles plunge. There were the rock islands where I had sunned and swum with friends through the years. Across a dry run, the nettled twist in the trail where I once held the eyes of a fox, and beyond that, the remnants of a brick chimney, all that was left behind of some former cabin destroyed by a flood.

As I approached the stone stack, something glittering beneath it caught my eye. I hopped through fallen timber to investigate. In the empty space of the hearth, someone had cleared away the debris and laid down a mandala of pebbles, dried bracken, and bits of river glass. Leading up the far side of the trail from where I had come, someone had placed stones into something like a garden path, leading hikers up the hill.

The mandala curved along wisps of goldenrod and Christmas fern. Blue shards of glass flared at the edges of the pattern like comets. Foliated rocks—what I learned as a child to call "wishing stones"—formed the core of the whirling disk. Mandalas, and even more so the act of making one, represent the pursuit of unity with the universe. And because this mandala was made with scruff and scraps so specific to the Potomac, I could not help but think that whoever made it had laid out these things with a desire for wholeness with the river. That its maker had also set down a trail leading to it suggested an invitation to take part, and even to be part of this place.

Every so often over the years, I had thought of the disease my landlady diagnosed me with my first spring on the river. Potomac fever, as I had understood it then, was a term for an obsession with Washington, D.C., rooted in the desire for money and influence. For years, I dismissed the diagnosis; politicians and politicos contract Potomac fever, not historians and naturalists.

But as time has passed, I have wondered whether my landlady could detect a nascent, and at times frenzied, compulsion on my part to parse out the complexities of this city, to understand why this city appeared at first to be so placeless. I didn't yet know that the Potomac River has always been the remedy for whatever ails this city.

I think it was the surprise of the mandala, circling and stretching out from its center of striped stones, but I could feel myself then within that web of expanding time, my body at once rooting down and extending out. How had it come to me, this knowing that I am bound to this place? The closest words I've found for it are from Rarámuri scholar Enrique Salmon, who uses the term *kincentric ecology* to describe the total interconnectedness and integration of all life in a given place, both physical and spiritual. Recognizing your own interdependence gives rise to actions based in generosity and reciprocity; it's not self-interest at work, but mutualism, the certainty that for me to belong and to thrive, my neighbors must, as well.

Of course, it's all easier said than done, easier still felt than said. And in a city where the legacy of white supremacy bleeds so palpably into the present, it is more difficult still to maintain a practice of reciprocal relation with the world around you. Even in these moments where I am held by the blessed assurance of belonging here, it is impossible to hold at once the consciousness of my own interdependence and the silences encouraged by whiteness.

But this, perhaps, has been the greatest gift of the river: the knowledge that if I want to be a part of this place, then I must commit to untying the violent legacy of the past from the present and future. That when I think and act on matters of care, the community I address includes all things—all people, regardless of race or nationality; all organisms, regardless of species or strain; and all facets of land, regardless of humanity's perception of animation or sentience. And that each thing—white-water rivers running glossy with pollution, descendants of enslaved Africans, Indigenous peoples dispossessed of their lands, and Native lands dispossessed of their caretakers—demands repair in order for all citizens to live rooted in commonality and in care for their chosen homes, whether that is here on the Potomac or far away, on some other river.

Of course it has never been as simple as declaring an intention to care for others and being rewarded with the easy embrace of love. Even with the moral abstractions of "community" and "repair" in mind, I cannot forget that the Potomac is very much the Nation's River, the waterway that reflects our country's history of white violence, colonial rule, and capital-ism. I cannot forget, either, how easy it has been for me at times to accept facile binaries and to retreat into the lonely estrange-ments of whiteness.

bell hooks described "a culture of belonging" as a practice of place where the past "is a resource that can serve as a foun-dation for us to revision and renew our commitment to the present, to making a world where all people can live fully and well." If Americans broadly, and Washingtonians specifically, are ever to seek a culture of belonging within their places, then it is critical that any examination of the nation's past be guided by constructive reparations—a movement to build a flourishing society by acknowledging and restituting past acts of violence and discrimination. In pursuit of constructive reparations, the past is no longer a fetter, holding us in the same position of racial division and civic enmity. Instead, it is a new root from which we might grow a society guided by the ethics and values of the places where we live, not the nation we are bound to.

From my pocket, I produced the raccoon skull and jawbone, and the one tiny tooth. Studying the lines and arcs of the man-dala, I placed the bones along the edges of the design so that it continued to stretch out into the space around it. I moved the skull around, searching for the right angle or corner, but wher-ever I laid it, it seemed to foreclose the sense of outward move-ment that emanated from the mandala's center, connecting it to the place around it. Eventually, I positioned the skull just off to the side, a slight imperfection that I nevertheless thought right.

In retrospect, this interruption in the circle was the most accurate addition I could have made. For a design that rep-resents total unity with a place, a break in that connection sym-bolized every time that I have erred or I have simply been who I am. For all the days and hours in which I have felt myself to be working in right reciprocity, living up to the civic and social responsibilities of belonging to a community, here arrives the gospel truth: There will never be a sense of permanent belonging for me here. This place is not mine and it never will be. It is, instead, ours, those of us who live in this city and care for it, and to share in that—that is the miracle.

※

By MIDAFTERNOON, THE SUN TOUCHED the crowns of the trees on the ridge behind me. The day had only just begun, and here it was, already dying. Slants of light sifted down to the surface of the river, where they weakened and dissolved. As the sun dropped farther into the forest, it became chilly, and the landscape began to turn bleak. Time to turn around and head home.

Walking with the current, I imagined myself as a partner to the river, the two of us just out for an afternoon stroll, and I felt a curious ease with the fact of our difference. I followed a mallard pair downstream for a while, then past Turkey Run I stalked a fox before losing the tracks in the chaos of a fern glade. Quite dim now, it began to snow again, or maybe the wind was blowing hardened crystals off the trees. The snowflakes were delicate, and when they caught a rare streak of sunlight, they were diamonds in the air. Here was the copse that flushed with morels that one spring, the curve in the trail thick with blue cohosh, the sycamore that fell seven years ago, so decayed that its whiteness had vanished.

At the mouth of Wood Duck Run there is a sandy beach, where I stood for a time in cold shadow, looking out over the Potomac. Without turning around, I could tell the sun had not yet dropped behind the ridge. Across the water, mansions were lined up on top of the District palisades, their glass fronts pointed south to the sunset. Hundreds of panes blazed on the hills, orange squares caught in the last light. For a minute or two, I stared at these windows, watching them flicker and glow, and then, in an instant, go dark. The sun had set. The longest night of the year had begun.

From here, I might have hurried home, rushed to reach the car before nightfall and beat the evening traffic. I was meeting friends for dinner and still had to clean myself up before getting over to Mount Pleasant. But I lingered. It is always hard to say good-bye to the river, even if I know I will see it again tomorrow. In the morning, I may find that it has swollen or shriveled, or else turned green or red or blue from ice or earth or sun. It may yet freeze over or disappear in drought. The uncertainty is what haunts me; the mystery is what thrills.

The lights could go out on this city in a second. Precarity and division define this place as surely as coalition and care. "Where it is and what it is, and what it promises to be, let it stand, now and forever," Frederick Douglass concluded his "Lecture on Our Nation's Capital." Our time is not so dissimilar from Douglass's, and I long to see this city become what it promises to be: not a place that "belongs alike to all," as Douglass described it, but a place to which all belong. The future is faint, an inscrutable twilight we might mistake for daybreak, or else the other way around. I cannot know what the future holds for this city, whether it will stand now and forever, or collapse under the weight of the past.

A chickadee whistled its fee-bee song, and another sang back its own name. I saw them on a maple branch above my head and observed them, tiny and brave, fly off together along the bank. I watched a heron glide southeast over the Potomac in the direction of the city. It floated inches above the water, then pulled off into the sky, where the outline of the Washington Monument and the Rosslyn skyline were just visible. It is a sight I have seen a hundred times, and I hope to see it a hundred times more. Sometimes I think it all might have come to me in another city or on another river, but I can never know because this is my place.

Acknowledgments

MY FIRST DEBT is to the land and its inhabitants. I wrote this book while living on settler-occupied land belonging to the Piscataway, Nacotchtank, Massowomeck, Catawba, and Cherokee peoples. Late in the process of drafting this book, I dug an arrowhead point from my garden. Wait—whose garden? That sliver of rock was a reminder that the mention of debt or the statement of gratitude is a cruel insufficiency; a portion of this book's proceeds will be donated to the Piscataway Land Trust.

To early editors and readers, thank you. To Patrick Madden and Joey Franklin at *Fourth Genre* and Debra Marquart at *Flyway,* where versions of these chapters have found a home, thank you for giving space on your pages to my words. To Caitlin Taylor Rae, former editor of the *Southern Humanities Review,* thank you for publishing an essay of mine from a time when I was learning to break from academic writing and find my feet with new verbs; publication of that essay was a seed I did not know I had planted.

Thanks beyond measure to Laura Hart, a champion among editors and friends; your care and patience with this book have inspired me at every turn down this long road. It is largely a testament to your good questions and attentive resolve that this book became a book, and did not instead become a confused jumble of unfinished essays in Google Docs. You have my endless gratitude for tending with me the plant that sprouted from the seed of that *SHR* essay way back when. Thank you to Erika Goldman at Bellevue Literary Press for giving my book a place to call home, and promoting books that live at the intersections and edges of science and art. Thank you to Joe Gannon for his expertise with book production, and Molly Mikolowski for her excellent work with marketing, publicity, and sales. Thank you to Carol Edwards for copyediting, and Amelie Littell for proofreading. And a final Bellevue thanks to Tree Abraham, who designed a book cover that mirrors the Potomac's mercurial nature.

To friends and colleagues from the Bread Loaf Environmental Conference: Your words lifted and guided me. Thanks to Elizabeth Rush for conversations around the workshop table and out in the fields carved open by glaciers. Special gratitude is also due to Natalie Levin, Kimberly Coburn, and Nicole Stockburger, who read early versions of the manuscript and offered their careful critiques.

To dear, old friends: Samantha Luu, Jasmine Jackson-Irwin, Meredith Hamrick, Jaycie Vos, Gayatri Surendranathan, Grace Tatter, Rebecca Murray, Marisa Sedlak, and many others, thank you for always asking questions, for believing I could write another book. Thank you to my Chapel Hill community, particularly to all with whom I have shared a drink and a laugh on the front porch of the Love House at the Center for the Study of the American South. To my fellow canoers, swimmers, hikers, arborists, foragers, herbalists, and rock skippers of the town of Glen Echo, the Sycamore Island Canoe Club, and this little slip of the Potomac between the falls: It's the pleasure of a lifetime. To my students: You make me laugh more than I deserve for all the homework I assign you; I love writing, learning, and running with you.

To Emily Myers: You introduced me to the Potomac in 2017 in a way I had never met it before. Your facilitation of my reintroduction to the river may not have been purposeful, but your introduction to your grandmother (and my future neighbor) was. I would never have written this book, never had my heart open to this river had we not met. What an absurdity to thank landlords, but I have had such generous ones. Thank you to Marie Ridder, paragon of an old world of Washington, who has watched the Potomac flow by her home for nearly seventy-five years and taught me a thing or two about it. Marie gave this book its name, the least interesting thing she will be remembered for. Thank you to Galina Sergen and Reza Aghamiri for sharing your home in Park View, and teaching me about a neighborhood I came to love; I learned so much from you about what it means to really know D.C.

To my family, your curiosity and kindnesses are your greatest gifts. My parents and siblings are an invisible presence on every page; I could not have written a book about my love for D.C. had I not learned what love for our shared home in North Carolina could look like first. My most heartfelt thanks to my sister, Elizabeth, who drew the beautiful frontispiece map for this book and, in this way, became a visible presence in its pages. Eli, darling—your love allows me to be the mole in the ground I want to be; you are my lizard in the spring, my chickadee in the tree. Annie Dog—your companionship brings me such ease, I can hardly speak, and your presence assures me I need not to.

To the plants who know this river better than I could ever try to tell it: Thank you. Thank you, bluebells. Thank you, sochan. Thank you, ironweed and pawpaws, sycamores and jewelweed. Thank you, little yellow passionflower. Thank you, hemlocks on the hills. Thank you, water willows in the rills. Above (and still, too, below) all, my greatest thanks are due to all those who love the Potomac River and have fought for its right to be only what it is: a river.

Notes

Preface

12   **Because this book is concerned:** As a settler, my aim in including Indigenous histories and practices within this book is not to lay claim to a field of knowledge that is not my own. Communally conferred knowledge and customs of Indigenous peoples offer strong opposition to the deadliest forms of power in practice in our world, lessons critical to all of us. I include stories of Indigenous peoples and places in this book because not to include them would be an act of complicity with the erasure of the continued presence of Native Americans in Washington, D.C., and along the Potomac River.

13   **"You may know much":** Frederick Douglass, "A Lecture on Our National Capital" (Washington, D.C.: Smithsonian Institution Press, 1978), 38.

Sycamores

18   **The tree we call an American sycamore:** Jack Wennerstrom, *Leaning Sycamores: Natural Worlds of the Upper Potomac* (Baltimore: Johns Hopkins University Press, 1996), 40–41.

18   **"No one was white":** James Baldwin, "On Being 'White'. . . and Other Lies," *Essence,* April 1984, 90–92.

18   **Thomas Jefferson confirmed:** Thomas Jefferson, *Notes on the State of Virginia* (London: Printed for John Stockdale, 1787), 60.

18   **The sycamore was so prized:** Wennerstrom, 40–41.

19   **There was a sycamore tree:** Stuart Banner, "The Origin of the New York Stock Exchange, 1791–1860," *The Journal of Legal Studies* 27, no. 1 (1998): 113–40.

19   **The Burnside Sycamore:** Mike Yessis, "These Five 'Witness Trees' Were Present at Key Moments in American History," *Smithsonian Magazine,* August 25, 2017, https://www.smithsonianmag.com/travel/these-five-witness-trees-were-present-at-key-moments-in-americas-history-180963925/.

19   **"white tramp":** "Both Men Lynched at Emporia," *Richmond Dispatch,* March 25, 1900.

19   **In its limbs, the white elite:** "Baltimore Dedicates Historical Marker Remembering Lynching of Howard Cooper," Equal Justice Initiative, May 26, 2021, https://eji.org/news/baltimore-dedicates-historical-marker-remembering-lynching-of-howard-cooper/.

20   **a mob of two hundred:** "Lynch Law Again," *Richmond Dispatch,* February 19, 1880.

20   **"I feel most colored":** Zora Neale Hurston, "How It Feels to Be Colored Me," *World Tomorrow* 12, no. 5 (1928), 2.

20   **"exercise . . . authority over all places":** James Madison, "The Same Subject Continued: The Powers Conferred by the Constitution Further Considered," *The Federalist,* no. 43, January 23, 1788.

21   **"always the continent of Democracy":** Walt Whitman, "Our Old Feuillage," in *Leaves of Grass,* 1892, "Death-Bed" Edition (Philadelphia: David McKay, 1891), 138.

22   **Given the small number of citizens:** Throughout this book, I do not describe people living in Washington, D.C., as American citizens, but simply as District residents or inhabitants. Until the people of Washington, D.C. have representation in Congress on par with Americans in other states, they are not citizens, but subjects of the federal government.

22   **If you speak of the place:** Brandi Thompson Summers, *The Spatial Aesthetics of Race in a Post-Chocolate City* (Chapel Hill: University of North Carolina Press, 2019), xiii.

23   **"Since the city's inception":** Chris Myers Asch and George Derek Musgrove, *Chocolate City: A History of Race and Democracy in the Nation's Capital* (Chapel Hill: University of North Carolina Press, 2017), 3.

23   **"men breathe freer here":** Frederick Douglass, "A Lecture on Our National Capital" (Washington, D.C.: Smithsonian Institution Press, 1978), 38.

24   **By the time of the March on Washington:** Asch and Musgrove, 2.

24   **Five years later:** Ibid., 355–72.

24   **"implies a kind of natural expression":** Ta-Nehisi Coates, "The Case for Reparations," *The Atlantic,* June 2014, https://www. theatlantic.com/magazine/archive/2014/06/the-case-for-reparations/361631/.

25   **"murder capital":** Asch and Musgrove, 406.

26   **The Latino and Asian populations:** Alex Baca and Nick Finio, "Gentrification in D.C. Isn't Just a Black and White Issue," Greater Greater Washington, May 25, 2020, https://ncrc.org/greater-greater-washington-gentrification-in-dc-is-not-just-a-black-and-white-issue/.

26   **In 2021, after several noncommittal decades:** Megan Flynn, "House Democrats Pass D.C. Statehood, Launching Bill into Uncharted Territory," *Washington Post,* April 22, 2021.

28   **"The poor man should feel rich":** Frederick Douglass, "A Lecture on Our National Capital," 11.

31   **I did not know that the bridge:** Philip Kennicott, "Capital Crossings," *Washington Post,* April 1, 2021.

34   **To borrow from Henry David Thoreau:** Henry David Thoreau, "Slavery in Massachusetts," in *Essays* (New Haven: Yale University, 2003), 172.

34 **"peculiar sensation, this double-consciousness":** W. E. B. Du Bois, *The Souls of Black Folks: Essays and Sketches* (New York: Gramercy Books, 1994), 2.

34 **Dr. Anna Julia Cooper, a longtime resident of D.C:** Anna Julia Cooper, *A Voice from the South* (Xenia, Ohio: Aldine Printing House, 1892), 134.

36 **and so, lost in the city:** I echo here Edward P. Jones, *the* Bard of Washington, D.C., as far as I am concerned. *Lost in the City,* his 1992 short story collection, has been a constant touchstone as I have tried to find my own way in this city.

36 **In 1954, the only creatures:** Interstate Commission on the Potomac River Basin, "A Deep Dive into Potomac History," accessed December 1, 2020, https://storymaps.arcgis.com/stories/58a788ead106439db4d51b0e042f4a39.

38 **"The life of a nation":** Frederick Douglass, *Address by Hon. Frederick Douglass, delivered in the Congregational Church, Washington, D.C., on the twenty-first anniversary of emancipation in the District of Columbia* (Washington, D.C.: s.n., 1883), https://www.loc.gov/item/90898291/.

39 **"a place where people trade":** Eugene Scheel, "Indians Left Their Mark in Naming Landmarks," *Washington Post,* April 8, 2004.

Bald Eagles

41 **"supreme power and authority":** Jimmy Stamp, "Who Designed the Seal of the President of the United States?" *Smithsonian Magazine,* January 23, 2013, https://www.smithsonianmag.com/arts-culture/who-designed-the-seal-of-the-president-of-the-united-states-5162560/.

42 **"There was a strange stillness":** Rachel Carson, *Silent Spring* (New York: Houghton Mifflin, 1962), 2.

42 **Though the implications:** Krista Schlyer, *River of Redemption: Almanac of Life on the Anacostia* (College Station: Texas A&M University, 2018), 106–8.

43   **This number was compared:** Ibid., 111–12.

43   **"may well make it necessary":** Carson, 119.

43   **In 1967, bald eagles:** Schlyer, 114.

44   **In 1977, there were:** Tamara Dietrich, "Bald Eagles Have Come Back from the Dead in the Chesapeake Bay," *Baltimore Sun,* July 13, 2019.

47   **This was the case in 2016:** Jedediah Britton-Purdy, *This Land Is Our Land: The Struggle for a New Commonwealth* (Princeton, New Jersey: Princeton University, 2018), 6.

49   **"the set of assumptions":** Cheryl I. Harris, "Whiteness as Property," *Harvard Law Review* 106, no. 8 (1993): 1707.

49   **Today, it is a national landmark:** Schlyer, 113.

50   **"There was once a town":** Carson, 3.

50   **"this town does not actually exist":** Ibid.

50   **The letter that first:** Christopher C. Sellars, *Crabgrass Crucible: Suburban Nature and the Rise of Environmentalism in the Twentieth Century* (Chapel Hill: University of North Carolina Press, 2012), 256–57.

50   **"suburbanite who derives":** Carson, 86.

51   **"They love it because":** Judith Voirst, "Q. Is There a Silver Spring and If so, Why?," *Washingtonian,* July 1967, 68.

51   **"get away from certain neighbors":** Ibid.

52   **Black workers used buses:** David S. Rotenstein, "Silver Spring, Maryland Has Whitewashed Its Past," History News Network (blog), October 15, 2016, https://historynewsnetwork.org/article/163914.

52   **"the natural heart":** Advertisement, Silver Spring Chamber of Commerce, *Washington Evening Star,* September 10, 1927.

52   **When her domestic duties:** Lida Maxwell, "Queer/Love/Bird Extinction: Rachel Carson's Silent Spring as a Work of Love," *Political Theory* 45, no. 5 (2017): 682–704.

52 **Park spaces were understood:** Jess Row, *White Flights: Race, Fiction, and the American Imagination* (Minneapolis: Graywolf, 2019), 115.

53 **"all the special things":** Frank Graham, Jr., *Since Silent Spring* (Boston: Houghton Mifflin, 1970), 12.

55 **I was surprised to learn:** This statistic is calculated by measuring for four characteristics of an effective park system: the number of residents who live within ten minutes' walking distance of a public park, the size of an average park's acreage, the diversity and number of amenities (e.g., basketball hoops and marked trails), and the per capita investment.

57 **"the wrong side of the park":** Eliza Cava, "Francis Newlands, Racial Segregation, and the Land of Woodend," Nature Forward Conservation (blog), September 15, 2020, https://conservationblog.anshome.org/blog/francis-newlands-racial-segregation-and-the-land-of-woodend/.

57 **"perpetually dedicated and set apart":** Code of the District of Columbia § 10–140, Rock Creek Park—Establishment, September 27, 1890, 26 Stat. 492, ch. 1001, § 1.

Ephemerals

64 **The rock cliffs immediately:** Callan Bentley and Ken Rasmussen, "Travels in Geology: Touring the Capital Geology of Washington, D.C.," *Earth Magazine,* November 9, 2018, https://www.earthmagazine.org/article/travels-geology-touring-capital-geology-washington-dc.

65 **With species converging:** Stanwyn G. Shelter and Sylvia Stone Orli, "Annotated Checklist of the Vascular Plants of the Washington-Baltimore Area. Part I. Ferns, Fern Allies, Gymnosperms and Dicotyledons," Department of Botany, National Museum of Natural History, Smithsonian Institute, 2000.

65   **Across the three square miles:** Jeffrey P. Cohn, "The Wildest Urban River: Potomac River Gorge," *BioScience* 54, no. 1 (January 2004): 8–14.

68   **Tasked with surveying:** Joel Achenbach, *The Grand Idea: George Washington's Potomac and the Race to the West* (New York: Simon & Schuster, 2004), 26.

68   **Throughout the remainder:** Robert P. Watson, *George Washington's Final Battle: The Epic Struggle to Build a Capital City and a Nation* (Washington, D.C.: Georgetown University Press, 2021), 24–26.

69   **"Potomac River then":** Mark A. Mastromarino, ed.,*The Papers of George Washington*, Presidential Series, vol. 9, September 1791– February 1792 (Charlottesville: University Press of Virginia, 2000), 255.

69   **Washington envisioned the Potomac:** Achenbach, 37–39.

69   **Blinded by riparian monomania:** Ibid., 29–31.

70   **"bind those people to us":** W. W. Abbot, ed., *The Papers of George Washington,* Confederation Series, vol. 2, July 1784–May 1785 (Charlottesville: University Press of Virginia, 1992), 122.

70   **As the first step:** Frederick Gutheim, *The Potomac* (Baltimore: Johns Hopkins University Press, 1949), 8–10.

71   **"there is such an intimate":** Robert F. Haggard and Mark A. Mastromarino, eds., *The Papers of George Washington*, Presidential Series, vol. 10, March 1792–August 1792 (Charlottesville: University Press of Virginia, 2002), 229–30.

71   **In the last years of his life:** Watson, 24.

72   **"the mere whim of the President":** Ibid., xvii.

72   **"the very dirtiest Hole":** Stewart Mitchell, ed., *New Letters of Abigail Adams 1788–1801* (Boston: Houghton Mifflin, 1947), 257.

73 **"sandwiched between two":** Frederick Douglass, "A Lecture on Our National Capital" (Washington, D.C.: Smithsonian Institution Press, 1978), 22.

74 **By 1800, the year President John Adams:** Chris Myers Asch and George Derek Musgrove, *Chocolate City: A History of Race and Democracy in the Nation's Capital* (Chapel Hill: University of North Carolina Press, 2017), 47–49.

74 **"negro-raising states":** Alfred L. Brophy, "Considering William and Mary's History with Slavery: The Case of President Thomas Roderick Dew," *William & Mary Bill of Rights Journal* 16, no. 4 (2008): 1091–1139.

74 **"the best place in town":** Jesse Holland, *Black Men Built the Capitol: Discovering African-American History in and Around Washington, D.C.* (Guilford, Connecticut: Globe Pequot, 2007), 26.

75 **The residents of Alexandria:** Asch and Musgrove, 86–93.

77 **"army of liberation":** W. E. B. Du Bois, *John Brown* (Philadelphia: George W. Jacobs Company, 1908), 289.

77 **Brown's raid was short:** Frederick Douglass, and Daniel Murray Pamphlet Collection, *John Brown: An address* (Dover, New Hampshire: Morning Star Job Printing House, 1881), https://www.loc.gov/item/07012896/.

78 **At the meeting of the Shenandoah:** Du Bois, 275.

Ramps

81 **Within this intimate woodland community:** Robert N. Muller, "The Phenology, Growth and Ecosystem Dynamics of *Erythronium americanum* in the Northern Hardwood Forest," *Ecological Monographs* 48, no. 1 (Winter 1978): 1–20.

82 **When people forage for ramps:** Amy B. Trubek, *The Taste of Place: A Cultural Journey into Terroir* (Berkeley: University of California Press, 2008), 1.

83   **"weeds have become a delicacy":** Gina Rae La Cerva, *Feasting Wild: In Search of the Last Untamed Food* (Vancouver: Greystone Books, 2020), 30.

87   **"To name the world as gift":** Robin Wall Kimmerer, "The Serviceberry: An Economy of Abundance," *Emergence Magazine,* October 26, 2022, https://emergencemagazine.org/essay/the-serviceberry/.

88   **Shaw was ground zero:** Christina Sturdivant Sani, "An Oral History of Gentrification in Shaw and U Street NW," *Washington City Paper,* August 29, 2019, https://washingtoncitypaper.com/article/1820/an-oral-history-of-gentrification-in-shaw-and-u-street-nw/.

89   **A century ago, Bladgen:** David Weible, "The Hidden History Inside D.C.'s Blagden Alley," The National Trust for Historic Preservation (blog), June 20, 2016, https://savingplaces.org/stories/the-hidden-history-inside-washington-dc-blagden-alley#.YHIeexRKhpQ.

89   **"the most despicable in the country":** Terri Sapienza, "Bohemian Carriage House," *Garden & Gun,* February/March 2013, https://gardenandgun.com/articles/homeplace-bohemian-carriage-house/.

91   **Gentrifiers' search for diverse, placeful living:** Brandi Thompson Summers, *Black in Place: The Spatial Aesthetics of Race in a Post-Chocolate City* (Chapel Hill: University of North Carolina Press, 2019), 8–15.

91   **She describes how white newcomers:** Ibid., 86–110.

92   **Though the consumerist and even emotional demands:** Ibid., 8–15.

92   **It is one of many painful paradoxes:** Sabihya Prince, *African-Americans and Gentrification in Washington, D.C.: Race, Class and Social Justice in the Nation's Capital* (New York: Taylor & Francis, 2016), 10.

93 **"the bounty yielded up":** Edna Lewis, *The Taste of Country Cooking* (New York: Knopf, 1976), xx.

94 **"'GGJ,' a good government job":** Martin Austermuhle, "When Blacks Fled the South, D.C. Became Home for Many from North Carolina," DCist, September 23, 2016, https://wamu. org/story/16/09/23/when_blacks_fled_the_south_dc_became_ home_for_many_from_north_carolina/.

94 **Segregation in rural areas was not:** Chris Myers Asch and George Derek Musgrove, *Chocolate City: A History of Race and Democracy in the Nation's Capital* (Chapel Hill: University of North Carolina Press, 2017), 246.

95 **"surrounded by people who were from":** Isabel Wilkerson quoted in Austermuhle, "When Blacks Fled the South, D.C. Became Home for Many from North Carolina."

96 **"sleep over a volcano":** Isabel Wilkerson, *The Warmth of Other Suns* (New York: Vintage Books, 2010), 124.

Anacostia

100 **From their village at the confluence:** Krista Schlyer, *River of Redemption: Almanac of Life on the Anacostia* (College Station: Texas A&M University, 2018), 165–72.

100 **"goodly River called Patomack":** Paul Metcalf, *Waters of Potowmack* (Charlottesville: University Press of Virginia, 2002), 9.

101 **By 1670, colonizers and their pathogens:** Schlyer, 165–72.

101 **Within the Piscataway Indian Nation:** Neely Tucker, "Anacostia River: From Then Till Now," *Washington Post,* September 29, 2011.

102 **In 1619, the year that the first twenty Africans:** Schlyer, 32.

102 **Tobacco agriculture extended up and down:** John R. Wennersten, *Anacostia: The Death & Life of an American River* (Baltimore: Chesapeake Book Company, 2008), 19–21.

103 **By 1762, newspapers reported:** Schlyer, 33–34.

104 **"not worthy of improvement:** Wennersten, 212.

104 **"destroyed some 2,600 acres":** Ibid.

104 **Disease clouded the riverbanks:** Ibid., 123–29.

105 **Washington expanded dramatically:** Schlyer, 39–41.

105 **By the beginning of World War II:** Ibid.

106 **In December 1966, twenty-five members:** Ibid.

106 **For the children of Kenilworth:** Ibid., 43–44.

107 **"a model of beauty here in the capital":** LBJ quoted in Jacob Fenston, "From Sewage Dump to Beach: Washington's Rivers May Be Safe to Swim Within 5 Years," DCist, July 23, 2019, https://wamu.org/story/19/07/23/from-sewage-dump-to-beach-washingtons-rivers-may-be-safe-to-swim-within-5-years/.

108 **Marion Barry, D.C.'s magnetic mayor:** Wennersten, 178–79.

109 **"toxic soup":** Ibid., 189.

109 **Fecal coliform counts in the Anacostia rose:** Ibid., 193–95.

109 **"Georgetown on the Potomac boomed":** George Gurley quoted in ibid., 181–82.

111 **Centuries ago, in the Anacostia's former sandbanks:** Schlyer, 183–90.

112 **the Anacostia Watershed Society (AWS):** Ibid., 203.

112 **Each year, AWS measures the river's health:** Fenit Nirappil, "Can Tens of Thousands of Mussels Help Save the Polluted Anacostia River?" *Washington Post,* October 23, 2019.

113 **"Stop calling me resilient":** Tracie L. Washington quoted in Malini Ranganathan and Eve Bratman, "From Urban Resilience to Abolitionist Climate Justice in Washington, D.C.," *Antipode* 53, no. 1 (June 2019): 115–37.

114   **These development projects levy critical questions:** Isabelle
Anguelovski, "Is Gentrification in Washington DC's Anacostia
Whitewashing Black Culture?" Barcelona Laboratory for
Urban Environmental Justice and Sustainability (blog),
September 2, 2019, http://www.bcnuej.org/2019/09/02/is-
gentrification-in-washington-dcs-anacostia-whitewashing-
black-culture.

115   **"Environmental Justice protects the right":** Principles of
Environmental Justice, People of Color Environmental
Leadership Summit, October 24–27, 1991, https://www.ejnet.
org/ej/principles.html.

115   **"reconstructing the internal life":** Robin D. G. Kelley, *Freedom
Dreams: The Black Radical Imagination* (New York: Beacon Press,
2003), 114–15.

Honeysuckle

118   **A relative newcomer to this continent:** Japanese Honeysuckle,
Invasive Plant Species Assessment Working Group, Purdue
University, last modified October 2006, https://www.entm.
purdue.edu/iisc/pdf/plants/more/japanese_honeysuckle.pdf.

119   **But by the 1980s, honeysuckle:** Japanese Honeysuckle, North
Carolina Extension Gardener Plant Toolbox, accessed
December 1, 2021, https://plants.ces.ncsu.edu/plants/lonicera-
japonica/.

119   **"alien species whose introduction":** Executive Order 13112,
Section 1: Definitions, February 3, 1999.

119   **In Illinois, Indiana, Connecticut, and New Hampshire:** Japanese
Honeysuckle, Invasive Plant Species Assessment Working
Group, Purdue University.

119   **"unemployment, damaged goods and equipment, power
failures":** National Invasive Species Council 2001, *Meeting the
Invasive Species Challenge: National Invasive Species Management
Plan,* 2.

121   **At the conclusion of the Revolutionary War:** Joel Achenbach, *The Grand Idea: George Washington's Potomac and the Race to the West* (New York: Simon & Schuster, 2004), 5.

121   **"No estate in America is more pleasantly situated than this.":** Mark A. Mastromarino, ed., *The Papers of George Washington,* Presidential Series, vol. 9, September 1791–February 1792, (Charlottesville: University Press of Virginia, 2000), 253–58.

121   **"The Maryland shore, on the opposite side":** Isaac Weld, *Travels Through the States of North America, and the Provinces of Upper and Lower Canada, During the Years 1795, 1796, and 1797* (London: Printed for John Stockdale, 1807), 92.

121   **"perhaps the most beautiful view in the world":** Julian U. Niemcewicz, *Under Their Vine and Fig Tree: Travels Through America in 1797–1799, 1805, with Some Further Account of Life in New Jersey,* trans. Metchie Budka (Elizabeth, New Jersey: Grassman Publishing, 1965), 99.

121   **When commercial development threatened the land:** Janet A. McDonnell, "Preservation and Partners: A History of Piscataway Park," Resource Stewardship and Science, National Capital Area, National Park Service and Organization of American Historians, December 2020, http://npshistory.com/ publications/pisc/adhi.pdf.

123   **The Potomac was the center of their lives:** Gabrielle Tayac, "Keeping the Original Instructions," in *Native Universe: Voices of Indian America,* eds. Gerald McMaster and Clifford E. Trafzer (Washington, D.C.: National Geographic Society, 2008), 77.

123   **The seasonal demand to follow game:** James H. Merrell, "Cultural Continuity Among the Piscataway Indians of Colonial Maryland," *William and Mary Quarterly* 36, no. 4 (October 1979): 548–70.

123   **But because the Piscataway farmed crops:** Gabrielle Tayac, "Spirits in the River: A Report on the Piscataway People," Smithsonian Institution, National Museum of the American Indian, Washington, D.C., June 1999.

123 **Buried beside the cedar:** Rebecca Sheir, "Rediscovering the Piscataway Hub of Moyaone," DCist, December 16, 2011, https://wamu.org/story/11/12/16/rediscovering_a_sacred_site_on_the_potomac_the_piscataway_hub_of_moyaone_0/.

124 **"negro mongrels":** J. Douglas Smith, "The Campaign for Racial Purity and the Erosion of Paternalism in Virginia, 1922–1930: 'Nominally White, Biologically Mixed, and Legally Negro,'" *Journal of Southern History* 68, no. 1 (2002): 65–106.

124 **"performed ceremonial dances at the site":** McDonnell, "Preservation and Partners: A History of Piscataway Park."

124 **As part of the expanding American Indian Movement:** Tayac, "Spirits in the River."

124 **A critical part of dispelling this myth:** Ibid.

125 **Through the early 1960s, as various white interest groups:** McDonnell, "Preservation and Partners: A History of Piscataway Park."

125 **Today, his grave is a pilgrimage site:** Sheir, "Rediscovering the Piscataway Hub of Moyaone."

126 The **daylily, for example, was introduced to this continent:** Common Daylily, Invasive.org, November 11, 2010, https://www.invasive.org/alien/pubs/midatlantic/hefu.htm.

127 **Similarly, wineberries were introduced to North America:** Wineberries, Invasive.org, November 11, 2010, https://www.invasive.org/alien/pubs/midatlantic/ruph.htm.

127 **The three invasive plants I had harvested:** Harold Mooney, "Invasion Dynamics: From Invasion Biology to Invasion Science," *BioScience* 67, no. 9 (2017): 860–61.

128 **The answer lies in post–World War II England:** Ellie Irons, "Re-Patterning with Kudzu: Reckoning in Search of Regeneration," *Anthropocene Curriculum,* February 15, 2021, https://www.anthropocene-curriculum.org/contribution/repatterning-with-kudzu-reckoning-in-search-of-regeneration.

128 **"illegal aliens":** Alien Species Prevention and Enforcement Act of 1992, Public Law 102–393, 102 Cong. (October 6, 1992).

128 *invasive species* **left the academy:** National Invasive Species Act of 1996, Public Law 104-332, 104 Cong. (26 October 1996).

128 **In 1992, Bill Clinton signed the Alien Species Prevention and Enforcement Act:** Illegal Immigration Reform and Immigrant Responsibility Act of 1996, Public Law 104-208, 104th Cong. 1st sess. (September 30, 1996).

128 **During the same period, Clinton signed:** Emma Lansdowne, "Crisis of Invasion: Militaristic Language and the Legitimization of Identity and Place," *Invisible Culture,* issue 28 (March 2018), https://ivc.lib.rochester.edu/crisis-of-invasion-militaristic-language-and-the-legitimization-of-identity-and-place.

129 **In order for European settlers to make a moral claim:** Eve Tuck and K. Wayne Yang, "Decolonization Is Not a Metaphor," *Decolonization: Indigeneity, Education & Society* 1, no. 1 (2012), 7.

131 **The modern Land Back movement:** The Land Back Manifesto, NDN Collective, accessed December 1, 2021, https://ndncollective.org/.

Swimming

137 **"Photographs can abet desire":** Susan Sontag, *On Photography* (New York: Picador, 1977), 16.

137 **"All photographs are memento mori":** Ibid., 15.

139 **There are hundreds of these images:** See: Harris & Ewing Collection, Library of Congress, 1905–1945; National Photo Company Collection, Library of Congress, 1850–1945.

140 **"one of the most trying climates in the United States":** "Report of Pollution of Tidal Basin," *Washington Evening Star,* December 11, 1915.

140 **The city's public health service:** Perry Gerard Fisher et al., *Historic Structures Report: Tidal Basin Inlet Bridge, Washington, D.C.* (Washington, D.C.: KressCox Associates, 1986), 32.

140 **In view of the Bureau of Engraving and Printing:** "Tidal Basin Beach Officially Opens," Histories of the National Mall, accessed December 10, 2023, https://mallhistory.org/items/show/211.

141 **In July 1919, the line to access:** "2,000 Stand for Hours in Line for Chance to Bathe in Tidal Basin," *Washington Post,* July 7, 1919.

141 **On one particularly scorching day in July:** "20,000 at Tidal Basin: Attendance Records Shattered at Improved Bathing Beach," *Washington Post*, June 14, 1920.

141 **After dancing for hours in the Park's pavilion:** Madelyn Rosenberg, "Summer Pastimes," *Arlington Magazine,* August 5, 2013, https://www.arlingtonmagazine.com/summer-pastimes/.

142 **Eventually, its amusements included over a dozen attractions:** Richard A. Cook, "A History of Glen Echo Park," Glen Echo-Cabin John History, 1997, https://glenecho-cabinjohn.com/GE-04.html.

142 **Built in 1931 at a cost of:** Ibid.

143 **"every available island":** "Thus The Birch Canoe Was Builded—," *Washington Evening Star,* April 26, 1908.

143 **"The Thousand and One Sources of Pleasure for the Camper":** "Summer Camps Along Virginia Shore of the Potomac," *Washington Evening Star,* August 8, 1915.

144 **"a photograph is both a pseudo-presence and a token of absence":** Sontag, 12.

146 **When the Tidal Basin Bathing Beach closed:** Jenna Goff, "Cooling Off in the Tidal Basin," Boundary Stones (blog), WETA, July 21, 2015, https://boundarystones.weta.org/2015/07/21/cooling-tidal-basin.

147 **White anxieties about integrated swimming:** Jeff Wiltse, *Contested Waters: A Social History of Swimming Pools* (Chapel Hill: University of North Carolina Press, 2007), 133.

147 **The threat of white mob violence:** Gillian Brockell, "The Deadly Race Riot 'Aided and Abetted' by the Washington Post a Century Ago," *Washington Post,* July 15, 2019.

147 **During the hot summer of 1919:** Betsy Schlabach, "Sex, Swimming, and Chicago's Racial Divide," *Black Perspectives,* October 3, 2017, https://www.aaihs.org/sex-swimming-and-chicagos-racial-divide/.

147 **"race war":** Brockell, "The Deadly Race Riot 'Aided and Abetted' by the Washington Post a Century Ago."

147 **In 1924, the House finally approved:** "Senate Cuts Out Appropriation for Bathing Beaches," *Washington Post,* February 19, 1925.

148 **Newspapers circulated the convenient fiction:** Goff, "Cooling Off in the Tidal Basin."

148 **Across the river, Arlington Beach:** "Fun in the Sun: Summers of Arlington's Past," Arlington Public Library (blog), July 22, 2020, https://library.arlingtonva.us/2020/07/22/fun-in-the-sun-summers-of-arlingtons-past/.

148 **acronym KKK:** "Summer Camps Along Virginia Shore of the Potomac," *Washington Evening Star,* August 8, 1915.

149 **"officials envisioned the distinctly American phenomenon":** Heather McGhee, *The Sum of Us: What Racism Costs Everyone and How We Can Prosper Together* (New York: Random House, 2021), 23.

149 **By the late 1930s, white Washingtonians:** Martha H. Verbrugge and Drew Ingling, "The Politics of Play: The Struggle Over Racial Segregation and Public Recreation in Washington, D.C., 1945–1950," *Washington History* 27, no. 2 (2015): 56–69.

149   **Francis and Banneker immediately became:** Lauren Ober,
      "D.C. Swim League Busting the Myth That Black People Don't
      Swim," DCist, July 24, 2015, https://wamu.org/story/15/07/24/
      dc_swim_league_works_to_get_african_american_kids_into_
      the_water/.

150   **For Black children growing up outside of Northwest:** Verbrugge
      and Ingling, "The Politics of Play," 56–69.

150   **The Watts Branch of the Anacostia:** Jacob Fenston, "From
      Sewage Dump to Beach: Washington's Rivers May Be Safe to
      Swim Within 5 Years," DCist, July 23, 2019, https://wamu.org/
      story/19/07/23/from-sewage-dump-to-beach-washingtons-
      rivers-may-be-safe-to-swim-within-5-years/.

151   **From 1931 to 1951, at least nine Black children drowned:** The
      Memorial Pool, The City of Alexandria, accessed December 10,
      2023, https://www.alexandriava.gov/rpca/basic-page/charles-
      houston-recreation-center-memorial-namings.

151   **The Watkins brothers:** "Body of One Boy Found in Hunting
      Creek After He and Brother Drown," *Washington Evening Star,*
      July 19, 1948.

151   **"neither could swim":** "Funeral Rites Set Thursday for Brothers
      That Drowned," *Washington Evening Star,* July 20, 1948.

151   **Under duress from Black organizers:** "Civil Rights Tour:
      Recreation—Anacostia Pool, Swimming for All," DC Historic
      Preservation Office, DC Historic Sites, accessed December 10,
      2023, https://historicsites.dcpreservation.org/items/show/914.

152   **When Black children arrived on the morning of June 23 to
      swim:** Martha H. Verbugge, "Exercising Civil Rights/Public
      Recreation and Racial Segregation in Washington, DC, 1900–
      1949," in *DC Sports: The Nation's Capital at Play,* eds. Chris Elzey
      and David K. Wiggins (Fayetteville: University of Arkansas
      Press, 2015), 108–9.

152 **After the tragic drowning of the Johnson brothers:** The Memorial Pool, The City of Alexandria, accessed December 10, 2023, https://www.alexandriava.gov/rpca/basic-page/charles-houston-recreation-center-memorial-namings.

152 **1952, a Black teenager seeking relief:** "Playground Segregation Challenged," *Washington Post,* August 19, 1948.

152 **Later in the 1960s, protests called "swim-ins":** Lori Wysong, "Wishing in a Fountain: The Protest for More D.C. Pools," Boundary Stones (blog), WETA, July 1, 2019, https://boundarystones.weta.org/2019/07/01/wishing-fountain-protest-more-dc-pools.

153 **As they fled from the city:** McGhee, 28.

153 **Inspired by that spring's successful sit-ins:** Matt Blitz, "On the 60th Anniversary of the Fight to Desegregate Glen Echo, Activists Look Back—and Ahead," DCist, June 30, 2020, https://dcist.com/story/20/06/30/glen-echo-park-civil-rights-movement-protest-history/.

153 **The Nonviolent Action Group:** Cook, "A History of Glen Echo Park."

155 **"drained-pool politics":** McGhee, 28.

156 **In 2023, D.C. Water finished construction:** Jacob Fenston, "Time to Lift the Ban on Swimming in the Potomac and Anacostia Rivers, Advocates Say," DCist, March 22, 2022, www.npr.org/local/305/2022/03/23/1088192692/time-to-lift-the-ban-on-swimming-in-the-potomac-and-anacostia-rivers-advocates-say.

Pawpaws

162 **"The world has signed a pact with the devil":** Annie Dillard, *Pilgrim at Tinker Creek* (New York: Harper & Row, 1974), 183.

163 **In a recent comprehensive report from the United Nations:** "UN Report: Nature's Dangerous Decline 'Unprecedented'; Species Extinction Rates 'Accelerating,'" Sustainable Development, United Nations, May 6, 2019.

163 **By the year 2100, over one half:** Edward O. Wilson, *The Future of Life* (New York: Vintage Books, 2002), 31.

163 **Even as the exact data surrounding extinction:** Fred Pearce, "Global Extinction Rates: Why Do Estimates Vary So Wildly?" *Yale Environment 360,* August 17, 2015, https://e360.yale.edu/ features/global_extinction_rates_why_do_estimates_vary_so_ wildly.

163 **Endlings—the last individuals of a species:** Camille T. Dungy, "Losing Language," *Emergence Magazine,* June 25, 2019.

163 **"I'm trying to imagine what it would be like":** Robin Wall Kimmerer, *Braiding Sweetgrass: Indigenous Wisdom, Scientific Knowledge, and the Teachings of Plants* (Minneapolis: Milkweed Books, 2013), 208–9.

165 **Prior to colonization, the beaver population:** Jack Wennerstrom, *Leaning Sycamores: Natural Worlds of the Upper Potomac* (Baltimore: Johns Hopkins University Press, 1996), 141.

165 **"I conceived all my hopes and future fortunes" and subsequent Fleet quotes:** Frederick Gutheim, *The Potomac* (Baltimore: Johns Hopkins University Press, 1949), 34–42.

166 **By the time the steel trap had been invented in 1823:** Wennerstrom, 141.

166 **Lonely George, the previously mentioned Hawaiian tree snail:** Julia Jacobs, "George the Snail, Believed to Be the Last of His Species, Dies at 14 in Hawaii," *New York Times,* January 10, 2019; Natasha Geiling, "Lonesome George, the Last Tortoise of His Kind, Is Put on Posthumous Display in NYC," *Smithsonian Magazine*, September 26, 2014, https://www.smithsonianmag. com/travel/lonesome-george-last-tortoise-his-kind- posthumous-display-nyc-180952833/.

167   **Beavers are a keystone species:** Ben Goldfarb, *Eager: The Surprising, Secret Life of Beavers and Why They Matter* (White River Junction, Vermont: Chelsea Green Publishing, 2018), 55.

167   **Beavers once submerged approximately 234,000 square miles:** Ibid., 36.

168   **Prior to colonization, wetlands comprised 220 million acres:** Ibid., 55.

168   **The beaver I had seen from that outcropping:** Wennerstrom, 142.

168   **Indeed, almost all the beavers now living on the East Coast:** Goldfarb, 55.

169   **The profuse flora of the floodplain:** Wennerstrom, 135.

170   **Today, there are an estimated thirty million white-tailed deer:** Tim Heffernan, "The Deer Paradox," *The Atlantic,* November 2012, https://www.theatlantic.com/magazine/archive/2012/11/the-deer-paradox/309104/.

170   **Prior to colonization, the Nacotchtank and Piscataway peoples:** Gutheim, 43.

170   **The abundance of carnivorous predators:** Wennerstrom, 134.

170   **"as for deers, buffaloes, bears, turkeys":** Gutheim, 39.

170   **Colonizers did not recognize the forests:** Roderick Nash, *Wilderness and the American Mind* (New Haven: Yale University Press, 1967), 12.

170   **"the laws have also descended to the preservation":** Thomas Jefferson, *Notes on the State of Virginia* (London: Printed for John Stockdale, 1787), 144.

171   **By 1700, what remained of black bears, wolves, and cougars:** Wennerstrom, 133.

171   **The extinction of a species from a certain ecological community:**
Rodolfo Dirzo, Hillary S. Young, Mauro Galetti, Gerardo
Ceballos, Nick J. B. Isaac, and Ben Collen, "Defaunation in the
Anthropocene," *Science* 345, no. 6195 (2014): 401–6.

171   **Deer numbers, already high from forest cutting and farming:**
Wennerstrom, 134.

171   **By 1890, the U.S. Biological Survey:** White-tailed Deer
Education Curriculum Guide, Maryland Department of
Natural Resources, 2013, https://dnr.maryland.gov/wildlife/
Documents/WT_Deer_curriculum_Guide.pdf.

172   **But in areas where the population exceeds the carrying capacity:**
Wennerstrom, 135.

172   **In Rock Creek Park, for example, from 1990 to 2010:**
"Population Dynamics at Rock Creek Park," Rock Creek Park,
Explore Natural Communities, accessed December 10, 2023,
https://www.explorenaturalcommunities.org/parks-places/
rock-creek-park/stewardship-and-ecological-threats/plants-
and-animals/population-dynamics.

172   **Pawpaw leaves and twigs have a distinctive petroleum-distillate
odor:** Elizabeth Matthews, "Pawpaw: Small Tree, Big Impact,"
National Capital Region Network of the National Park Service
(blog), December 27, 2017, https://www.nps.gov/articles/
pawpaw.htm.

173   **it is doubtful the public would support the release of wolves:**
Sarah A. Hendricks et al., "Natural re-colonization and
admixture of wolves (*Canis lupus*) in the US Pacific Northwest:
challenges for the protection and management of rare and
endangered taxa," *Heredity* 122, no. 2 (2019): 133–49.

173   **Eastern cougars are no longer a potential option:** "Cougars
Officially Declared Extinct in Eastern U.S.," *Yale Environment
360,* January 23, 2018, https://e360.yale.edu/digest/cougars-
officially-declared-extinct-in-eastern-u-s-removed-from-
endangered-species-list.

174   **"One of the penalties of an ecological education":** Aldo Leopold,
      A Sand County Almanac (New York: Oxford University Press,
      1949), 68.

Drought

179   **hyperobjects are things so vastly distributed:** Timothy Morton,
      Hyperobjects: Philosophy and Ecology After the End of the World
      (Minneapolis: University of Minnesota Press, 2013), 1.

180   **"the gap between knowing something":** Eve Kosofsky Sedgwick,
      Touching Feeling: Affect, Pedagogy, Performativity (Durham: Duke
      University Press, 2003), 166.

182   **The Massowomeck and Manahoac peoples built:** Don Peterson,
      *Native American Fish Traps in the Potomac River, Brunswick,
      Maryland* (Brunswick, Maryland: Bellwether Press, 2018).

182   **"all water has a perfect memory":** Toni Morrison, "The Site of
      Memory," in *Inventing the Truth,* ed. William Zinsser (New York:
      Houghton Mifflin, 1995), 99.

182   **By 1936, overfishing had nearly exterminated Potomac fish
      populations:** "Eels Are Nearly Extinct in the Potomac,"
      Potomac Conservancy (blog), November 22, 2019, https://
      potomac.org/blog/2019/11/22/where-did-the-eels-go.

183   **In October 1930, during the very worst drought:** Carl J. Lauter,
      "The Effect of 1930 Drought on Washington Water Supply,"
      American Water Works Association 24, no. 1 (January 1932):
      73–77.

183   **The upper Potomac was reduced to a chain of fetid puddles:**
      Eugene Scheel, "Drought Survivors of 1930 Recall the Ultimate
      Dry Spell," The History of Loudoun County, Virginia (blog),
      November 2007, https://www.loudounhistory.org/history/
      drought-survivors-recall-1930/.

183   **The National Fish and Wildlife Service reported:** "Wild Ducks
      on the Potomac Afflicted with Disease," press release, U.S.
      Department of Agriculture, November 1, 1930.

183 **In Loudoun and Fauquier Counties:** Scheel, "Drought Survivors of 1930 Recall the Ultimate Dry Spell."

184 **Though there have been only three major droughts:** National Integrated Drought Information System, Maryland, 1895– Present, https://www.drought.gov/states/maryland#historical-conditions.

185 **On one day in August 2015, while the recorded temperature:** Jacob Fenston, "What Are D.C.'s Hottest Neighborhoods? Science Wants to Know," DCist, August 30, 2018, https:// wamu.org/story/18/08/30/d-c-s-hottest-neighborhoods-science-wants-know/.

185 **Residents of these Anacostia River–adjacent neighborhoods:** Malini Ranganathan and Eve Bratman, "From Urban Resilience to Abolitionist Climate Justice in Washington, D.C.," *Antipode* 53, no. 1 (2021): 115–37.

185 **Children living in Ward 8 are hospitalized:** Morgan Baskin, "Doctors Blame D.C.'s High Asthma Rates in Part on Poor Housing," *Washington City Paper,* May 22, 2019.

185 **Current projections from D.C.'s Department of Energy & Environment:** "Climate Ready D.C.: The District of Columbia's Plan to Adapt to a Changing Climate," Department of Energy & Environment, 2019, https://doee.dc.gov/sites/default/files/ dc/sites/ddoe/service_content/attachments/CRDC-Report-FINAL-Web.pdf.

187 **Skepticism about the name and frequency:** Richard L. Stanton, *Potomac Journey: Fairfax Stone to Tidewater* (Washington, D.C.: Smithsonian Institution Press, 1993), 163.

187 **In 2019, D.C.'s DOEE reported:** "Climate Ready D.C.: The District of Columbia's Plan to Adapt to a Changing Climate."

188 **The 1936 flood killed two hundred people:** Carole L. Herrick, *Ambitious Failure: Chain Bridge: The First Bridge Across the Potomac River* (Falls Church, Virginia: Higher Education Publications, Inc., 2012), 282–91.

188   **After 1936, the canal was in such a state of disrepair:** Stanton,
      163.

189   **In Washington, Black workers from the Civilian Conservation
      Corps:** "Flood of 1936," *Histories of the National Mall*, accessed
      December 10, 2023, https://mallhistory.org/items/show/343.

189   **Meanwhile, President Franklin D. Roosevelt:** Herrick, 289–91.

189   **"the turbulent brown water":** Stanton, 165.

189   **Newsreel footage taken after the waters subsided:** "After the
      Floods in the United States," Pathé Gazette, video, 1936,
      https://www.youtube.com/watch?v=W56BhIblK70.

190   **Even before the floods, white Washingtonians:** Chris Myers
      Asch and George Derek Musgrove, *Chocolate City: A History
      of Race and Democracy in the Nation's Capital* (Chapel Hill:
      University of North Carolina Press, 2017), 321–24.

190   **The original 4,500 families of Southwest D.C. were forced:** Asch
      and Musgrove, 321–24.

192   **If global temperatures rise 3°C or higher:** Picturing Our Future,
      Washington, D.C., Coastal Risk Screening Tool, Climate
      Central, 2021, https://www.climatecentral.org/climate-matters/
      picturing-our-future-CM.

194   **"inescapably vivid in repeated mental shuttle passes":** Sedgwick,
      166.

Tiber

196   **The vast grounds surrounding the Old Solders' Home:** The
      park surrounding the Soldiers' Home also lent its name to
      the neighborhood. In Park View, the park in view is the Old
      Soldiers' Home grounds.

196   **But in the mid-twentieth century:** Emily Wax, "Can Soldiers'
      Home Residents and Urban Gentrifiers Overcome Barbed
      Wire?" *Washington Post*, March 1, 2013.

197   **Wherever streams are channeled into:** "Daylighting Streams: Breathing Life into Urban Streams and Communities," American Rivers Daylighting Report, May 2016, https://www.americanrivers.org/wp-content/uploads/2016/05/AmericanRivers_daylighting-streams-report.pdf.

197   **This entire city was built on the bones of buried creeks:** Linda Poon, "Lessons from a 'Historic' Flash Flood May Soon Be Normal," *Bloomberg News,* July 10, 2019.

198   **Staring out at the old path of the Tiber:** Garnett P. Williams, "Washington, D.C.'s Vanishing Springs and Waterways," Geological Survey Circular 752, United States Department of the Interior, 1977.

199   **"inside-the-Beltway kind of guy":** "Interview with Bernie Sanders," *Hardball with Chris Matthews,* MSNBC, February 25, 2016.

199   **Most Washingtonians are aware that the city:** Carl Abbott, "The Myth That Washington Was a Swamp Will Never Go Away," *Smithsonian Magazine,* March 9, 2017, https://www.smithsonianmag.com/history/draining-swamp-guide-outsiders-and-career-politicians-180962448/.

199   **the "swamp" of the metaphor:** Ted Widmer, "Draining the Swamp," *The New Yorker,* January 19, 2017.

200   **A few blocks south of here, near Union Station:** Williams, "Washington, D.C.'s Vanishing Springs and Waterways."

200   **In June 1783, Continental army veterans marched:** Kenneth R. Bowling, "New Light on the Philadelphia Mutiny of 1783: Federal-State Confrontation at the Close of the War for Independence," *The Pennsylvania Magazine of History and Biography* 101, no. 4 (1977): 419–50.

201 **Other congressional members pointed out the tension between:**
George Derek Musgrove and Chris Myers Asch, "Democracy
Deferred: Race, Politics, and D.C.'s Two-Century Struggle for
Full Voting Rights," State Research D.C., March 2021, https://
static1.squarespace.com/static/5a04c080f14aa19fe2f7b0f9/
t/6077205094518b024362ef6a/1618419793470/
Democracy+Deferred.pdf.

201 **"It has cost me many a Sleepless Night":** Samuel Osgood to
Samuel Adams, January 5, 1788, in *The Documentary History
of the Ratification of the Constitution,* eds. John Kaminski et al.
(Madison: State Historical Society of Wisconsin, 2009), 621.

202 **But in 1801, Congress finally decided to enforce the clause:** Chris
Myers Asch and George Derek Musgrove, *Chocolate City: A
History of Race and Democracy in the Nation's Capital* (Chapel Hill:
University of North Carolina Press, 2017), 67.

202 **After emancipation, thousands of formerly enslaved people
moved:** Musgrove and Asch, "Democracy Deferred."

203 **Under the leadership of charismatic businessman:** "The Tiber
Creek Sewer Flush Gates, Washington, D.C.," *Engineering News
and American Railway Journal,* February 8, 1894.

203 **Shepherd was a productive but unscrupulous leader:** It is ironic,
or perhaps now quite fitting, that the men responsible for
draining the Washington swamp (by tunneling up the Tiber)
were also some of the most corrupt leaders the city has ever
seen.

203 **Drawing on racist stereotypes of Black people as children:** Kate
Masur, *An Example for All the Land: Emancipation and the Struggle
for Equality in Washington, D.C.* (Chapel Hill: University of North
Carolina Press, 2011), 232–50.

204 **In 1874, Congress accepted the committee's recommendations:** Steven J. Diner, "Democracy, Federalism, and the Governance of the Nation's Capital, 1790–1974," *Studies in D.C. History and Public Policy No. 10* (Washington, D.C.: Center for Applied Research and Urban Policy, University of the District of Columbia, 1987), 24–29.

204 **"Under this bill":** "The Crime Against Suffrage in Washington," *The Nation,* June 27, 1878, 415.

204 **"abominable and disgraceful":** Morgan quoted in Edward Ingle, *The Negro in the District of Columbia* (Baltimore: Johns Hopkins Press, 1893), 81.

204 **"negro domination":** Editorial, *Washington Post,* February 1, 1878.

205 **With the ferment of the civil rights movement:** Asch and Musgrove, *Chocolate City,* 347–51.

205 **Senator Robert Byrd of West Virginia:** "John McMillan Dies, Opposed Home Rule as Congressman," *Washington Post,* September 4, 1979; "Robert C. Byrd—A 'Villain' to Poor of D.C.?" *Charleston Gazette,* May 12, 1965.

205 **In 1956, an upper-class cadre of white Washingtonians:** Musgrove and Asch, "Democracy Deferred."

206 **President Johnson supported home rule:** "School Election Bill Signed," *Washington Post,* April 23, 1968; "D.C. Delegate Bill Signed by Nixon," *Washington Post,* September 23, 1970.

206 **The greatest obstruction to past bills:** "John McMillan Dies, Opposed Home Rule as Congressman."

207 **Because the federal government oversees the District's courts:** Martin Austermuhle, "D.C. Inmates Serve Time Hundreds of Miles from Home. Is It Time to Bring Them Back?," DCist, August 10, 2017, https://wamu.org/story/17/08/10/d-c-inmates-serving-time-means-hundreds-miles-home-time-bring-back/.

207   **Included in the law are also a number of exceptions:** District of Columbia Home Rule Act, Public Law 93-198.

207   **Over the last three decades:** "Congressional Intervention," D.C. Statehood, D.C. Government, accessed December 10, 2023, https://statehood.dc.gov/page/congressional-intervention.

209   **Turning around to face the white-stoned Capitol:** Valeria Federici, "Taming the Waters on the National Mall," National Gallery of Art (blog), October 26, 2021, https://www.nga.gov/blog/taming-the-waters-on-the-national-mall.html.

210   **Less than twenty-four hours after the attempted coup:** "Why Statehood for D.C.," D.C. Statehood, D.C. Government, accessed December 10, 2023, https://statehood.dc.gov/page/why-statehood-dc.

211   **I didn't know that a barbed-wire fence:** Colleen Grablick, "After Six Months, the Capitol Fencing Is Slated to Come Down," DCist, July 7, 2021, www.npr.org/local/305/2021/07/08/1014192779/after-six-months-the-capitol-fencing-is-slated-to-come-down.

212   **Having won the limited right to home rule:** George Derek Musgrove, "Statehood Is Far More Difficult," *Washington History* 29, no. 2 (Fall 2017), 5–6.

212   **In the wake of the failed ratification of the DCVRA:** Musgrove and Asch, "Democracy Deferred."

212   **With partisan power teetering on a knife's edge:** Bill McKibben, "Vermont Is a Great State, and D.C. Would Be, Too," *The New Yorker,* March 24, 2021, https://www.newyorker.com/news/daily-comment/vermont-is-a-great-state-and-dc-would-be-too.

213   **Other arguments rest:** Michaela Lefrack, "Greetings from Douglass Commonwealth," *What's with Washington?* (podcast series), WAMU, October 27, 2020, https://wamu.org/story/20/10/27/51st-greetings-from-douglass-commonwealth/.

213 **Still other arguments are blatantly racist:** Abdallah Fayyad, "Call Republican Opposition to D.C. Statehood What It Is: Racist," *Boston Globe,* March 3, 2021.

Bones

223 **"people are trapped in history":** James Baldwin, "Stranger in the Village," *Harper's Magazine,* October 1953, 42.

223 **"a ball of contradictions" and "a mess of ironies":** Gil Scott-Heron, "Washington, D.C.," on the album *Moving Target,* 1982.

226 **the term *kincentric ecology*:** Enrique Salmon, "Kincentric Ecology: Indigenous Perceptions of the Human-Nature Relationship," *Ecological Applications* 10, no. 5 (2000): 1327-32.

228 **"a culture of belonging":** bell hooks, *Belonging: A Culture of Place* (New York: Routledge, 2009), 5.

228 **"in pursuit of constructive reparations":** Olúfẹ́mi O. Táíwò, *Reconsidering Reparations* (Oxford: Oxford University Press, 2022), 140.

230 **"Where it is and what it is, and what it promises to be":** Frederick Douglass, "A Lecture on Our National Capital" (Washington, D.C.: Smithsonian Institution Press, 1978), 20.

Bellevue Literary Press is devoted to publishing literary fiction and nonfiction at the intersection of the arts and sciences because we believe that science and the humanities are natural companions for understanding the human experience. We feature exceptional literature that explores the nature of consciousness, embodiment, and the underpinnings of the social contract. With each book we publish, our goal is to foster a rich, interdisciplinary dialogue that will forge new tools for thinking and engaging with the world.

To support our press and its mission, and for our full catalogue of published titles, please visit us at blpress.org.

Bellevue Literary Press
New York